Elementary School Social Studies:

Research As a Guide to Practice

Second Printing
with updated position statment

Virginia A. Atwood
Editor

NATIONAL COUNCIL FOR THE SOCIAL STUDIES

Library of Congress Catalog Card Number : 86-63064
ISBN-0-87986-054-5
Copyright © 1986, 1991 by
NATIONAL COUNCIL FOR THE SOCIAL STUDIES
3501 Newark Street N.W.
Washington, D.C. 20016-3167

TABLE OF CONTENTS

Part I
Introduction

Part II
What Research Says About Children Learning Social Studies

Part III
Related Concerns

CONTRIBUTORS

Beverly J. Armento is Associate Professor of Social Studies Education at Georgia State University in Atlanta and Director of the Specialized Center for Learning Theory and Economic Education there. She was president of the National Association of Economic Educators from 1985 to 1986 and has been active in NCSS, CUFA and AERA. Her writing and research have emphasized concept learning and the general application of developmental and learning theories to the design of effective instruction.

Virginia A. Atwood is Professor of Education at the University of Kentucky in Lexington. She teaches classes in early childhood and elementary social studies and classroom management and discipline. She chaired the NCSS Early Childhood/Elementary Advisory Committee and currently serves on the NCSS Board of Directors. Her writing and research focus on strategies for teaching in elementary schools and teacher education.

JoAnne Buggey is a teacher in the Department of Curriculum and Instruction at the University of Minnesota. She has taught all elementary grades, served as a social studies consultant, and conducted inservice workshops nationwide. She has developed a wide variety of social studies curriculum materials and teacher's guides.

Wayne Dumas is Chair of the Department of Curriculum and Instruction and Professor of Education at the University of Missouri-Columbia. He is co-author of 4 books, is the author or coauthor of over 50 articles in professional journals, and is actively involved in research in teacher education and international political and social education. He chaired the NCSS Teacher Education and Certification Committee in 1984 and was the 1985 chair of the NCSS Teacher Education Special Interest Group.

Sharon Flores has been actively involved in economic education for at least ten years. She teaches 5th grade at The Lovett School in Atlanta and for several years has implemented an award-winning classroom "business" there to teach economic concepts. Flores is an active participant in Georgia State University's Master Teachers of Economic Education Program and has conducted numerous economic education workshops for teachers throughout the country.

Carole Hahn is Professor of Social Studies education and director of the Division of Educational Studies at Emory University in Atlanta. She teaches elementary social studies methods courses. She is a past president of NCSS and chaired the NCSS Publications Board, College and University Faculty Assembly, and Committee on Sexism and Social Justice. She has done research and writing on the diffusion of social studies innovations, sex equity, economics education, and teaching from a global perspective.

Richard K. Jantz is Professor of Education at the University of Maryland, College Park. He has authored children's social studies text and teachers' text materials at the primary grade level and a research chapter on early childhood social studies, and published in such journals as *Social Education, Theory and Research in Social Education, Journal of Negro Education, Research Quarterly, The Gerontologists, International Journal of Aging and Human Development, The Elementary School Journal* and *The Reading Teacher.*

Theodore Kaltsounis is a past president of NCSS and Professor of Education and Associate Dean of the College of Education at the University of Washington, Seattle. A former Fulbright scholar, he has written numerous articles and books, including *Teaching Social Studies in the Elementary School* and *States and Regions.* Kaltsounis taught at all levels and participated in a number of social studies curriculum development projects.

Kenneth Klawitter is a principal in Spring Grove Area School District, Spring Grove, Pennsylvania, after having taught for 11 years in the Central York School District of York, Pennsylvania. He has served as a special education teacher and department chair at both the elementary and secondary level. Since completing his doctoral studies at the University of Maryland in 1983, he has been active conducting research and writing in the areas of reading, concept formation and information processing.

James B. Kracht is a professor in the Department of Educational Curriculum and Instruction and also in the Department of Geography at Texas A & M University. His primary responsibilities are social studies education and geographic education. He currently serves as first vice president of the National Council for Geographic Education and is also a member of GENIP (Geographic Education National Implementation Project).

Linda S. Levstik is Assistant Professor of Elementary and Social Studies Education at the University of Kentucky. Active in promoting the use of local resources in teaching history, she is a consultant to "Reflections of the Past," a National Endowment for the Humanities supported project promoting the use of archival materials in the classroom. Her publications include articles and curriculum materials designed to enhance the teaching of history at the elementary level.

Gary R. McKenzie is Associate Professor of Education at the University of Texas in Austin where he teaches instructional design, elementary social studies and a field-based practicum course for experienced teachers. He has averaged a demonstration lesson a week in classrooms from kindergarten to 8th grade. His research has focused on effects of questions on higher order thinking, but he is presently studying the origin and influence of developmental stage theory on assumptions in primary social studies.

Walter C. Parker is Assistant Professor of Education in Social Studies at the University of Washington. He was a social studies teacher and department chairperson in Northglenn, Colorado, and later worked as a staff development coordinator. He has served on the NCSS Urban Social Studies and Citizenship Education committees and authored with John Jarolimek the NCSS/ERIC bulletin *Citizenship and the Critical Role of the Social Studies.*

Lynda Stone is a doctoral candidate in the Department of Curriculum and Teacher Education, School of Education, Stanford University, and currently is Visiting Lecturer in the Philosophy of Education at the University of New Hampshire. A long-tenured social studies teacher, she remains interested in global and citizenship education and in qualitative research in social studies classrooms. She is working on a dissertation that looks at the broad forms of knowledge for which we educate.

Cynthia Szymanski Sunal is Professor of Curriculum and Instruction at West Virginia University and Adjunct Research Professor in Family Studies, Appalachia Educational Laboratory. She has been a Fulbright Professor to Nigeria and was a classroom teacher for 10 years. She has chaired the NCSS Early Childhood/Elementary Advisory Group.

Thomas Weible is Professor and Chair of the Department of Elementary Education at Iowa State University. He has authored more than 30 articles and 2 books and teaches the graduate elementary social studies courses at ISU.

PREFACE

Thus far during the 1980s, we have witnessed both the expression of intense public interest in schools and general displeasure with schools' performance. Many local and national commissions and committees have issued reports and made recommendations, based on data analyses and the biases of each particular group. A back-to-basics approach has continued to receive support in many quarters, reinforced and abetted by state legislation mandating standardized testing of narrowly defined basic skills. On the heels of the administration of these tests came reports of elementary schools further reducing or abandoning social studies and science in the primary grades in order to spend more time teaching reading and computing skills—the skills most often measured by the standardized tests and reported by the press. Choosing a somewhat different approach to "educational reform," some state legislatures have specified the time to be spent on each subject at each grade level. While this step helped to ensure that the usual array of elementary subject areas would be taught, some teachers have felt discouraged from integrating subjects—for example, using social studies experiences to facilitate language arts, or using historical novels to supplement basal readers. Obviously, these two approaches to reform are likely to achieve different results, some of which will surely be unintended, and the sum of which will be inadequate.

The whole reform process has included some glaring inconsistencies. For example, there is an obvious and troublesome contradiction between commonly stated goals of education and what children are being taught. Professional educators and business people alike declare the need to educate students to be critical thinkers, rational decision makers, and cooperating team members who are knowledgeable of different cultural, political and economic systems. This view of schooling supports the utilization of a broad curriculum. Further, contrary to former Commissioner of Education Ernest Boyer's plan for delaying until grade 6 the teaching of subjects other than reading, language and mathematics, research confirms the importance of early learning and accents the danger of limiting the primary curriculum to basic skills narrowly defined. Too many students now are having reading difficulties because of what reading specialists call lack of prior knowledge, and too often students are asked to do computational exercises that appear unrelated to life outside of the mathematics period. Thus, Boyer's suggestion, which is surely shared by many other people, ignores the failure of the recent heavy emphasis on low-level basic skills, as well as disregards what we know about child development.

It is apparent that social studies educators must do a better job of advocating, to both the public and teachers, the importance of high quality social studies curricula for young children. Part of our task is to provide a sound rationale for planned and regular attention to social studies. In addition, we must make readily accessible the most current and valid data on how and when children develop concepts, skills and attitudes associated with social studies. The major purpose of this bulletin is to begin to perform these tasks.

The introductory chapter describes the status of social studies in elementary schools and presents a rationale for elementary social studies. The bases on which curricular and instructional decisions should be made are also discussed. Walter C. Parker and Theodore Kaltsounis survey the research on citizenship and law-related education and draw implications for school practice. International and multicultural education are defined and delineated by Lynda Stone as she critiques research in these related areas.

The chapters that follow discuss and summarize current research findings on how and when children's concepts, skills and attitudes develop in various social sciences that comprise social studies. JoAnne Buggey and James Kracht posit that, although there is general agreement that geography should be a fundamental part of elementary school social studies curricula, agreement does not exist on how and when geography concepts should be included. Since research seems to support the belief that children can learn what is systematically taught them by well-prepared teachers, Buggey and Kracht provide three illustrative lessons. History is the other discipline that tends to dominate elementary school social studies curricula. Linda S. Levstik laments the fact that little research has focused on teaching history to young children. She discusses implications for teachers in current research and gives examples of history in action. Richard K. Jantz and Kenneth Klawitter focus on content from anthropology and sociology appropriate for elementary school social studies and instructional strategies that research demonstrates to be effective. They conclude that "when exposed to the content from these two disciplines, children appear to develop a more positive attitude towards social studies."

The authors of most chapters advocate instruction that aims at higher level outcomes, such as concept development and problem-solving skills. Guided by that purpose, the work of developmentalists, Piaget's work in particular, is frequently cited to inform curriculum development and instructional decisions. The chapter by Beverly J. Armento, which focuses on economic education, is a good example. Certainly focusing on the requirements for obtaining higher level cognitive outcomes is consistent with the stated goals of NCSS for elementary school social studies. However, most goal statements for social studies also include information acquisition and lower level cognitive processing. Gary R. McKenzie suggests, quite correctly, I think, that it is these latter outcomes the masses of teachers attempt to teach and standardized tests tend to measure. To that end, McKenzie describes specific strategies that research has shown to be effective, particularly with children from low socioeconomic families. Some will view the data and opinions reported by McKenzie and the constructionists' data and views reported by Armento and others to be contradictory; others will recognize a need for both. Certainly different perspectives supported by research data should be thoughtfully considered, and for that purpose different views have been included.

Three chapters address issues of a more general nature. However, these issues have an impact on the quality and quantity of social studies taught and learned in elementary schools. Thomas Weible and Wayne Dumas discuss the status of elementary teacher certification standards relative to social studies and social science course requirements. Cynthia Szymanski Sunal reviews literature on parent involvement in schools and suggests implications for social studies programs. Finally, Carole Hahn prescribes a procedure for actively advocating elementary school social studies that can be used by either individuals or state councils.

This bulletin includes no claim to a final solution to the problem of establishing a sound and substantial social studies program in elementary schools across the United States. It is hoped that the publication will serve as a catalyst to discussion, to debate and—most important—to action toward that end. This will happen only if readers gain insight, raise questions, experiment with suggested classroom applications, and design research to fill the gaps of knowledge or test conclusions drawn by the authors.

I want to thank the chapter authors, the major contributors to this bulletin. In addition, I also would like to express my gratitude to several others. The members of the NCSS Special Interest Group on Early Childhood and Elementary Social Studies shared my deep concern for the status of social studies in elementary schools and provided encouragement and support for the project. Carole Hahn helped formulate the initial outline, suggested authors and critiqued drafts of several chapters. Judy Finkelstein, Barbara Hatcher, Dorothy Skeel, Frankie Daniel, Mary Jacque Northup and Angene Wilson also reviewed chapters and made many insightful and useful suggestions to authors.

Finally, this bulletin is dedicated to Chase Rogers and all the other children who ask "Why?" and are seldom completely satisfied with the answers they receive. May we be as diligent in providing opportunities to learn as they are in seeking to learn!

Virginia A. Atwood

SOCIAL STUDIES FOR EARLY CHILDHOOD AND ELEMENTARY SCHOOL CHILDREN PREPARING FOR THE 21ST CENTURY

A Report from NCSS Task Force on Early Childhood/Elementary Social Studies[*]
Approved by NCSS Board of Directors, June 1988

This position paper will discuss the definition, rationale, and goals for social studies in the early childhood/elementary years; the developmental characteristics that should be considered in planning a social studies program; an overview of the basic research for elementary social studies; a look at the current status of social studies in the elementary school; and a discussion of preservice and in-service education for teachers of early childhood/elementary social studies.

Society is characterized by increasingly rapid social and technological change. Society's ability to orchestrate change frequently outstrips its ability to reflect on the ramifications of what it has done. Are children developing skills to absorb new information in light of the information explosion? Are they learning structures for understanding and adapting to changes in technology, the marketplace, and their own family organization? Are they beginning to learn about interdependence and the relationship of technology to social conditions?

When they leave the classroom, many children do not return immediately to the family setting but go to a day-care facility where they again interact with others from a variety of backgrounds. Nearly all the children spend more hours each week watching television than they spend in any other activity besides sleeping. As they sit passively watching, they are bombarded by messages. They take in spotty, disconnected information about war, the homeless, Ethiopia, the president, and the Soviets. Are they learning any structures for interpreting this information and fitting it into a larger framework? Commercial television networks see children as an economic force and press them to make consumer decisions. Are children learning to evaluate these messages, or do they continue to sit passively as they are manipulated?

The social studies in the early childhood/elementary years are crucial if we expect the young people of this nation to become active, responsible citizens for maintaining the democratic values upon which this nation was established. Unless children acquire the foundations of knowledge, attitudes, and skills in social studies in the important elementary years, it is unlikely that teachers in the junior and senior high schools will be successful in preparing effective citizens for the 21st century.

I.   What problems do young children encounter as they enter school?

Consider a kindergarten class in any one of thousands of school systems in the United

States. How do the children in the class experience the world? Their classroom mirrors the larger society with its diverse ethnic, religious, and socioeconomic backgrounds. Are the children learning structures for accepting and appreciating diversity at this critical age in the development of lifelong attitudes? Mere contact with diversity, without understanding, can intensify conflict. Does their classroom mirror the larger society in this sense also?

In classroom, day-care center, home, and neighborhood, kindergartners encounter rules and laws. Do they understand the reasons for these institutions? Can they distinguish between legitimate authority and raw power? Are they learning to act as rule makers as well as rule obeyers and to see the necessity of personal involvement in the democratic process?

The kindergarten class of 1988 will graduate in the year 2001 as citizens who live in a world characterized by a staggering volume of information, varying sets of values, and a growing interdependence among nations. However, children will not automatically become citizens when they graduate or reach voting age; they are citizens now, with rights, responsibilities, and a confusing array of choices before them. The abilities for making personally and socially productive decisions do not just happen. They require that the knowledge, skills, and attitudes of social studies be introduced early and built upon throughout the school years.

II.   What should be the definition of and rationale for social studies for early childhood/elementary children?

The social studies are the study of political, economic, cultural, and environmental aspects of societies in the past, present, and future. For elementary school children, as well as for all age groups social studies have several purposes. The social studies equip them with the knowledge and understanding of the past necessary for coping with the present and planning for the future, enable them to understand and participate effectively in their world, and explain their relationship to other people and to social, economic, and political institutions. Social studies can provide students with the skills for productive problem solving and decision making, as well as for assessing issues and making thoughtful value judgments. Above all, the social studies help students to integrate these skills and understandings into a framework for responsible citizen participation, whether in their play group, the school, the community, or the world.

The energy, curiosity, and imagination of young children lead them to action and interaction within their environment from a narrow, unilateral perspective. They live in a family, play in a peer group, and make decisions about how they will relate to other people, what to do in their free time, with whom to play, what books to read, and how to spend money. The larger social world penetrates their lives through television and other media, travel, family, and friends; but young children lack the conceptual base to integrate the new knowledge these experiences bring. They also lack the skills to account for other perspectives in solving problems or to anticipate long-range consequences when making decisions.

A planned K–12 social studies program directs and focuses these natural characteristics to help children understand and function in their personal and social worlds. These learnings must be developed systematically from an early age, so that children move from egocentric, random observations and experiences to a broader and more structured conceptual organization. Many times, teachers suggest that at the primary level everything they do is related to social studies, but it is important to recognize that an effective social studies program cannot be just a haphazard collection of unrelated activities. It must be organized systematically around concepts from history and the social sciences.

Active, curious children need, want, and are able to learn skills that are taught and reinforced in social studies classes. These skills are required for processing information so that they can make generalizations and integrate new information into a developing system of knowledge.

Children formulate many of their attitudes and values toward society in the early years. The development of these attitudes and values occurs primarily outside the school setting. However, the social studies program should provide a setting for children to acquire knowledge of history and the social sciences and to be exposed to a broad variety of opinions, facilitating the formulation, reassessment, and affirmation of their beliefs.

The social studies program enables children to participate effectively now in the groups to which they belong and not to look only to their future participation as adults. The school itself serves as a laboratory for students to learn social participation directly and not symbolically. Democratic and participatory school and classroom environments are essential to this type of real-world learning.

If the social studies are not part of the elementary curriculum, we cannot expect our children to be prepared to understand or participate effectively in an increasingly complex world. They need to encounter and *re*encounter, in a variety of contexts, the knowledge, concepts, skills, and attitudes that form the foundation for participation in a democratic society. Otherwise, we are in danger of disrupting the critical balance between individual and community needs. Social studies are intended to help children understand, evaluate, and make decisions regarding these often competing claims. The problem lies in developing a learning environment and pedagogy that are intellectually and developmentally appropriate.

III. What are the goals for early childhood/elementary social studies that no other subject in the elementary curriculum can achieve?

It is understood that teaching social studies in the elementary schools is an essential part of the framework of an overall K–12 social studies program. The elementary school years are important in that they are the ones in which children develop a foundation for the entire social studies program and a beginning sense of efficacy as participating citizens of their world.

Basic skills of reading, writing, and computing are necessary but not sufficient to participate or even survive in a world demanding independent and cooperative problem solving to address complex social, economic, ethical, and personal concerns. Knowledge, skills, and attitudes necessary for informed and thoughtful participation in society require a systematically developed program focusing on concepts from history and the social sciences.

Knowledge. Social studies provide a sense of history, a sense of existence in the past as well as the present, a feeling of being in history. Even though young children find the concept of time difficult, they need to understand how the present has come about and to develop an appreciation for the heritage of this country. Huck and Kuhn (1968) state that even though children have difficulty with time concepts, they can develop an appreciation for their historical heritage through factual presentation of history, biographies of famous people, and historical fiction.

Geographic concepts are equally difficult, but the social studies provide continuing opportunities for children to understand the spatial relationships of their immediate environment as well as those of areas of the world. Scholars found that children need systematic instruction to develop map and globe skills (Rice and Cobb 1978; Crabtree 1968, 1974; Savage and Bacon 1969; Cox 1977). Children need to develop an understanding of and an appreciation for their physical and cultural environments and to consider how resources will be allocated in the future.

Concepts from anthropology and sociology provide knowledge and understanding of how the multiplicity of cultures within society and the world has developed. Children need to recognize the contributions of each culture and to explore its value system. Acquisition of concepts about racial and ethnic groups is complex, but early, planned, and structured activities can result in positive attitudes in children (Katz 1976, 234).

Knowledge from sociology, economics, and political science allows children to understand the institutions within the society and to learn about their roles within groups. Although children easily learn concepts from economics such as work, exchange, production, and consumption, they need useful and powerful economic knowledge and the formal development of critical-thinking skills. Economic content in the early years should relate to events in children's lives as they examine buying, selling, and trading transactions, the process of making goods and services, and the origin of materials and products in their everyday lives (Armento 1986).

Skills. The skills that are primary to social studies are those related to maps and globes, such as understanding and using locational and directional terms. However, other skills that enhance students' abilities to learn, to make decisions, and to develop as competent, self-directed citizens are more meaningful and useful when developed within the context of social studies. Skills that are shared with other parts of the curriculum but may be most powerfully taught through social studies include communication skills such as writing and speaking; research skills such as collecting, organizing, and interpreting data; thinking skills such as hypothesizing, comparing, drawing inferences; decision-making skills such as considering alternatives and consequences; interpersonal skills such as seeing others' points of view, accepting responsibility, and dealing with conflict; and reading skills such as reading pictures, books, maps, charts, and graphs.

For children to develop citizenship skills appropriate to democracy, they must be capable of thinking critically about complex societal problems and global problems. Teachers must arrange the classroom environment to promote data gathering, discussion, and critical reasoning by students. Another important aspect of citizenship is that of decision maker. Children must acquire the skills of decision making, but also study the process that occurs as groups make decisions. Continually accelerating technology has created and will continue to create rapid changes in society. Children need to be equipped with the skills to cope with change.

Attitudes. The early years are ideal for children to begin to understand democratic norms and values (justice, equality, etc.)—especially in terms of the smaller social entities of the family, classroom, and community. Applying these concepts to the nation and the world is easier if one understands and appreciates them on smaller but manageable scales.

Although not uniquely in social studies, children can achieve a positive self-concept within the context of understanding the similarities and differences of people. Children need to understand that they are unique in themselves but share many similar feelings and concerns with other children. They need to understand how as individuals they can contribute to society.

Children can also develop, within the context of social studies, positive attitudes toward knowledge and learning and develop a spirit of inquiry that will enhance their understanding of their world so that they will become rational, humane, participating, effective members of a democratic society.

IV. What are the developmental characteristics of children that should be considered in planning a social studies program?

First, we need to consider that children of all ages come to school from different socioeconomic and cultural backgrounds. They come with different value systems, experiences, and learning styles, and with different feelings about themselves and the people around them. As we discuss the general characteristics of children, we recognize these individual differences.

A report from the National Association for the Education of Young Children (NAEYC) provides a helpful summary of the significant literature on the development characteristics of children.

Most five-year-olds can begin to combine simple ideas into more complex relations. They have a growing memory capacity and fine motor physical skills. They have a growing interest in the functional aspects of written language, such as recognizing meaningful words and trying to write their names (NAEYC 1986). They need an environment rich in printed materials that stimulates the development of language and literacy skills in a meaningful context. They also need a variety of direct experiences to develop cognitively, physically, emotionally, and socially. Since five-year-olds come to school with an interest in the community and the world outside their own, curriculum can expand beyond the child's immediate experience of self, home, and family (NAEYC 1986).

Six-year-olds are active learners and demonstrate considerable verbal ability. They are interested in games and rules and develop concepts and problem-solving skills from these experiences. Hands-on activity and experimentation are necessary for this age group (NAEYC 1986). Seven-year-olds become increasingly able to reason, listen to others, and show social give-and-take. Spatial relationships and time concepts are difficult for them to perceive. Flexibility, open-mindedness, and tolerance of unfamiliar ideas essential in social studies are formed to a remarkable extent by the interactions of the four- to eight-year-olds (Joyce 1970). Eight-year-olds combine great curiosity with increased social interest. They are able to learn about people who live elsewhere in the world. During these early grades, children can learn from the symbolic experiences of reading books and listening to stories; however, their understanding of what they read is based on their ability to relate the written word to their own experience (NAEYC 1986).

Research indicates that by age nine or ten children have well-established racial and ethnic prejudices and these are highly resistant to change (Joyce 1970); therefore, teachers must go beyond studies of other cultures and celebrations of their holidays and include studies of families, music, shelter, customs, beliefs, and other aspects common to all cultures (NAEYC 1986).

Nine-year-olds may be somewhat self-conscious and prefer group activities to working alone. They are beginning to understand abstractions as well as cause-and-effect relationships. Most are operating at a concrete level but need real experiences of society and social institutions such as those provided in social studies. Ten-year-olds may be experiencing bodily changes and rapid growth spurts. These changes cause periods of frustration and anger. Generally, ten-year-olds are interested in and enthusiastic about places and problems in the news. They want to know what events caused these problems, where they occurred, and the reasons for them. Most of the skills for learning social studies have been introduced by this time and they are able to apply them to new situations.

Eleven-year-olds are generally in a period of transition between childhood and adolescence. More decision making is required of them. They tend to be sociable and need opportunities to express feelings and opinions. The developmental research suggests that children at this age do not have the ability to view issues from the perspective of a whole society (Selman 1975), but need to be confronted with the types of analytical questions about history, society, and social and political behavior so important in social studies learning. Political attitudes develop very early and undergo major changes during the elementary school years. Attitudes developed by the end of elementary school are away from a personalized, benevolent government toward a more abstract, realistic idea (Greenstein 1969). The social studies also inform attitudes with accurate information from the humanities and the social sciences.

As we consider these characteristics, it becomes obvious that social studies must be an essential part of the elementary curriculum to provide the essential elements for continuing the democratic way of life. There may not be a more urgent need in the elementary school.

V.   What is the research base for elementary school social studies?

What guidance does research offer in the selection of content and learning experiences for social studies to enable children to achieve the goals previously described—especially for children who will be citizens of the 21st century? Frequently, curricular patterns are not grounded either in research or in an understanding of how children learn. In fact, the social studies are often left out of the curriculum at the primary level since some educators fail to see sufficient evidence to support their inclusion (Goodlad 1984; Clegg 1977). Yet we cannot dispute the importance of an educated citizenry in maintaining, preserving, and refining a democratic society, and research points out the critical nature of early and varied learning in elementary social studies (cf. Rice 1966; Hess and Torney 1967; Atwood 1986).

Social studies concepts, based as they are in human interactions, are complex. As a result of these complexities, some would suggest that young children not be introduced to the concepts until they are mature enough to understand them. After a decade of research on early learning in social studies, Rice (1966, 3) concluded that children could learn more difficult and abstract social studies concepts much earlier than is expected in the traditional social studies curriculum. What is equally important, however, is not so much that children are capable of earlier and more complex learning, but that, if the early learning does not occur, the optimum teaching time for some concepts may pass, making it much more difficult for students to entertain new ideas or to think critically about old ones.

There seem to be crucial years for certain concepts—times when students are most receptive or have developed a tolerance for or interest in emotionally powerful topics long before these topics are introduced in the curriculum. What, then, does research indicate about the process of learning particular social studies concepts?

Research findings related to the previously described goals—the development of concepts related to social studies content, the development of civic understanding, and the development of a social perspective that enables children to function at all levels of community to which they belong—highlight the significance of elementary social studies. This is not intended as an exhaustive review of the research but rather to emphasize certain studies. More comprehensive reviews can be found in William B. Stanley's *Review of Research in Social Studies Education: 1976-1983* (1985), Virginia A. Atwood's *Elementary School Social Studies: Research as a Guide to Practice* (1986), and Linda Rosenzweig's *Developmental Perspective on the Social Studies* (1983). Social studies also benefit from a wide range of research in other disciplines, notably those of psycho- and sociolinguistic studies considering linkages between language and conceptual development (cf. Nelms 1987), work in cooperative learning (cf. Slavin, in press; Slavin 1981), and research in social science disciplines that inform social studies.

Time and space. History and geography, keystones of elementary as well as secondary social studies, are linked to conceptions of time and space. Yet these concepts are difficult even for some adults. Some scholars have argued, in fact, that Western society makes it especially difficult to develop a sense of time as it relates to history because Western society does not provide clear and present needs for such concepts (Poster 1973). Others have noted the culture-boundedness of time conceptions, including Western, linear concepts of time. In any case, both time and space are abstract concepts formulated on relationships that are equally abstract and certainly provide difficulties for young children. This acknowledgment of the difficulty of acquiring sophisticated time and space concepts has led to some reluctance to introduce historical and geographical content in the elementary curriculum. Recent research indicates that this reluctance may be unfounded.

- Young children who are active participants in a highly structured and sequential series of geographic inquiries can learn complex analytic processes and concepts of geography (Crabtree 1974; GENIP Committee on K–6 Geography 1987; Muessig 1987).
- Evidence indicates that children do possess complex spatial information and can abstract information from map symbols (Hewes 1982; Hatcher 1983; Park and James 1983; Liben, Moore, and Golbeck 1982).
- Children can learn cardinal directions as early as kindergarten (Lanegran, Snowfield, and Laurent 1970).
- The type of discourse used in history teaching appears to influence student interest. Children who encountered historical data in the form of biography and historical fiction exhibited interest in and enthusiasm for history and for further investigation in more traditional sources (Levstik 1986).
- Historical and geographical understanding may not be linked to the developmental patterns associated with acquiring physical time concepts (Kennedy 1983).

Economic understanding. Armento (1986) indicates that "part of the role of social studies during elementary school years is to use children's informal learning as a basis for formal development of critical-thinking skills and for the construction of useful and powerful economic knowledge."

- By age seven, children have formulated fairly accurate conceptions of work, wants, and scarcity and evidence the capability of developing a method for making decisions (Armento 1986).
- Pictures and other concretizing tools can greatly benefit children with learning disabilities and those who have not enjoyed a broad variety of experience (Armento 1986).

Social perspective. The focus on relationships between people and their environments in elementary social studies is derived from the assumption that young children need to understand both their own uniqueness and their relationship to the world. Social knowledge is constructed as students attempt to build coherent systems for thinking about and explaining their immediate environment and the elements that make up the larger world environment (Turiel 1983). Their social judgments are not random responses; rather, they are the result of the application of analysis and reason in the social world and are influenced by such factors as peer groups, adults, social and educational environments, experiences, and the institutions to which they are exposed. Social judgments also involve more than the child's "getting along" in the home or school environment. They involve the child's ability to make decisions about such issues as race and ethnicity, citizen concerns of law and justice, and social welfare and economics, many of which make competing claims in a rapidly changing world. Research on how children acquire these understandings indicates that

- Children are more open to diversity in the early elementary years than in later years (Stone 1986). A fourth grader, for instance, is more likely to express interest in studying and visiting foreign countries than an eighth grader.
- Positive self-concepts, important in positively perceiving and judging social interactions, also form during these crucial early years (Stanley 1985, 77). Particular classroom environments seem to influence the ways children develop these interactions. Teachers who appear to enjoy teaching, who include great student-to-student interaction, shared decision making, and positive student-to-teacher interactions, foster more positive self-concepts in their pupils.
- Interest in and analysis of racial and ethnic differences begin early. Between the ages of six and nine, children begin to identify their own racial group as "better than the out-group" (Semaj 1980, 76).
- Acquisition of concepts about racial and ethnic groups is complex, but there is evidence that early, planned, and structured activities can result in improving positive attitudes in children (Katz 1976, 234).
- Elementary age children are already well aware of societal attitudes toward different groups (e.g., housing patterns, dating, and marriage mores). Research also indicates that elementary children can think critically about these patterns where they have sufficient experience and active involvement in discussion and inquiry (Ragan and McAulay 1973).

Civic Understanding. Research indicates that children are ready to deal with and already have ideas about civic understanding.

- As early as kindergarten, students engage in citizenship education, both covert and overt (Edwards 1986).

- Political feelings, evaluations, and attachments form well before the child learns the relevant supporting information (Greenstein 1969, 72).
- By eighth grade, children have already acquired basic orientations, and political socialization is generally well advanced by the end of elementary school (Hess and Torney 1967, 220).
- By the eighth grade, children have developed a sense of the need for consensus and majority rule in the democratic process. They have not recognized the role of debate, disagreement, and conflict in the operation of a democratic political system (Hess and Torney 1967, 216).
- A developed sense of justice and law appears to be requisite to democratic citizenship (Kohlberg 1976, 213). Particular types of classroom environments, including discussions in which students must actively think and communicate about another's reasoning, appear to facilitate this type of growth (Berkowitz 1981; Berkowitz and Gibbs 1983).

Needed research. There is much that research has not told us about teaching and learning social studies. We lack a sufficient body of basic research in many fields including research on teaching methodologies most appropriate for teaching specific social studies concepts, skills, and attitudes. We need studies of the effects of particular approaches to organizing social studies content—for instance, thematic versus chronological. These studies must take into account how children learn, another problem in need of investigation. There is also a need for further research on social studies and the exceptional child, both in terms of the exceptional child as learner and in helping other children understand and interact with exceptional children. Little has been done to investigate appropriate content and methodology for preschool and kindergarten social studies, although Carolyn Edwards' book, *Promoting Social and Moral Development in Young Children* (1986), is a thought-provoking start in that direction.

One of the most important conclusions one can draw from the available research on early learning in social studies is the critical importance of the elementary years in laying the foundation for later and increasingly mature understanding. There is reason to believe that teachers who miss these crucial opportunities to build interest, to introduce concepts from history and the social sciences, and to develop social perspectives and civic understanding may make it more difficult for citizens of the 21st century to cope with their future.

VI. What is the current status of social studies in the elementary school?

In schools throughout the United States, there are exciting classrooms where teachers challenge students to acquire the knowledge and skills necessary for making reasoned social commitments and decisions; where students hold mock trials and legislative debates to gain experience with the judicial process and the rules of debate; where they write classroom constitutions and hold elections to understand the role of the citizen in shaping political decisions; where they debate such social issues as welfare and social programs to develop an awareness of those in need of such programs; where they graph rainfall and temperatures around the country and can interpret the geographical patterns that result; where they develop travel brochures to interest students from other countries to visit their country; where they use milk cartons to build a city and can explain why certain land uses develop in areas of the city; where they hold a global olympics day to build an interest in international knowledge; or where someone role-plays a historical figure and holds a press conference for furthering knowledge of the humanity and motivations of these important persons. The overall status of social studies in elementary schools still needs improvement. We find teachers who feel unqualified to teach the content of social studies or who misinterpret them, confining instruction to a narrow focus on socialization skills or mere recall of facts from history, geography, and civics. We find that the time available for teaching the basic tools and concepts of the social sciences that can contribute to understanding human behavior receives an ever-shrinking slice of the school day. At best, this can provide only superficial treatment of this important learning. Student apathy—and even dislike—for a subject considered to be lifeless and useless is understandable in classrooms where strategies encouraging active involvement in grappling with human issues are absent; where forced marches through textbooks are frequent; and where the assumption prevails that memorization of names, places, and dates will somehow translate itself during adulthood into civic involvement. This type of curriculum does not prepare students for a future characterized by rapid change, increasing diversity, and global interdependence.

Elementary school social studies, especially in the primary grades, continue to suffer a decline in emphasis (Goodlad 1984; Gross 1977; Hahn 1985). Average instructional time ranges from approximately 20 minutes per day at the primary level to 34 minutes in the upper elementary grades (Lengel and Superka 1982). Some schools report very little or no social studies instruction at all in grades K–3 (Atwood 1986). This low priority is coupled with the belief of many elementary teachers that, although they are well qualified to teach reading and mathematics, they are less prepared to teach social studies (Eslinger and Superka 1982). Students themselves often characterize social studies as difficult, uninteresting, and largely irrelevant to their present and future lives. This comes as no surprise in light of reports that the dominant classroom pattern is characterized by lecture and recitation, reading textbooks, and completing worksheets. Goodlad's 1984 study confirms earlier reports that, even when students express a high interest in social studies topics, classroom treatment tends to reduce these topics to recitation of dates and places and displaces opportunities to explore relationships, draw inferences about human behavior, and make in-depth cultural comparisons.

Goodlad found that at the primary level the social studies curriculum is blurred by lack of common agreement about what is to be taught. A predominant theme appears to be an effort to help students understand themselves and others in the context of family and community. These topics are punctuated by occasional—and often superficial—attention to other cultures.

At the upper elementary level, history, geography, and civics become solidly established in the curriculum. The major emphasis is on the United States with additional time allocated to world history and geography. However, pressure increases to memorize more and more low-level information (Atwood 1986). Although teachers list thinking and decision-making skills prominently among goals for students, actual practice reveals vastly different priorities. Essay tests are rare, and opportunities to engage in the problem-solving and inquiry activities that are key ingredients in citizen efficacy are notably absent from most classrooms. The prevailing inattention to international topics and in-depth cultural comparisons leaves little mystery as to why more than 50 percent of the students in Goodlad's study perceived other countries and their ideologies as threatening to the United States. He concludes that many elementary teachers have not identified the curricular components necessary for understanding the United States in a global context. Relying solely on reading textbooks, completing worksheets, taking tests, and listening eliminates the active, participatory power of social studies that is essential to the education of citizens in a democracy.

Newmann (1986) notes that a trend toward minimal civic participation among adults can be expected to continue. Most people's only foray into the public arena is voting or temporary involvement in single-issue politics. Strikingly absent is a feeling of personal trusteeship of general civic welfare. The current agenda of most schools lack the components for converting into reality the stated goal of producing active, informed citizens. In a complex, interdependent world, students remain ethnocentric. In a participatory political culture, they receive scant opportunity to learn participation. In an era of rapidly expanding knowledge, they have few chances to develop the structures necessary for sifting and evaluating the vast amount of information constantly streaming at them through the media.

VII.   How should we prepare teachers of early childhood and elementary social studies?

Effective early childhood/elementary social studies as described earlier in this paper will not just happen. If the status of early childhood/elementary social studies education is to change, then the education of teachers who have the responsibility for teaching those children will be a critical factor. Teacher education in social studies has the task of educating teachers with sufficient content knowledge in history and the social sciences; knowledge about and skill in different teaching techniques; an ability to locate, evaluate, and use appropriate resources to supplement the text; sufficient knowledge regarding the characteristics and abilities of young children; and an enthusiasm for teaching social studies that comes from an understanding of the importance of social studies in the early years and an appreciation for and understanding of social studies content.

NCSS has adopted Standards for the Preparation of Social Studies Teachers (1988) to address these goals. It leaves to the individual states and teacher-education institutions to design specific programs around these standards. The NCSS standards specify that "candidates for initial licensure as social studies teachers should have gained substantial understanding of the information, concepts, theories, analytical approaches and differing values perspectives, including global and multicultural perspectives, important to teaching social studies. Problem-solving, critical-thinking, and application skills should be stressed." The standards recognize, however, that teaching social studies to children requires more. The standards further state that "courses in social studies methods should prepare prospective teachers to select, integrate, and translate knowledge and methodology from history and social science disciplines in ways appropriate to students in the school level they will teach and give attention to the goals unique to the social studies and those shared jointly with other areas of the school curriculum. Students should also be able to teach social studies utilizing a variety of curriculum approaches and in different types of settings."

Early childhood and elementary school teachers must be well versed in learning and motivation theories. They need to understand cognitive and psychosocial development and its relationship to the teaching and learning processes. They need to be able to integrate concepts, processes, and examples from science, literature, mathematics, music, art, and social studies. They must understand the effects of sociopolitical and economic variables on families and, consequently, on children. It is critical for prospective teachers to observe and work with children in order for them to assimilate, synthesize, and substantiate all that is learned in a program.

The goals of social studies dictate that elementary school teachers have certain experiences, skills, values, and knowledge. Multicultural experiences for prospective elementary teachers are crucial. Studies have shown that the numbers of minority children in schools are growing while the numbers of minority teachers are declining; these phenomena affect elementary social studies in two ways. Teachers need to be well grounded in multicultural education so that they can teach about it, and they need to be sensitive to the needs of minority children. Jantz and Klawiller (1985, 82) state that attitudes about race crystallize during the later elementary years and "the attitudes expressed by teachers and peers are important in the elaboration of racial attitudes."

VIII. What type of continued professional development is needed for early childhood/elementary social studies teachers?

Teaching must be seen as continuous learning. Initial certification only commences the process. Continued professional development should be shaped and controlled by the continuously evolving research related to teaching methodologies, child development, learning principles, and new technological developments that may be used in instruction. Teachers must remain knowledgeable of changing demographic patterns of the nation and accompanying changes in student characteristics. New knowledge in history and the social sciences, current issues, controversial issues, and evolving social conditions requires the constant attention of the teachers.

Programs of individual professional growth may include such experiences as attendance and participation in conventions, in-service courses and workshops, travel and exchange programs, postgraduate studies, participation in professional organizations, reading of desirable professional literature, and self-evaluations (Dobkin, Fischer, Ludwig, and Kobliner 1985).

Professional development within the local school district should provide: (1) a well-organized teacher development and evaluation program; (2) support staff for instructional improvement; (3) appropriate social studies materials and resources; (4) a functioning social studies curriculum committee; (5) a K–12, systemwide, articulated social studies program that is regularly reviewed and updated; (6) opportunities for teachers to participate in professional social studies organizations at a local, state, and national level; and (7) a professional library that contains social studies periodicals, research studies, social studies texts, and related literature.

State and national professional organizations should be involved in the professional growth activities of teachers. Of the many contributions these professional organizations make, the publication of significant literature is one of the most important. These organizations should also act as a voice for improving education in general.

Professional growth programs will influence and control teachers' abilities throughout their professional careers. It is imperative that each individual make a personal commitment to professional growth and through that commitment provide effective and exciting social studies for early childhood/ elementary children.

IX.   Appropriate number of daily minutes for social studies teaching in the elementary school

Given the importance of social studies in the elementary school, NCSS recommends that 20 percent of the academic day which includes reading/language arts, science, mathematics, and the arts, be devoted to social studies instruction.

X.   Summary

If the young people of this nation are to become effective participants in a democratic society, then social studies must be an essential part of the curriculum in the early childhood/elementary years. In a world that demands independent and cooperative problem solving to address complex social, economic, ethical, and personal concerns, the social studies are as basic for survival as reading, writing, and computing. Knowledge, skills, and attitudes necessary for informed and thoughtful participation in society require a systematically developed program focused on concepts from history and the social sciences.

REFERENCES

Armento, B. J. "Research on Teaching Social Studies." In *Handbook of Research on Teaching,* edited by M. C. Wittrock. 3d ed. New York: Macmillan, 1986.

Association of American Colleges. "Integrity in the College Curriculum: A Report to the Academic Community." *Chronicle of Higher Education* 29, no. 22 (1985): 12 -30.

Atwood, V. A., ed. *Elementary Social Studies: Research as a Guide to Practice.* Washington, D.C.: National Council for the Social Studies, 1986.

Berkowitz, M. W. "A Critical Appraisal of the Educational and Psychological Perspectives on Moral Discussion." *Journal of Educational Thought* 15 (1981): 20-33.

Berkowitz, M. W, and J. C. Gibbs. "Measuring the Developmental Feature of a Moral Discussion." *Merrill-Palmer Quarterly* 29 (1983): 339-440.

Carnegie Corporation Task Force on Teaching as Profession. *A Nation Prepared: Teachers for the Twenty-first Century.* New York: Carnegie Forum on Education and the Economy, Carnegie Corporation of New York, 1986.

Carnegie Foundation for the Advancement of Teaching. "College: The Undergraduate Experience in America." *Chronicle of Higher Education* 33, no. 10 (1986): 16-22.

Clegg, A. "Three Midwest Cities: The Status of Social Studies Education." *Social Education* 41 (November/ December 1977): 585-587.

Cox, W. "Children's Map-reading Abilities with Large-scale Urban Maps." Doctoral dissertation. Madison: University of Wisconsin, 1977.

Crabtree, C. *Teaching Geography in Grades One through Three: Effects of Instruction in the Core Concept of Geographic Theory.* Project No. 5-1037. Washington: Department of Health, Education, and Welfare, Office of Education, 1968.

_____. *Children's Thinking Skills in the Social Studies.* Part 1: *Some Factors of Sequence and Transfer in Learning Skills of Geographic Analysis.* Los Angeles: University of California, 1974.

Dobkin, S. W., J. Fischer, B. Ludwig, and R. Kobliner, eds. *A Handbook for the Teaching of Social Studies.* 2d ed. Newton, Mass.: Allyn and Bacon, Inc., 1985.

Downey, M. "Teaching the History of Childhood." *Social Education* 50 (April/May 1986): 262-267.

Edwards, C. P. *Promoting Social and Moral Development in Young Children.* New York: Teachers College, Columbia, 1986.

Eslinger, M. V., and D. P. Superka. "Teachers." In *Social Studies in the 1980s: A Report of Project SPAN,* edited by Irving Morrissett. Alexandria, Va.: Association for Supervision and Curriculum Development, 1982.

Freeman, E., and L. Levstik. "Recreating the Past: Historical Fiction in the Social Studies Curriculum." *Elementary School Journal* 88, no. 14 (1988): 329-337.

Gander, M. J., and H. W. Gardiner. *Child and Adolescent Development.* Boston: Little, Brown and Co., 1981.

Geographic Education National Implementation Project (GENIP) Committee on K–6 Geography. *K–6 Geography: Themes, Key Ideas, and Learning Opportunities.* Washington, D.C.: Geographic Education National Implementation Project, 1987.

Goodlad, J. I. *A Place Called School.* New York: McGraw-Hill, 1984.

Greenstein, F. I. *Children and Politics.* New Haven, Conn.: Yale University Press, 1969.

Gross, R. E. "The Status of the Social Studies in the Public Schools of the United States: Fact and Impressions of a National Survey." *Social Education* 41 (November/December 1977): 574-579.

Hahn, C. L. "The Status of the Social Studies in the Public Schools of the United States: Another Look." *Social Education* 49 (March 1985): 220-223.

Hatcher, B. "Putting Young Cartographers 'On the Map.'" *Childhood Education* 59 (1983): 311-315.

Hess, R. D., and J.V. Torney. *The Development of Political Attitudes in Children.* Chicago: Aldine, 1967.

Hewes, D. W. "Preschool Geography: Developing a Sense of Self in Time and Space." *Journal of Geography* 81 (1982): 94-97.

Holmes Group. *Tomorrow's Teachers.* East Lansing, Mich.: Holmes Group, Inc., 1986.

Huck, Charlotte S., and Doris Young Kuhn. *Children's Literature in the Elementary School.* New York: Holt, Rinehart and Winston, 1968.

Jantz, R. K., and K. Klawiller. "Early Childhood/Elementary Social Studies: A Review of Recent Research." In *Review of Research in Social Studies Education: 1976-1983,* edited by W.B. Stanley. Washington, D.C.: National Council for the Social Studies, 1985.

Joyce, B. R. "Social Action for Primary Schools." *Childhood Education* 46, no. 5, 1970.

Katz, P. A. *Toward the Elimination of Racism.* New York: Pergamon Press, 1976.

Kennedy, K. J. "Assessing the Relationship between Information Processing Capacity and Historical Understanding." *Theory and Research in Social Education* 11, no. 2 (1983): 1-22.

Kohlberg, L. "This Special Section in Perspective." *Social Education* 40 (April 1976): 213-215.

Lanegran, D. A., J. G. Snowfield, and A. Lavent. "Retarded Children and the Concepts of Distance and Direction." *Journal of Geography* 69 (1970): 157-160.

Lengel, J. G., and D. P. Superka. "Curriculum Patterns." In *Social Studies in the 1980s. A Report of Project SPAN,* edited by Irving Morrissett. Alexandria, Va.: Association for Supervision and Curriculum Development, 1982.

Levstik, L. "The Relationship between Historical Response and Narrative in a Sixth Grade Classroom." *Theory and Research in Social Education* 41, no. 1 (1986): 1-15.

Levstik, L., and C. Pappas. "Exploring the Development of Historical Understanding." *Journal of Research and Development in Education* 21, no. 1 (1987): 1-15.

Liben, L. S., M. L. Moore, and S. L. Golbeck. "Preschooler's Knowledge of Their Classroom Environment: Evidence from Small-scale and Life-size Spatial Task." *Childhood Development* 53 (1982): 1275-1284.

Muessig, R. "An Analysis of Developments in Geographic Education." *The Elementary School Journal* 87, no. 5 (1987): 571-589.

NAEYC. "Position Statement on Developmentally Appropriate Practice in Early Childhood Programs Serving Children from Birth through Age 8." *Young Children* (September 1986): 4-19.

NCSS. "Standards for the Preparation of Social Studies Teachers." *Social Education* 52 (January 1988): 10-12.

Nelms, B. F. "Response and Responsibility: Reading, Writing, and Social Studies." *Elementary School Journal* 87, no. 5 (1987): 571-589.

Newmann, F. M. "Priorities for the Future: Toward a Common Agenda." *Social Education* 50 (April/May 1986): 240-250.

Park, D. C., and C. Q. James. "Effect of Encoding Instructions on Children's Spatial and Color Memory: Is There Evidence of Automaticity?" *Child Development* 54 (1983): 61-68.

Poster, J. B. "The Birth of the Past: Children's Perception of Historical Time." *History Teacher* (1973): 581-598.

Ragan, W., and J. McAulay. *Social Studies for Today's Children.* 2d ed. New York: Appleton-Century-Crofts, 1973.

Rice, M. J. *Educational Stimulation in the Social Studies: Analysis and Interpretation of Research.* Athens: Research and Development Center in Education Stimulation, University of Georgia, 1966.

Rice, M. J., and R. L. Cobb. *What Can Children Learn in Geography? A Review of the Research.* Boulder: SSEC, 1978.

Rosenzweig, L. *Developmental Perspectives on the Social Studies.* Bulletin 66. Washington, D.C.: National Council for the Social Studies, 1983.

Savage, T. S., Jr., and P. Bacon. "Teaching Symbolic Map Skills with Primary Grade Children." *Journal of*

Geography 68 (1969): 326-332.

Selman, R. L. "A Developmental Approach to Interpersonal and Moral Awareness in Young Children: Some Theoretical and Educational Implications of Levels of Social Perspective Taking. In *Values Education,* edited by J. Meyer, B. Barnham, and J. Cholvat. Waterloo, Ontario: Wilfrid Laurier University Press, 1975: 233-249.

Semaj, L. "The Development of Racial Evaluation and Preference: A Cognitive Approach." *Journal of Black Psychology* 6 (1980): 59-79.

Slavin, R. E. "Synthesis of Research on Cooperative Learning." *Educational Leadership* 38, no. 8 (1981): 655-659.

_____. "Cooperative Learning: Where Behavioral and Humanistic Approaches to Classroom Motivation Meet." *Elementary School Journal.* In press.

Stanley, W. B. *Review of Research in Social Studies Education: 1976-1983.* Washington, D.C.: National Council for the Social Studies, 1985.

Stone, L. C. "International and Multicultural Education." In *Elementary Social Studies: Research as a Guide to Practice,* edited by V. Atwood. Washington, D.C.: National Council for the Social Studies, 1986.

Thornton, S., and R. Vukelich. "Effects of Children's Understanding of Time Concepts on Historical Understanding." *Theory and Research in Social Education* (1988): 69-82.

Turiel, E. *The Development of Social Knowledge: Morality and Convention.* New Rochelle: Cambridge University Press, 1983.

VanderZanden, J. W. *Human Development.* New York: Alfred A. Knopf, 1985.

* Task Force

"Nucleus Committee"
Dorothy J. Skeel, Chair, Peabody College of Vanderbilt, Nashville, Tennessee
Virginia A. Atwood, University of Kentucky, Lexington, Kentucky
Buckley Barnes, Georgia State University, Atlanta, Georgia
Maria Cruz, Dade County Public Schools, Miami, Florida
Edith Guyton, Georgia State University, Atlanta, Georgia
Linda Levstik, University of Kentucky, Lexington, Kentucky
Patricia Van Decar, Georgia Southern College, Statesboro, Georgia

Members:
Susan Austin, Research for Better Schools, Philadelphia, Pennsylvania
Phyllis Clarke, Boulder Valley Public Schools, Boulder, Colorado
Carol Hamilton Cobb, Metropolitan Nashville Schools, Nashville, Tennessee
Lois "Frankie" Daniel, Millcreek Elementary School, Lexington, Kentucky
Francis Davis, Dougherty County Schools, Georgia
Wayne Dumas, University of Missouri, Columbia, Missouri
Judith M. Finkelstein, Price Laboratory School, Northern Iowa University, Cedar Falls, Iowa
Charles J. Fox, Kansas City Schools, Kansas City, Kansas
Michael Hartoonian, Wisconsin Department of Public Instruction, Madison, Wisconsin
Lillian G. Katz, University of Illinois, Champaign-Urbana, Illinois
Willard M. Kniep, Global Perspective in Education, Inc., New York, New York
Ellen Kronowitz, California State University, San Bernardino, California
Morris Lamb, Southern Illinois University at Carbondale
Margit McGuire, Seattle Pacific University, Seattle, Washington
Mabel McKinney-Browning, American Bar Association, Chicago, Illinois
Debra Miller, Belmont Street Community School, Worcester, Massachusetts
Charles Mitsakos, Winchester Public Schools, Winchester, Massachusetts
Raymond Muessig, Ohio State University, Columbus, Ohio
Jack Nelson, Rutgers University, New Brunswick, New Jersey
Mary Jacque Northup, Plainview Schools, Plainview, Texas
Anna S. Ochoa, Indiana University, Bloomington, Indiana
Linda W. Rosenzweig, Chatham College, Pittsburgh, Pennsylvania
Huber M. Walsh, University of Missouri-St. Louis, Missouri
Myra Zarnowski, Queens College, New York, New York

CHAPTER 1

ELEMENTARY SOCIAL STUDIES: CORNERSTONE OR CRUMBLING MORTAR?

Virginia A. Atwood

I know of no safe depository of the ultimate powers of the society but the people themselves; and if we think them not enlightened enough to exercise their control with a wholesome discretion, the remedy is not to take it from them, but to inform their discretion by education.

Thomas Jefferson
(Padover, 1939, pp. 89–90)

In 1979 the National Council for the Social Studies (NCSS) and 11 other professional associations collectively issued a statement to reaffirm the importance of a balanced curriculum. A catalyst for this hallmark effort was the public outcry that every child should complete school with knowledge of and competency in the basic skills. *The Essentials Statements* acknowledged the validity of the public's concern but challenged it to "reject simplistic solutions and declare a commitment to the essentials of education." Further, the statement argued that

a definition of the essentials of education should avoid three easy tendencies: to limit the essentials to "the three R's" in a society that is highly technological and complex; to define the essentials by what is tested at a time when tests are severely limited in what they can measure; and to reduce the essentials to a few "skills" when it is obvious that people use a combination of skills, knowledge, and feelings to come to terms with their world. By rejecting these simplistic tendencies, educators will avoid concentration on training in a few skills at the expense of preparing students for the changing world in which they must live. (p. 1)

The NCSS went a step further and specified the essentials of exemplary social studies programs that "[not only contribute] to the development of students' capacity to read and compute, but also link knowledge and skills with an understanding of and commitment to democratic principles and their application" (NCSS, 1981). Essentials were enumerated in five categories: knowledge, democratic beliefs, thinking skills, participation skills, and civic action. Through this statement, the NCSS reaffirmed its belief that effective programs must be

organized according to a professionally designed scope and sequence and must begin in preschool.

While this stance is not new, or unique to the NCSS, a great deal of evidence suggests that social studies is frequently not included in the elementary school curriculum, particularly in the primary grades. Indeed, Morrissett, Hawke, and Superka (1980) found that in some districts, K–3 social studies was literally fighting for existence. They concluded that the back-to-basics movement was the primary cause and noted that the public had not protested the de-emphasis of the social studies. Shaver, Davis, and Helburn (1978) agreed: "It seems clear that, particularly in the primary grades, both social studies and science are losing instructional time . . . because of the increasing emphasis on the 'basics,' defined as reading and arithmetic" (p. 8). A two-week conference of 55 social studies leaders yielded a broader list of causes, including: inadequate teacher preparation in the social science disciplines, inadequate inservice for incorporating social studies content, overcrowded curricula, school and district tests that do not include social studies learnings, and lack of enthusiasm for social studies on the part of administrators (Gross & Dynneson, 1980).

Others would blame the neglect of social studies in elementary schools on teacher preparation. In a later chapter in this bulletin, Weible and Dumas report that only 17 states require for certification instruction in methods and materials in teaching social studies. While some teacher education programs in the other 33 states presently have a social studies methods and materials requirement, many experienced elementary teachers in those states have never had such a course. Relatively few elementary teachers in the 50 states have been encouraged to participate in state and national social studies organizations. Perhaps the latter situation is largely the result of having instructors for the undergraduate social studies methods courses who themselves do not have advanced training in social studies education and are not active in the state and national councils. The net result is a message to elementary teacher education students that social studies is not very important.

Whatever the causes, or however prevalent the apathy, quality social studies—the kind described in *The Essentials Statements*—is, indeed, endangered in far too many elementary schools.

STATUS REPORTS

Gross (1977) acknowledged the difficulty of precisely determining the status of social studies in elementary schools, primarily because accurate breakdowns of time allotments do not exist. "Nevertheless," stated Gross, "in both our state and district responses [to questionnaires] we were informed over and over again that elementary teachers are backing away from the social studies" (p. 198). Informal reports from Montana and California indicated that 70 percent or more of K–4 teachers were doing little or nothing with social studies. Surveys of two school districts in Colorado revealed elementary teachers spent an average of only one hour per week in social studies instruction. Gross cited a Florida study (Prince, 1976) that found that less than half of the K–5 teachers surveyed regularly taught social studies. Hahn (1985) reassessed the status of social studies to determine if the generalizations drawn by Gross were still applicable. Her survey, conducted in the winter of 1982–83, confirmed a still-declining attention to social studies in elementary schools in 22 of 46 states represented in the study; in another 18 states, time spent on social studies remained at the 1975 level. Hahn concluded that "in general the answer to the question, 'How fares the social studies in elementary schools?' is 'Not well, especially in the primary grades' " (p. 220).

The problem of accurately assessing time spent on social studies instruction (Gross, 1977) is compounded when studying primary grades, particularly kindergartens. In addition to the perennial problem of definition, or what is included in social studies, many kindergarten teachers reportedly integrate social studies into other curriculum areas. A preliminary analysis of survey data for kindergarten teachers in Kentucky and Iowa indicated a large portion of teachers (Kentucky, 75 percent; Iowa, 60 percent) followed this practice, rather than scheduling a separate time block for social studies (Atwood & Finkelstein, 1986).

Jean Hutt (1985) presented a case study of a school district where elementary school principals and the superintendent proposed weekly time allotments for each subject area. At grades 1 and 2, social studies was allocated 75 minutes, the same amount of time allocated for spelling and listening, and only 15 minutes more than was allocated for vocal music and physical education. While the designated time for spelling increased in grades 3 through 6 to 125 minutes a week, it remained at 75 minutes for social studies in grades 3 and 4; equal time was given the two subjects in 5th and 6th grades.

In 1976, the National Science Foundation sponsored three related studies on the status of precollegiate social studies, mathematics and science education in the United States. Three different methodologies were used in the studies: a review of the literature, consisting primarily of a summary of previous reviews; a direct observation case study approach at eleven sites, with each site including a high school and its feeder schools; and a national survey of teachers and administrators. An NCSS task force subsequently reviewed these studies and prepared an interpretive report on the status and needs of social studies education (Shaver, Davis, & Helburn, 1978; see summary in Shaver, Davis, & Helburn, 1979). The NSF-sponsored studies seemed to place the responsibility for the status of elementary school social studies primarily on the classroom teacher.

> The reports remind us emphatically that the teacher is the key to what social studies will be for any student. The day-to-day classroom experiences of students emerge from teachers' beliefs about schooling and social studies in particular, their knowledge of the subject area and the available materials and techniques, and how they decide, consciously or not, to put these together for instruction. Teachers do not control budgets and so they have difficulty in introducing new programs that depend on financial expenditures. But they typically participate in the selection of textbooks and they are the arbiters of what goes on in their classrooms. They can, therefore, effectively veto curricular changes of which they do not approve. (Shaver, Davis, & Helburn, 1979, p. 151)

The NSF studies further concluded that social studies curricula consist primarily of content from history, government and geography at the elementary level, with large-group, teacher-controlled recitation and lecture being the dominant modes of instruction. Further, the studies revealed that teachers tend to perceive the textbook as the central instrument of instruction, source of knowledge and basis for testing. About 50 percent of the teachers surveyed reported using only one text, and approximately 20–35 percent reported using textbooks that were over five years old. Also, elementary teachers tended to view investigative teaching and learning as being too demanding of students at this level of intellectual development and self-discipline. "Instructional time is considered too valuable to squander by having students formulate problems and pursue answers. Moreover, teachers typically have experienced few models of inquiry teaching, in either pre-college or college courses" (Shaver, Davis, & Helburn, p. 151). Fifty to sixty percent of the teachers reported that help would be needed if inquiry teaching was to be implemented.

From students' perspective, according to the report by Shaver, Davis, and Helburn (1979), the content and mode of social studies instruction are generally uninteresting. It is not surprising, then, that teachers expressed concern about student apathy toward the subject. However, students apparently have not been expected to learn because of their own interest and curiosity, or because the knowledge and skills being taught were seen as useful for solving problems important to them. Rather, motivation has been expected to come from an awarding of grades, a desire for approval, or the belief that doing one's lessons is the thing to do at school. Teachers expressed concern that external factors such as these are no longer motivating students, if they ever did. Teachers expressed distress, too, that students are increasingly unwilling to accept authority or textbook "truths," or to complete assignments they believe are not worth doing. However, teachers did not seem to relate their own textbook/subject matter focus and passive learning by their students to the lack of student motivation. While students tended to be viewed as highly dependent learners by their teachers, aspirations of teachers for their students were apparently high. Shaver, Davis, and Helburn deduced that teachers were genuinely interested in their students' well-being and personally liked them.

Attitudes Toward Social Studies

Several investigators have surveyed students' subject preferences or attempted to determine correlates of student attitudes toward social studies. Greenblat (1962) asked 300 3rd, 4th and 5th graders to rank their favorite school subjects. Art, mathematics and reading ranked highest. Science, music and social studies shared an intermediate position of preference, followed by writing, language and health. However, statistically, student preferences for social studies were not significantly higher than for the least preferred subjects or significantly lower than for art, mathematics and reading.

A study of correlates of attitudes toward social studies by Haladyna, Shaughnessy, and Redsun (1982) included 1800 students in grades 4, 7 and 9. Since minorities were underrepresented in the sample, the authors cautioned against generalizing the results to minority students. For the 4th grade sample, the variable most highly related to attitudes toward social studies was the students' view of the importance of the subject matter. Frequency of class projects or work sessions was also highly positively related. Fatalism (e.g., "I'm not the type to do well in social studies") and self-confidence in one's ability to learn social studies were moderately related to attitudes about social studies. Teacher variables had a low to moderate correlation to student attitudes toward social studies, with teacher enthusiasm for the subject being the most positively correlated.

The significance of students' assessment of the importance of the subject is supported in a study by Schug, Todd, and Beery (1984). A midwestern school district was chosen for a "best case" approach to investigate student attitudes toward social studies. As part of that study, 23 6th graders and 23 high school seniors were interviewed. Seventeen percent of the students judged social studies to be their most important subject, while 31 percent chose English. Mathematics and reading were each rated most important by 20 percent of the students, and 11 percent judged science to be the most important. Almost half (48 percent) of the 6th graders gave career preparation as the reason a particular subject was chosen as most important. Another 37 percent ranked a subject as most important because they thought it provided skills important to their future lives.

Shug et al. also asked students to identify their favorite subject and their least favorite subject. While only 11 percent of the students interviewed indicated that social studies was their favoriate subject, only 15 percent mentioned it as their least favorite. Mathematics and English topped the list of favorite subjects and the list of least favorite subjects. Primary reasons that students gave for preferring a particular subject were that they enjoyed the subject (57 percent) and they were "good at it" (30 percent). Relative to other subjects, then, it would seem that social studies is judged to lack importance, while not being particularly enjoyable or difficult. When students were asked what they found interesting about social studies, 48 percent of the 6th graders identified the study of the past, and 35 percent identified the study of other cultures. These responses should be viewed in the context of the typical 6th grade social studies curriculum, which is a study of cultures around the world—past and present.

Why were the favorite subjects of students more interesting than social studies? A total of 35 percent said that there was more opportunity in the former for active learning. Another 17 percent said there was more variety in these subjects. Note that these responses seem to reflect more on teaching strategies than on the content being taught. When asked what they found uninteresting about social studies classes, 44 percent said the classes were boring and 18 percent commented on the redundancy in the program.

The point that social studies curricula contain undesirable repetition or unneeded instruction was recognized by Rice two decades ago (1966). In reviewing research conducted from 1955 to 1965, he found that children had substantial knowledge of social studies content prior to instruction. For example, 2nd graders' knowledge of content ranged from 33 percent to more than 84 percent before instruction.

Summary of Status Reports

The available published reports (some of which are somewhat dated) on social studies instruction in elementary schools provide a depressing picture. Indications are that social studies is often not taught in elementary schools. When it is taught, all too often the major thrust seems to be toward transmitting low-level information from history, geography and government. Lecture and recitation involving class-size groups tend to dominate. Inquiry is likely to be considered too time consuming, potentially disruptive, and too demanding of students. Not surprisingly, students tend to view social studies as being of little importance or use. Further, they tend to find it uninteresting—even boring.

While status surveys provide information about the majority of classrooms, they frequently fail to uncover pockets of excellence. Any social studies educator can identify elementary teachers in his or her geographic area who teach social studies regularly and make it challenging and exciting for students. Such teachers' strategies are frequently dominated by investigative activities that focus on major concepts and problem-solving skills. Observations of these classrooms suggest that students find the experience both interesting and relevant. A challenge to the profession is to encourage these persons and increase their number.

Additionally, the intensive attention currently being given to education will likely cause changes. The effects of the "reforms" are difficult to predict and will need to be carefully monitored.

SOCIAL STUDIES FOR YOUNG CHILDREN

Should social studies be an integral part of the elementary school curriculum? What is its raison d'être? These questions may be answered on two levels: (1)

What is the rationale for teaching this subject; that is, what are the expected educational outcomes? (2) Why is it important to begin social studies experiences and studies at an early age?

Expected Educational Outcomes

The literature is replete with debates about the definition and goals of social studies. Joyce and Alleman-Brooks' (1980) argument is typical: "Obvious explanation for the decline of the social studies [is] our reluctance to reach even nominal agreement regarding the identity of this school subject" (p. 61). Yet, their survey of authors of elementary social studies methods textbooks provided somewhat contradictory data by showing a "high incidence of agreement regarding the significance of many of these goals" (p. 65).

Joyce and Alleman-Brooks point out that even coauthors of texts did not always agree. An example given from one author was: "Social studies is the familiarization of the world in terms of past and present social and physical phenomena that affect the planet's inhabitants"; and from the coauthor: "Social studies is a skill combined multidisciplinary field drawing upon the social sciences and related areas with a major focus upon contemporary problems vital to children, youth, and society" (p. 68). While these two statements are not synonymous, one can argue that they are more consistent than contradictory. One can point out, for example, that social and physical phenomena that affect the planet's inhabitants surely include contemporary problems vital to people and society. Or, if one is to become familiar with past and present social and physical phenomena that affect people of the world, multidisciplinary content and skills will likely be utilized.

How much *real* discord exists in the profession over definition, and how much is a semantic game—a game in which teachers have little interest? Is the debate over definition and goals to blame for the status of social studies in schools? Is a "lack of agreement" on specific goals for social studies ultimately a factor in determining student preference for the subject? Are most classroom teachers even *aware* of a debate?

On the other hand, perhaps the long quest for a profession-wide definition of social studies is functional. Shaver (1977) defended the exercise when he argued that "the definitions we attach to terms do affect how we think. In that sense, definitions are often persuasive. Word meanings lead us to believe and to act in certain ways" (p. 114). In the Foreword to Barr, Barth, and Shermis' important and comprehensive document *Defining the Social Studies* (1977), former NCSS president Howard Mehlinger posits that social studies

> has also profited from the lively intellectual debate that the identity crisis has provoked among social studies disciples. On balance, who can say whether the field would have been better served if no identity crisis had existed or whether the inability to resolve the primary question—what is social studies—has kept the field alive, flexible, and responsive to changes in society? (p. iii)

After patiently exploring and observing the field for several years, Barr, Barth, and Shermis (1977) began to describe similarities and repetition in conceptions of the social studies. They concluded that:

the field of social studies has reached a point in its evolution where it is possible to develop a definition of the social studies comprehensive enough to include all factors in the field, and yet flexible enough to permit differentiation of various points of view. The authors are prepared to argue that, far from a seamless web of illogical inconsistencies, there is logic and order to the field and that there are sufficient areas of agreement at least to attempt a generic definition. (p. 10)

They further maintained that "there is now general agreement that the primary, overriding purpose of the social studies is citizenship education" (p. 67), and there is also "fairly concrete agreement in the field on the basic objectives required to achieve good citizenship" (p. 68). The required components include: knowledge, information-processing skills, values and beliefs, and social participation.

Considering these components individually, most people in the field, according to Barr et al., accept that the knowledge base for the social studies will be drawn from the social sciences, the humanities, and other areas concerned with the human condition—past, present and future.

Most social studies educators—indeed, educators in general—believe that information-processing skills are needed to acquire, organize, interpret and evaluate information (Barr et al., 1977). The "Essentials" statement (1981) also includes decision-making and interpersonal skills, which are in the information-processing domain.

Although some parents and lay people still express concern about which values and beliefs are taught to children and how they are taught, Barr et al. contend that most people in the field believe that there are identifiable processes for examining values and these process skills should be taught in schools. The NCSS goes a step further and identifies democratic beliefs as an essential; "exemplary school programs do not indoctrinate students to accept these ideas blindly, but present knowledge about their historical derivation and contemporary application essential to understanding our society and its institutions" (NCSS, 1981, p. 163).

The fourth area of agreement found by Barr, Barth, and Shermis was social participation, applying what has been learned and what is believed to the actual participatory activities. This component reflects the belief that civic participation can and should be taught in schools.

In *The Decline of Democracy* (1978) Ralph Buultjens seemed to concur. In this work, he attributed the decline, in part, to a weakness in education. He asserted, "There is little continuing or serious concern for educating students or citizens about the condition or the responsibilities of democracy" (p. x). It becomes clear that social studies teachers must recognize the importance of teaching students to be effective social and civic participants. In what other field are professionals as able to provide students with the knowledge and skills to become good citizens? Social studies educators are in the best position to help accomplish this important and broad purpose of education. Furthermore, the work must begin early if it is to be highly successful.

Early Education

While the work of developmentalists, like Piaget, emphasizes the importance of early learning generally, research also supports early instructional experiences that teach specific concepts, skills and attitudes to young children. In an 18-year follow-up study, Lozar and Darlington (1982) found that enrichment of early childhood programs for low socioeconomic children resulted in the following long-lasting effects: increased school competence, development of abilities, more favorable attitudes toward school, higher staying power in school, and positive impacts on families of these children.

In a publication cited previously, Rice (1966) reviewed a decade of social studies literature pertinent to the hypothesis that "early and continuous intellectual stimulation of children, age 3 through 12, through structured sequential learning activities will result in higher levels of ultimate achievement than would otherwise be obtained" (p. 1). He concluded that "children can learn more difficult and abstract social studies content at an earlier level than is represented in the traditional social studies curriculum" (p. 3). Rice cited a large-sample survey of children in grades 2 through 8 that indicated that political attitudes are formed prior to the time formal instruction in government usually occurs. These findings suggest that elementary school years are more important for citizenship training than previously thought. Research on attitudes about race (Katz, 1976; 1983; Kleinke & Nicholson, 1979; Semaj, 1980), gender equity (Reilly, 1979; Butzin, 1982), and government and government workers (Greenstein, 1969; Hess & Torney, 1967) also supports the need to give early attention to the goals of social studies.

Cognizant of the condition of social studies education and attentive to "desired states," Morrissett, Superka, and Hawke (1980) urged "state and local social studies councils and state department of education personnel [to] press for state and local requirements for social studies instruction [with] special emphasis . . . placed on strengthening elementary-level social studies programs" (p. 576). Knight (1978) went a step further and insisted that teachers with the highest level of competence should instruct the child in initial school experiences, and that primary teachers should receive the greatest rewards in order to attract the best talent. Otherwise, he argued, the eagerness and confidence of children beginning school will dissolve into disenchantment and disrespect.

Thus, not only should social studies be salvaged, but a high quality program should begin in the early childhood years. Considering the need for a viable social studies program for young children that begins the preparation for effective citizenship, and the status of social studies at the elementary level, a reexamination of what social studies should be taught at this level, and how it should be taught, seems warranted.

BASIS FOR CURRICULUM DECISIONS

A group of elementary school teachers enrolled in a graduate curriculum class were asked to identify the factors they used to decide what to teach and how to teach it. Responses were candid and included: the teacher next door, tradition, expediency, state-mandated basic skills tests, pressure from parents, adopted textbooks, cost, the time needed to plan and develop materials, and potential management problems. After being cued that perhaps more idealistic factors should also be taken into account, additional responses included: developmental and social needs of the children, anticipated future needs of society, learning styles of the children, interests of the children and teacher, and current events. In what seemed to be an afterthought, one teacher added "research findings" to the list.

While each of these factors, at one time or another, may provide some basis for choosing a particular topic, instructional strategy, or set of instructional materials, some have more potential for contributing to a sound program and should be more consistently employed in curriculum decision making. Much has been written, for example, verifying developmental stages of cognitive and social growth, and demonstrating the legitimacy of planning learning experiences consistent with these stages (see, for example, Bybee & Sund, 1982; Labinowicz, 1980; Wadsworth, 1978). Research reports and reviews of research have the potential to inform educators about the probable effectiveness of particular strategies, organizational patterns, and space and time utilization (see, for example, Atwood & Leitner, 1985; Medley, 1979; Rowe, 1974; Rosenshine, 1976). However, instructional and curricular decision making is a multifarious problem. As Barclay (1983b) notes:

> We have overwhelming knowledge that the effects of intelligence, socio–economic status, and effort and motivation are strongly influenced by psychological support systems within the learning environment. Specifically, we know that success in academic learning is less likely when a student's environment is characterized by failure, fear, anxiety, and defeat. (p. 230)

Aptitude, past performance, learning style, academic self–confidence and a number of other variables unique to individuals likely affect learning also. While this bulletin does not focus on research into these variables, it is important to note that research related to children learning social studies has typically looked at groups rather than individuals. Results of research on groups of children should be considered along with research data on individual children in order to make the best decisions about individual children's curricular and instructional needs. The seminal work by Barclay (1983a; 1983b) has been particularly fecund in developing a model that enables educators to match intervention strategies with functional needs and characteristics of individual children.

And what about research on how to teach specific knowledge, concepts, and skills in elementary social studies? How adequate is the research base? How useful is it to teachers and curriculum developers? While it has been suggested that classroom teachers are "not much aware of educational research" (Shaver, Davis, & Helburn, 1978, p. 19), Shaver (1979) declared that "teachers are losing little in decision–making power by their inattention to the research literature" (p. 27).

In fact, several sources have suggested that research in social studies is in disarray (Shaver, Davis, & Helburn, 1978; Shaver, 1979; Herman, 1980). The most frequent criticisms include: a lack of systematic research programs and cumulative studies; lack of replication of promising studies; and too little variation of research methodologies in studies that address the same type of questions.

While these criticisms are not groundless, we now know more about how to optimize learning than we have ever known before. Rather than ignoring the limited research base that exists, a more productive approach would be to pull together the results of related studies, compare results, attempt to explain or further investigate conflicting findings, tentatively draw implications for practice based on existing research, and identify research questions most in need of study.

Herman (1980) outlined four reasons why an adequate research base is needed in social studies education:

- Research tests conjectures.
- Research promotes improvement.
- Research stimulates additional research.
- Research lends credence to a field.

When a reservoir of research findings exists in the field of law, medicine, agriculture, or [other] human endeavor, that field enjoys more confidence and respect from both those inside and outside the field than enterprises like witch-doctoring and fortune-telling with inadequate research bases. The social studies desperately needs the confidence supplied by a research base. (pp. 27–28)

The major purpose of this bulletin is to acknowledge and examine the existing research base—to answer the question: What do we know about what and how children learn in social studies? The authors have done more than merely summarize the research literature. They have attempted to clarify, to highlight particularly salient findings, to identify significant incompatible conclusions, and to register concerns about the research base reviewed. They also have attempted—cautiously, I think—to draw implications from the research for classroom teachers, teacher educators and curriculum developers.

This endeavor is viewed as an important step in removing elementary social studies from the endangered list. It is considered an important step in achieving the major goal of providing children with opportunities to develop the knowledge, information-processing skills and beliefs requisite to participatory citizenship.

REFERENCES

Atwood, V. A., & Finkelstein, J. M. (1986). *Social studies in kindergarten: A status report.* Manuscript submitted for publication.

Atwood, V. A., & Leitner, J. T. (1985). Time and space: Tools for effective teaching. *Education, 106,* 15–21.

Barclay, J. R. (1983a). A meta-analysis of temperament-treatment interactions with alternative learning and counseling treatments. *Developmental Review, 3,* 410–443.

Barclay, J. R. (1983b). Moving toward a technology of prevention: A model and some tentative findings. *School Psychology Review, 12,* 228–239.

Barr, R. D., Barth, J. L., & Shermis, S. S. (1977). *Defining the social studies.* Arlington, VA: NCSS.

Barth, J. L. (1983). *Elementary and junior high/middle school social studies curriculum activities and materials* (2nd ed.). Lanham, MD: University Press of America.

Butzin, S. M. (1982). Learning experiences to promote sex equity. *Social Education, 46,* 48–53.

Buultjens, R. (1978). *The decline of democracy.* Maryknoll: Orbis Books.

Bybee, R. W., & Sund, R. B. (1982). *Piaget for educators* (2nd ed.). Columbus: Charles E. Merrill.

Greenblat, E. L. (1962). An analysis of school subject preferences of elementary school children of the middle grades. *The Journal of Educational Research, 55,* 554–556.

Greenstein, F. I. (1969). *Children and politics.* New Haven, CT: Yale University Press.

Gross, R. E. (1977). The status of the social studies in the public schools of the United States: Facts and impressions of a national survey. *Social Education, 41,* 194–205.

Gross, R. E., & Dynneson, T. L. (1980). Regenerating the social studies: From old dirges to new directions. *Social Education, 44,* 370–374.

Hahn, C. L. (1985). The status of the social studies in the public schools of the United States: Another look. *Social Education, 49* (3), 220–223.

Haladyna, T., Shaughnessy, J., & Redsun, A. (1982). Correlates of attitudes toward social studies. *Theory and Research, 10,* 1–26.

Herman, W. L. (1980). Toward a more adequate base in social studies education. *Journal of Research and Development in Education, 13,* 24–35.

Hess, R. D., & Torney, J. V. (1967). *The development of political attitudes in children.* Chicago: Aldine.

Hutt, J. (1985). In defense of social studies: A case study. *Social Education, 49,* 312–314.

Joyce, W. W., & Alleman-Brooks, J. (1980). Resolving the identity crisis in elementary and middle school social studies. *Journal of Research and Development in Education, 13,* 60–71.

Katz, P. A. (1983). Developmental foundations of gender and racial attitudes. In R. Leahy (Ed.), *The child's construction of social inequality.* New York: Academic Press.

Katz, P. A. (1976). *Towards the elimination of racism.* New York: Pergamon Press, Inc.

Kleinke, C. L., & Nicholson, T. A. (1979). Black and white children's awareness of de facto race and sex differences. *Developmental Psychology, 15,* 84–86.

Knight, G. R. (1978). Reschooling society: A new road to Utopia. *Phi Delta Kappan, 60,* 289–91.

Labinowicz, E. (1980). *The Piaget primer.* Menlo Park, CA: Addison-Wesley.

Lazar, I., & Darlington, R. (1982). Lasting effects of early education: A report from the consortium for longitudinal studies. *Monographs of the Society for Research in Child Development, 47,* 1–151.

Medley, D. M. (1979). The effectiveness of teachers. In P. L. Peterson and H. J. Walbery (Eds.), *Research on teaching* (pp. 11–27). Berkeley, CA: McCutchan.

Morrissett, I. (Ed.). (1982). *Social studies in the 1980's.* Alexandria, VA: ASCD.

Morrissett, I., Superka, D. P., & Hawke, S. (1980). Recommendations for improving social studies in the 1980's. *Social Education, 44,* 570, 576–653.

National Council for the Social Studies. (1981). Essentials of the social studies. *Social Education, 45,* 163–164.

National Council for the Social Studies. (1980). *Essentials of education statement.* Washington, DC: Author.

Padover, S. K. (Ed.). (1939). *Thomas Jefferson on democracy.* New York: The New American Library.

Piaget, J. (1964). Development and learning. In R. E. Ripple and V. N. Rockcastle (Eds.). *Piaget rediscovered* (pp. 1–5). New York: Cornell University Press.

Prince, F. L. (1976). Social studies in comparison with other subjects in the elementary grades, a survey of teacher attitudes. *Trends in Social Education,* 26–30.

Rice, M. J. (1966). *Educational stimulation in the social studies: Analysis and interpretation of research.* Athens, GA: Research and Development Center in Educational Stimulation, University of Georgia.

Rice, M. J., & Cobb, R. L. (1978). *What can children learn in geography?* Boulder: SSEC, Inc.

Rosenshine, B. (1976). *Recent research on teaching behaviors and student achievement.* Unpublished paper. University of Illinois, Bureau of Educational Research.

Rowe, M. B. (1974). Relation of wait-time and rewards to the development of language, logic, and fate control: Part II—Rewards. *Journal of Research in Science Technology, 2,* 291–308.

Schug, M. C., Todd, R. J., & Beery, R. (1984). Why kids don't like social studies. *Social education, 48,* 382–387.

Semaj, L. T. (1980). The development of racial evaluation and preference: A cognitive approach. *Journal of Black Psychology, 6,* 59–79.

Shaver, J. P. (1977). Comments of James P. Shaver. In R. D. Barr, J. L. Barth, & S. S. Shermis (Eds.), *Defining the social studies* (pp. 114–117). Arlington, VA: NCSS.

Shaver, J. P. (1979). The usefulness of educational research in curricular/instructional decision-making in social studies. *Theory and Research in Social Education, 7* (3), 21–43.

Shaver, J. P., Davis, O. L., & Helburn, S. W. (1978). *An interpretive report on the status of pre-college social studies education based on three NSF-funded studies.* Washington, DC: NCSS.

Shaver, J. P., Davis, O. L., & Helburn, S. W. (1979). The status of social studies education: Impressions from three NSF studies. *Social Education, 43,* 150–153.

Wadsworth, B. J. (1978). *Piaget for the classroom teacher.* New York: Longman.

CHAPTER 2

CITIZENSHIP AND LAW-RELATED EDUCATION

Walter C. Parker and Theodore Kaltsounis

Interviewer: How do you become a Republican?
Child: Like if Reagan wanted you to be *his* Republican, he would want you to come to the Republican party.
Interviewer: How would he let you know he wanted you to be a Republican?
Child: Maybe from his speeches, or call you up. He would want you to come to *his* party and not someone else's.
Interviewer: What kind of party is it?
Child: Probably like a long table with a feast on it.

(Abraham, 1983)

Defined broadly, citizenship education includes the whole school curriculum and is the school's reason for being. The founders of our "democratic experiment" were convinced that the welfare of the republic was contingent upon a citizenry that was literate, knowledgeable about political institutions and processes, and committed to democratic values. Professor R. Freeman Butts (1979) put it this way:

Universal education was not primarily to serve the self-fulfillment of individuals, or to develop the mind for its own sake, or to prepare for a job, or to get into college. . . . The most fundamental purpose of universal schooling is the political goal of empowering the whole population to exercise the rights and cope with the responsibilities of a genuinely democratic citizenry. (p. 359)

Of course, schools are not society's sole agency of citizenship education. The family, church, media, and ethnic and occupational groups also play an important role. Nevertheless, schools are virtually the only structured source of citizenship education in the community. And, within the schools, social studies is the one subject area that has citizenship education as its stated, central focus (Barr, Barth, & Shermis, 1977; Shaver, 1977).

We can no longer be innocent, however, about the relationship of schools to the broader society in which they are embedded. Researchers in what is called "the new sociology of education" (e.g., Apple, 1982; Anyon, 1979; Bourdieu & Passeron, 1977; Willis, 1977) have demonstrated quite well the subordination of citizenship education in schools to potent forces of social and cultural reproduction. Consequently, a formal citizenship education program in schools,

while espousing the noble objectives of which Butts speaks, will not easily overcome the more pervasive, covert citizenship education program that helps perpetuate current social practices and beliefs.

Because citizenship in the elementary school is related intricately to the broader society, elementary teachers, as citizenship educators, are unavoidably *sociopolitical actors.* As such, they must wrestle with the stand they want to take toward the status quo. Shall they seek, through their citizenship education curriculum, to conserve the present state of affairs? Transcend it? Neither? Both? Similarly, authors of research syntheses, like ourselves, must wrestle with their stand, for there is no neutral ground.

We have chosen in this chapter to define the aim of citizenship education as the cultivation of the kind of citizen needed to meet the challenge of fulfilling the democratic experiment. This citizen, whom we shall call a "democratic citizen" (Parker & Jarolimek, 1984), is informed; skilled in forming, using, and critiquing knowledge claims; skilled in interpersonal communication and civic participation; committed to democratic values; and willing—even feeling compelled—to participate in democratic processes. Speaking more broadly, we see the aim as being the cultivation of the kind of citizen who, as in the classic Greek definition of citizenship education, is committed to intelligent, ethical, and active participation in civic life.

The democratic citizen's participation in public life is shaped by conditions and assumptions that require the individual to nurture and maintain three different types of perspectives. The first is a global perspective. From this perspective, one's thinking and loyalties are international as well as local and national. One understands interdependence, and that one's commitment to "liberty and justice for all" extends to people everywhere. The second is a pluralistic perspective. From this perspective, one regards cultural diversity within and among societies, as well as differences of opinion among people, as an acceptable, even desirable, fact of contemporary life. The third is a constructive or critical perspective. From this perspective, one perceives democracy as unfinished business, a process, a vision yet unfolding; consequently, the democratic citizen constantly examines the congruence of existing practices with democratic ideals and seeks to close the gaps.[1]

Another important dimension of citizenship education concerns law and the way individuals at various developmental levels relate to it. A good deal of interest in law-related education has been generated in the last several years, and a variety of classroom materials has been developed (Anderson, 1980). In this report, law-related education is addressed in the context of the developing citizen's conception of justice.

A great deal of research is relevant to the development of democratic citizens, including research addressed to law-related education. Consequently, it is not possible in one chapter to undertake an exhaustive review. A narrowed focus is necessary. To accomplish this, major studies were selected for review that fall into four areas of research and that are considered to be central to the study of citizenship education and most helpful to elementary teachers who want to cultivate democratic citizenship in their students:
- political socialization
- cognitive development
- moral development
- classroom climate.

Since this publication is addressed to practitioners, the end of the chapter expands on the implications of research for classroom practice and describes tested programs on citizenship and law-related education.

RESEARCH ON POLITICAL SOCIALIZATION

Political socialization is the process by which individuals develop a political identity composed of political perspectives, beliefs, knowledge, skills, and behaviors. Research has revealed regularities in this process that bear directly on the cultivation of democratic citizens. Most importantly, this research shows that a person's political identity is learned, that this learning begins before a child enters kindergarten, and that it progresses rapidly during the elementary years and continues into adulthood.

A seminal study of political learning on children (Greenstein, 1969) included over 600 4th through 8th grade students in New Haven, Connecticut schools. A paper-and-pencil questionnaire administered in the children's classrooms indicated that the children idealized political authorities and considered them benevolent. This was an emotional tie reserved primarily for the president and the mayor. This indiscriminate affection decreased as the children progressed from 4th to 8th grade. However, while idealization of authorities was decreasing with grade level, political knowledge was increasing. The 4th graders' affection for the president and mayor was accompanied by virtually no political information; but, by the 8th grade, the children had become "reasonably well informed about the major political institutions" (Greenstein, p. 55). The pattern was clear: The higher the child's grade, the more accurate the information the child possessed and the less idealized the view of political authorities.

Though older children were far more informed, only a small proportion of them had any sort of orientation—that is, any consistent, philosophic frame of reference from which issues could be judged. Only six percent of the 8th graders were able to generate the kinds of responses that might be given by adults, such as "The Republicans are for the rich people," and "The Democrats are too free with money" (Greenstein, 1969, p. 69). In spite of the lack of orientation among even the 8th graders, it is interesting that over half of the children at every grade identified with a political party. Greenstein explains this phenomenon the same way he explains children's idealization of political authorities:

> Here, as in children's assessments of the importance of political roles, we find that political feelings, evaluations, and attachments form well before the child learns the relevant supporting information. (p. 72)

Another ground-breaking study of children's political learning supports the key findings in the Greenstein study. Hess and Torney (1967) administered a questionnaire to some 12,000 children, grades 2 through 8, in eight cities across the United States. Like Greenstein, these researchers focused on children's beliefs and their acquisition. They also found that young children's involvement in the political system begins with strong, emotional ties to the country, governmental institutions, and political roles. The president is the major political authority in the child's developing political identity and is regarded personally as one who can provide individualized assistance to people by telephone or visits to the White House. Hess and Torney found the police officer more important in the child's world than the mayor. The officer is well liked and is regarded as personally "nurturant"—a helper in times of trouble.

Children's trust in the benevolence of the political system was expressed also by their view that the citizen's chief responsibility is to be a good person. As children grew older, the good citizen was also expected to vote and express interest in political issues. The sense of personal efficacy and the belief that the individual does make a difference, particularly through voting, increased with age. The children viewed conflict among government leaders and politicians as undesirable and

> by the end of the eighth grade, children have developed a sense of the need for consensus and majority rule in democratic processes. Typically, they have not recognized the role of debate, disagreement, and conflict in the operation of a democratic political system. (Hess & Torney, 1967, p. 216)

The findings of these and other studies of the development of children's political identities tend to hold firm even through major political upheavals such as those that occurred in the 1960s and the Watergate scandal. While trust in political authorities decreased markedly among adult citizens during this turbulent period, the benevolent leader phenomenon was sustained for 2nd through 4th grade students (Dawson, Prewitt, & Dawson, 1969). This supports the general notion that children must reach a particular level of development in order to cope better with the political information and become more aware of the political environment.

A summary of the research on children's political learning includes the following:

1. Political learning begins early and continues through early childhood, late childhood, and adolescence.
2. Different types of political learning take place at different points over the pre-adult years.
3. Basic attachments and identifications are among the first political outlooks to be acquired.
4. Early orientations toward political authorities seem to be indiscriminately positive and benevolent. They become less so as the child moves through late childhood and into adolescence.
5. Early conceptions of politics and government are highly personalized. The government, the president, the mayor, and other elements are understood initially in personal terms. This personalization fades and is replaced by more abstract perceptions by late childhood and early adolescence.
6. Affective orientations, or feelings, about political objects seem to be acquired before information or knowledge. One has feelings about the nation and the president (usually positive feelings) before one has much understanding of their functions.
7. During late childhood, children acquire information and knowledge about the political world. They begin to distinguish between different political roles and acquire the basic factual information needed to map out the political world.
8. During adolescence, individuals increase their capacity to deal with abstractions and to engage in ideological thinking and ends-means analysis. They become more interested in following political events and more involved in partisan and electoral politics (Dawson et al., 1969, pp. 59–60).

The understanding of children's citizenship learning provided by these initial studies has been expanded in recent years by researchers who approach the subject from a cognitive developmental perspective as well as by those who study the relationship of citizenship learning to classroom climate. We turn first to the cognitive developmental point of view.

RESEARCH ON COGNITIVE DEVELOPMENT

Research conducted by developmental psychologists is relevant to understanding the process by which qualities of democratic citizenship develop and, therefore, to the planning of curriculum and instruction. Jean Piaget (1928) was the seminal thinker among these developmental psychologists. Briefly, his research revealed that an individual's cognitive development progresses through a sequence of four stages: the sensorimotor stage (birth to 1½–2 years); the preoperational stage (1½–2 to 5–6 years); the concrete operational stage (6–7 to 10–11 years); and the formal operational stage (beginning at 11–12 years). Piaget maintained that each stage is a qualitatively distinct thought system—an integrated, whole world view. The stages are hierarchically arranged with each succeeding stage representing a more complex, inclusive, and powerful system of thinking. The stages form an invariant sequence of development. No one ever skips a stage, although development through the stages can be slowed or halted altogether.[2]

What enables an individual to progress satisfactorily through the stages to the formal operational level? Active experience and social interaction expose the individual to disequilibrating events (intellectual conflicts) from which the only satisfying "escape" is cognitive development; that is, the only resolution is through the construction of a wholly different intellectual structure. Thus, the conflicts inherent in interaction with the people and events in the growing child's environment stimulate a search for more effective ways to think about the world. In this view, children's minds develop as they interact with a stimulating environment. Through the process of assimilation and accommodation, knowledge is constructed by children as they act on the environment; intellectual development therefore takes place as a function of an individual's own constructive activity.

Failure to develop to the formal operational stage limits seriously a citizen's ability to understand the social world and participate intelligently in democratic processes. Citizens whose thinking develops only to the concrete operational stage can solve concrete but not abstract problems. They are limited therefore to thinking about the present, the known, the actual. Citizens thinking at the formal level are emancipated from this cognitive restraint. They can solve hypothetical, abstract problems that exist only in words, or in the future. They can focus on the *processes* of problem solving and data gathering, whereas their concrete counterparts cannot separate structure from content.

There is a general agreement among developmental psychologists that the development of political understandings corresponds to the Piagetian description of intellectual growth. Consequently, political understandings during the concrete and formal operational periods are predictably different in ways that reflect the distinct characteristics of these two stages of thought. For example, Siegel (1977) studied the development of children's concepts of justice and law. A questionnaire was administered to 450 black and white children ranging in age from eight to sixteen years; it asked about the children's reactions to the assassination of Martin Luther King, Jr. Responses to each of the questions revealed formal operational thinking by the older children. In response to the question "When the killer is found, how do you think he should be treated?" the older children indicated that the killer should receive a fair trial and be punished according to the law. The younger children, however, thought the killer should receive specific, often extralegal punishment—for example, the killer should be "turned over to the Negroes and let them take care of him," or "Let Mrs. King kill him," or "Dr. King was killed by him so the same thing should happen to him."

In response to questions like "Why do you think Dr. King was shot?" and "What made the person do it?" the older children more often gave political responses (e.g., "He was killed because he tried to do something for the Negroes."); while the younger, concrete-operational thinkers more often personalized the shooting, assigning motives to the killer (e.g., "He hated King," or "Because a riot might have went on in his neighborhood and wrecked his home and he thought Dr. King started it."). Specific punishments and personal motives are concrete representations of the event; the idea of justice mediated through a fair trial or political ideology is abstract. Siegel concluded that "both the development of the understanding of law and the increasing depersonalization of events and motives represent the growth of the child's ability to form abstractions about the political process" (p. 285).

In another study (Adelson, Green, & O'Neil, 1969), 5th, 7th, 9th, and 12th grade students were asked to imagine they were in a specific situation and then to make and justify a number of decisions about law, justice, and political authority. The older children were able to respond to aspects of their situation abstractly, while the younger children responded concretely, almost literally. Younger students usually emphasized the constraining and coercive side of the law—the side that kept people from committing cruel, antisocial acts. Older students were more likely to emphasize the beneficial, socially constructive side of the law. For example, when asked "What is the purpose of laws?" an 11-year-old responded, "Well, so everybody won't fight, and they have certain laws so they won't go around breaking windows and stuff and getting away with it." A 15-year-old responded. "To help keep us safe and free."

Given this dramatic developmental progression in political understandings between early childhood and late adolescence, two important concerns emerge for citizenship eduation in the elementary school years. First, how can learning activities be matched appropriately to the cognitive stages of students so that learning is maximized? Second, how can the transition from preoperational to concrete to formal thinking be facilitated (or at least not arrested)?

In an attempt to better understand each of these stages and, particularly, the nature of the cognitive reorganization involved in the transitions from one to the next, Abraham (1983) interviewed 3rd, 4th and 5th grade students about political party identification. The predictable differences in stage-related thinking were present. A concrete response to the question "Are all boys and girls in the world Republicans?" was "No, some can be born Republican, and some can be born Democrat." A response indicating transition to abstract thought was, "No, people have different beliefs."

However, Abraham (1983) found an interesting phenomenon as children move through the concrete operational period. Though considerable change in political thinking takes place between the 3rd and 5th grades, "this change does not occur in steady, grade-incremental progressions" (p. 227). Instead, a "back-and-forth" pattern characterized the movement of children through this period. On some questions, 4th and 5th graders tended to score at a lower cognitive level than 3rd graders, indicating alternating states of progression and regression during this period. Abraham speculates that this alternation reflects the dynamic state of these students' political thinking. Aware of the shortcomings of their former ideas, yet unaware of satisfactory ways of thinking anew about political phenomena, the children may be falling back to a familiar, though inadequate, cognitive mode. Whether the regression at this age is temporary, indicating a short-lived drop on a generally upward spiral of cognitive growth, or whether it becomes a relatively permanent fixation at a lower level of thought is of critical importance to their development as democratic citizens—particularly critical when we remember that not all adults exhibit formal operational thought. Abraham concludes "To avoid possible stagnation in political thinking, and to optimize children's cognitive performance in this area, it would appear that appropriate political instruction at this stage might be highly desirable" (p. 228).

RESEARCH ON MORAL DEVELOPMENT

Another group of cognitive developmental psychologists, led by Harvard professor Lawrence Kohlberg, has derived a theory of stage development that is focused on moral development, or one's reasoning about justice. Building on Piaget's structural approach to the development of thinking, Kohlberg (1969) and his associates have found that people's thinking about justice seems to progress through an invariant sequence of six stages arranged in three levels. Each stage is characterized by a different mode of reasoning about information and experience, not a particular set of beliefs or moral doctrine. Each succeeding stage of moral reasoning is more complex, capable of greater differentiation and integration of phenomena, and, consequently, appears to extend the individual's capacity to solve ethical problems.

Each level of moral reasoning, as with Piaget's levels of cognition, bears directly on the development of key qualities of democratic citizenship. At each level, individuals seem to have a distinctly different relationship to law, authority, and the concepts of justice, civil rights, and civic responsibility. The first, the "preconventional" level, is dominated by a pattern of reasoning that considers the immediate consequences of behavior. Right and wrong are defined in terms of punishment and reward, obedience, and the exchange of favors. At this level of moral reasoning, it is ethical to steal if you can get away with it; it is wrong if you are caught. Desirable relationships are characterized by the rule of reciprocity: You scratch my back and I'll scratch yours.

At the second, the "conventional" level, people value maintaining the rules and expectations of their groups for their own sake, even if doing so results in consequences less than rewarding from the preconventional view. Persons who reason at this level consider social approval paramount along with loyalty to the law and duty to family, friends, and country.

The third, the "postconventional" level, involves yet another reorganization of thought regarding right and wrong. At this level moral principles are paramount. They are valued for their own sake, apart from group loyalties and laws. Persons who reason below this level are incapable of a full understanding of the concept of "inalienable rights," for example, and of documents like national constitutions, the Bill of Rights, the Declaration of Independence, or the Universal Declaration of Human Rights—all of which are principled documents derived from postconventional thinking. A comprehension of these documents requires a complex, abstract conception of justice, or as Kohlberg has stated, "a disentangling of justice from the particular accepted rules of the culture" (1973, p. 373).

These modes of reasoning were discovered initially in interviews with 72 American boys, ages 10, 13, and 16 (Kohlberg, 1958). These boys were interviewed every three years until the 16-year-olds were 28, providing longitudinal data spanning preadolescence to adulthood. The data gathered were the subjects' responses to 10 hypothetical moral dilemmas. The dilemmas were similar structurally in that each pitted a common moral requirement (e.g., do not steal) against an unusual set of circumstances. For example, an often-used dilemma in the Kohlberg research involves a man stealing a drug to save his dying wife. Did the man act justly?

Because the Kohlberg research suggests that people progress developmentally in their relationship to law and authority, moral development can also be viewed as legal development (Tapp & Kohlberg, 1971). Accordingly, at the preconventional level, people conceive their relationship to the social order from a law-obeying perspective; at succeeding levels, people progress to a law-maintaining (conventional) and then a law-making (postconventional) perspective. Apparently it is not until individuals have attained the law-making mode of thinking that they are able to perceive law as a vehicle for social change rather than simply as the "firm hand" that controls antisocial behavior. It is apparently not until individuals have attained this level of thought that they could say knowingly, as did Aristophanes, "Wise men, though all laws were abolished, would lead the same lives."

National and cross-national studies support this stage-wise progression of legal perspectives (Tapp & Kohlberg, 1971). Interviews with 115 kindergarten-through college-level students from the United States revealed that preconventional thinking decreased markedly over the years on all questions asked. For example, a 2nd grader thought that if there were no rules, "people would go around killing other people, and they'd be stealing things, and they'd be kidnapping people. . . ." (level one). A college-level student replied, "If people were capable of acting responsibly and morally, nothing would happen (level three). When asked, "Can rules be changed?" 20 percent of the youngest group thought rules could not be changed (level one), while no students from the middle-school age and older responded negatively.

Cross-nationally, the data from students in Denmark, Greece, India, Italy and Japan corroborated the universality of the progression in legal thinking. Researchers concluded that preconventional subjects were oriented rigidly to obedience and punishment avoidance with no concern for group or societal welfare; conventional reasoners were also oriented rigidly, but to systems of law that are considered fundamental to group welfare and order. As Tapp and Kohlberg pointed out, the few who reasoned at the postconventional, law-making level

> viewed rules and laws as norms mutually agreed on by individuals for maximizing personal and social welfare. They judged laws should be obeyed either because of rational considerations or because they are coincident with universal principles of justice. This perspective offered a coherent, responsible guide to social change and the creation of new norms: Those that served no purpose or were unjust should be changed; those that violated fundamental individual rights and universal moral principles could be legitimately broken. (p. 85)

Both the national and cross–national studies concluded that conventional reasoning was the most common level of reasoning found in society. Most individuals move beyond level one, but normally only a small minority progresses from level two to three. In the U.S. sample, only college students (and only a minority of them) reasoned at level three.

Moral development is the aim of education, according to the Kohlberg school. Principled morality, it is argued, is critical to competent democratic citizenship. If students are to achieve the civic understandings and abilities necessary for participation in today's difficult world, it seems safe to say that they must be challenged to reason in ways that press beyond egocentricity and ethnocentricity.

Before leaving the subject of moral development, it should be noted that Kohlberg's work has been extended and qualified in important ways. For example, recent research suggests that the development of conceptions of justice and the development of conceptions of social conventions are distinct processes, not different stages on a single developmental course (Nucci, 1982; Turiel, 1983). Turiel (1978) found that people's reasoning about society and conventions develops through a series of seven stages, and Nucci (1984) found that this social development was independent of cognitive development as measured by Piagetian stage. These findings throw into question Kohlberg's assertion that formal operational thinking is prerequisite to advanced, level two reasoning. Other research points to inconsistencies in real–life situations and in issues involving authority versus issues involving justice (see Damon, 1980). Still other research has contrasted Kohlberg's principled or morality–as–fairness orientation with conceptions of morality as caring and responsibility (Gilligan, 1982; Noddings, 1981, 1984). Both Gilligan and Noddings have found the latter more typical of women, the former of men. Taken together, these qualifications of Kohlberg's conception of morality are demonstrating that the development of a sense of justice is just one dimension of a larger, multifaceted process of social development.[3]

RESEARCH ON CLASSROOM CLIMATE

Another body of research related to citizenship education is concerned with classroom climate. Just what is classroom climate? The construct remains somewhat vague, but refers generally to a collection of features that give a classroom a certain atmosphere—a context in which activity takes place and is given meaning. According to Ehman (1980), classroom climate exists at "the intersection of teacher behavior and classroom curriculum." Classroom climate neither refers to "*who* teaches, nor *what* is taught, as much as *how* teaching is carried out. . . ." (p. 108).

Classroom climate is important to citizenship education because it has been found to affect students' citizenship learning, including political efficacy, tolerance for the views of others, attitudes toward civil rights and duties, political interest, political participation, respect for the law, treatment of government authority, and support for democratic values. Classroom climate affects students in a covert rather than overt way. It is part of the "hidden curriculum" of the classroom in which routines, understandings, and arrangements teach a lesson of their own. This covert lesson occurs through decision-making procedures, student participation patterns, treatment or the lack of treatment of controversial issues, response to student opinions by teachers as well as other students, and other behavioral patterns which, taken together, constitute a distinctive sociopolitical atmosphere.[4]

Classroom climate can be conceptualized on a continuum from undemocratic to democratic, or from "closed" to "open." VanSickle (1983) points to a number of attributes of the democratic classroom climate. For one thing, students in a democratic classroom participate frequently. They often initiate questions and statements and respond to requests. This type of participation is distributed across all students. The student status system in the class is weak; consequently, active student participation in lessons is widespread and equitable rather than dependent on academic ability, social class, ethnicity, athletic skill, and gender. Furthermore, the decision-making process in democratic classrooms is, to a significant degree, decentralized. This means that students have more opportunities to influence their classroom environment—topics to be studied, instructional activities, rules and procedures, and daily classroom problems. Students in a democratic classroom generally cooperate, are considerate, and feel good about one another. There is less alienation; instead, students tend to feel that at least some others (including the teacher) care. This positive interaction is helped by the weak status system and is linked positively to increased student participation and influence on classroom decision making.

The research literature generally supports the claim that democratic classrooms foster desirable citizenship learning. For example, a study was conducted of over 2000 5th grade students in 71 randomly selected schools to determine the impact of teacher behavior on students' political values, particularly their tolerance for and interest in the ideas of their classmates (Hawley & Eyler, 1983). An adaptation of Flanders Interaction Analysis was used to observe teachers. Student attitudes and perceptions of their teachers were derived from questionnaires read to students. Findings of the study suggest that the teachers' respect for student ideas was significantly related to student interest in the ideas of others. Moreover, students who had substantial opportunity to interact with others on instructional tasks were more tolerant of the views of others. The researchers concluded that "teachers' modeling of behavior may be more important than the manifest content of instruction in learning political values" (Hawley & Eyler).

In a cross-national study involving 10 countries (including the United States), questionnaires were administered to more than 30,000 10-year-olds, 14-year-olds, and pre-university students (Torney, Oppenheim, & Farnen, 1975). All respondents were in representative samples of their respective school populations at each of the three age levels. The findings indicate that none of the countries successfully achieve the widely heralded objective of cultivating loyal, informed, critical, and actively participating democratic citizens. In Israel and the United States there was strong support for the national government, but below-average support for democratic values. In the Federal Republic of Germany and the Netherlands, the reverse was true. Across the countries in the study, classroom climate was found to affect citizenship outcomes more strongly than was specific classroom practice: "More knowledgeable, less authoritarian, and more interested students came from schools where [students] were encouraged to have free discussion and to express their opinion in class" (p. 18). Students who were exposed to "traditional" civic education programs with a strong emphasis on printed drills and the memorization of facts tended to be less knowledgeable about political content. Similarly, students who reported frequent participation in "traditional" patriotic rituals in the school or classroom were also less knowledgeable about political content and less democratic in their values.

These studies suggest fundamental characteristics of those climates that seem to foster desirable citizenship outcomes: Students are encouraged to express their opinions, and their teachers model respect for diverse opinions. Controversy and conflicting ideas are a part of the curriculum, and dealing with them is considered a welcome part of classroom life. It is important to note here that controversial issues have a positive impact on desirable citizenship outcomes only when these issues are discussed in a democratic climate—that is, a climate in which a wide range of student views is elicited and respected. The use of controversial issues in a closed climate tends, as would be expected, to produce negative attitudes in students.

The review of research on classroom climate included in this chapter is not exhaustive. Nevertheless, one can tentatively conclude from it that students' citizenship learning is influenced not only by the overt, planned social studies curriculum but by the covert, often unplanned climate of the classroom as well. Since the classroom climate can be altered, one can assume it can be altered in ways that might support rather than counter desirable citizenship learnings.

IMPLICATIONS FOR CLASSROOM TEACHING

What does the research reviewed in this chapter tell elementary teachers about how to provide for citizenship education? The following conclusions appear to be supported by the findings and can serve as general guidelines for teachers:

1. In every grade, from kindergarten through 12th, students are engaged in some sort of citizenship learning as a result of both the overt and covert curricula.

2. Citizenship learning begins early and is certainly a function of the elementary school. As a matter of fact, citizenship education may be more critical in the elementary grades than in later grades. As Hess and Torney (1967) point out:

> The most striking feature of political socialization in the elementary school is the extent to which basic orientations have been acquired by children by the end of the eighth grade. Many attitudes, concepts, and types of involvement approximate toward the end of the eighth grade the attitudes and orientations of the teachers. Although there are exceptions . . . , political socialization is well advanced by the end of the elementary school. (p. 220)

Since younger elementary school children are engaged primarily in forming emotional ties to political figures and ideal norms, it seems that these young children should be exposed to diverse role models—not only those who represent the government (e.g., George Washington, Abe Lincoln, etc.) but personalities who attempt to influence the government and render it more democratic (e.g., Martin Luther King, Jr., Susan B. Anthony, Andrew Jackson, etc.). Similarly, since children are developing loyalties to ideal norms, they should be exposed not only to the norms of national cohesion ("I'm proud to be an American") but to the other equally important norms of contemporary citizenship, like community and global responsibility, respect for diversity, social criticism, and civic courage.

Older children in the elementary school are also fully engaged in citizenship learning but, as shown earlier, more in a cognitive than an affective way. They are adding content to the loyalties developed earlier. Their curriculum should be primarily the study and critique of citizenship roles, group governance and procedures, constitutions, democratic values, and decision making of all sorts.

3. Children's minds, and consequently their citizenship, are developing in stages. Intellectually, they are constantly growing by acting on the stimuli contained in their experiences, constructing new knowledge and new ways of making sense of their environments. This natural process of cognitive growth must be facilitated if children are to grow into the sort of democratic citizens we most need—citizens capable of thinking critically about complex societal and global problems and participating competently in their solution. In other words, a primary goal of elementary citizenship education must be to lead the children through cognitive-stage development to formal operational thinking.

The citizenship education curriculum, therefore, needs to be rich in stimuli and managed by the teacher in a way that challenges students to construct new knowledge and new ways of thinking. This kind of curriculum is composed of learning activities that are challenging, active, and interactive. Students interact with their environment, gathering information and communicating about it with each other; they are analyzing, classifying, and organizing the information. In these learning activities, the important thing is "the students' search, not the teachers' answers" (Rest, 1974). The teacher's task is to arrange and rearrange the environment to promote data gathering, discussion, and critical reasoning by students. Doing this well requires that the teacher understand the developmental progression while striving to plan and conduct learning activities that encourage it.

4. Research also shows that requisite to the cultivation of democratic citizenship is a developed sense of justice and law. Kohlberg points out that "social education *is* moral education, and moral education is preparation for citizenship" (1976, p. 213). What is more, legal development appears to parallel moral development. Elementary teachers should provide the conditions conducive to this development. Basic among these conditions is frequent group discussion of moral dilemmas.

Research evidence suggests that the discussion of moral dilemmas can help promote an individual's development through the stages outlined by Kohlberg (Blatt & Kohlberg, 1975; Enright, Lapsley, Harris, & Shawver, 1983). These discussions need to be carefully planned and conducted so as to include the following features:

- A heterogeneous discussion group, the members of which reason at various moral stages. This helps to assure that each student will be exposed to moral reasoning at stages above his or her own.
- A teacher who is able to comprehend and pose arguments containing reasoning at various stages. As with heterogeneity of the group, this ability increases the probability that students will encounter reasoning at stages above their own and that the teacher can engage all students in moral discourse.
- A teacher who is able to create and maintain a discussion environment in which students are respected and all contributions are valued.

Edwin Fenton summarizes the nature of a moral dilemma discussion as follows:

> Teachers present dilemmas in a variety of forms: orally, written; by recordings, sound tapes, films, or videotapes; or as skits or role-playing exercises. The discussion leader then attempts to get students to confront the arguments one stage above their own. This confrontation takes place either when students who think at contiguous moral stages discuss reasoning or when the teacher poses a higher level argument through a probe question or a comment. (1976, p. 192)[5]

Recent research on moral discussions emphasizes that these discussions need to be "transactive" if moral development is to be facilitated (Berkowitz; 1981; Berkowitz & Gibbs, 1983). Discussions are transactive when discussants are actively thinking and communicating about one another's *reasoning,* as opposed to merely parroting other people's arguments or virtually ignoring other people's reasoning while engaged in "alternating monologues" (Berkowitz, 1984). Transactive discussion skills may be rare among a group of discussants, thus reducing the possibility that discussants will profit developmentally from the discussions. Consequently, if elementary teachers are to provide conditions conducive to moral development, they need to lead frequent moral discussions as well as training sessions in which students are taught the prerequisite discussion skills.

5. The climate of a classroom is influenced by the so-called "hidden curriculum." Elementary teachers should design this curriculum consciously so that it teaches lessons that complement, rather than contradict, the formal citizenship curriculum. Elementary teachers should, with their students, strive to build a climate that manifests the following five characteristics:
- Controversial issues are included in the formal curriculum;
- Students are given ample opportunity to express their views freely on all sides of issues and are encouraged to develop arguments both for and against their own opinions;
- The teacher listens to and models respect for diverse views;
- Student participation is widespread and equitable;
- The teacher provides opportunities for students to participate in decision making, thus influencing classroom policies and procedures.[6]

EXAMPLES

Drawing from these general guidelines, elementary teachers can design powerful learning activities at every grade level. The design of these activities requires the kind of inventiveness that has become the trademark of elementary teachers. Some examples are given below.

Direct Participation Experiences

As often as possible, students should be involved in actual citizenship activity. Broadly defined, this is activity related to the governance of any group—the city, the town, the classroom, the nation, the school, the family. There are a number of roles associated with group governance, and participation in each can provide students with opportunities to develop critical citizenship competencies while confronting controversial issues and diverse viewpoints.

Students can participate in classroom governance and be engaged in discussions of the controversies that lie therein by being involved in class meetings in which decisions are made about rules, seating arrangements, curriculum topics, instructional methods, and classroom maintenance schedules; by being asked to organize people and resources to accomplish a task; or by being asked to advocate a particular position at a class meeting. These same roles—decision maker, organizer, advocate—can be explored with academic as well as the nonacademic issues that arise daily in classroom life (Gillespie & Lazarus, 1976).

Similarly, students can take these roles in school governance where concrete, controversial issues also abound. An interesting model is the student government program at Cottage Lane Elementary School (Shaheen, 1980). This program involves the entire student body, 1st through 6th grades, in school governance. It seeks to implement many of the school-wide climate characteristics identified as promoting legal education:

1. Providing children with a broad range of opportunities to participate in the civic life of the community;
2. Helping the adults in the school model the behavior sought in the children;
3. Making school and classroom rules public information and involving children in rule-making, rule-evaluating, rule-enforcing, and rule-changing processes;
4. Working toward having the total school environment reflect the principles of a democratic, pluralistic society based on the rule of law (Shaheen, 1980, pp. 387–388).

Consistent with the developmental differences in younger students, there are two student councils at Cottage Lane, one for grades 1 through 3 and another for grades 4 through 6. Each class elects two delegates to the council, and a third is chosen by the principal and classroom teacher to assure a heterogeneous membership. These council members are delegates (not representatives) of their classrooms and consequently must vote as instructed by their classmates. So, the class meetings involving all students are a critical part of the program.

The school principal is important to the success of the Cottage Lane program. The principal is convenor and secretary to both councils, and chairs the younger council. Furthermore,

playing an advocate for individuals and small groups of children, the principal submits many agenda items. In this way, all children are encouraged to express their concerns, voice their problems, air their frustrations. (p. 390)

These classroom and council meetings seemed to be good opportunities for the discussion of controversial issues and moral dilemmas.

Role Study and Simulation

Besides direct participation in citizen roles, students need to develop understandings of these roles in many groups, from the immediate community to the global community. Field trips and guest speakers can provide students with concrete examples of these roles. As the students' concepts of decision makers, organizers and advocates come to include more and more examples, their thinking about these roles will increase in complexity and they will be challenged to differentiate among them, organizing and classifying them. So, students should study many decision makers in the school and community and, expanding outward, in the state, nation, and globe; they should interview advocates of various causes and diverse points of view on an issue; they should meet organizers of all sorts—from other classrooms, local interest groups, political parties, school clubs, and church groups.

Students should also have opportunities to simulate situations involving these roles. After a field trip to a city council meeting, students can simulate a meeting, taking the roles of council members, mayor, and advocates vying for their interests. After learning about a current international event, students can role-play the main actors, simulate their decision making, and discuss moral dilemmas they may be facing. Closer to home, the children can simulate the principal, parents, and faculty discussing a controversial school policy.

Decision-Making Exercises

Another way students can develop citizenship is by studying and practicing the decision-making process. Since decision making is a process distinct from the content of the decisions, the youngest concrete operational child will probably have difficulty studying it. It should, however, be possible for 4th through 6th grade students to study decision making. The exercises would need to concretize the process so that these students can grapple with it profitably. In addition, the exercises should be designed to stretch the students' minds with opportunities to differentiate, organize, classify, and critique.

A manual of well-designed decision-making activities is available that contains 25 activities for grades 4 through 9 (LaRaus & Remy, 1978). Each activity can be inserted into the existing social studies curriculum and used repeatedly with different content. The first unit of activities raises students' *awareness* of the decision-making process. One of these has students compile a log of alternatives they consider and decisions they make in a day.

The second unit helps students develop their decision-making *skills*. One of the six activities in the unit has students use three different methods of making group decisions and then compare them. In the third set of activities, students examine the *effects* of decisions and learn *criteria* for judging decisions. In one activity, students conduct interviews of classmates and adults to find out how they feel about national, state, local, and family decisions. The fourth unit lets students examine how decisions are *influenced* and practice influencing them. In an activity spanning three periods, students practice three steps in using information as an influence on decision making. The activity involves discussions and simulation, and provides students with an opportunity to study as well as to exert influence.

The manual includes needed student materials as well as bulletin board ideas and teacher inservice suggestions. Many of the activities are of the sort that promote cognitive and moral development. Others develop problem-solving skills that would be useful in the classroom meetings discussed earlier. As a source of ready-made citizenship activities, this one is quite helpful.

A Research-Based Law Curriculum

Elementary teachers in 5th and 6th grades should consider adapting a six-week law education curriculum developed and tested by Jacobson and Polonsky (1981). The curriculum is a collection of stimulating activities that the authors have found to have a positive effect on students' attitude toward the law and knowledge of legal concepts. The activities are compiled from a variety of legal education courses.

Some of the activities help students understand why societies develop laws. One activity involves field trips to libraries, theaters and bowling alleys to gather rules and regulations of all sorts. Another involves students in a simulation of a shipwrecked group stranded on an island faced with developing a legal system "from scratch." Other activities focus on law enforcement. One of these has students role-play police and citizens in simulated incidents, and another is a values inquiry into a town without police or law. Still other activities in this curriculum involve students in jury selection procedures and courtroom simulations of landmark civil liberties cases.

It should be noted that many law-related education programs have been developed for use with elementary children. A helpful resource is the special section on law-related education in the May 1980 issue of *Social Education*. Several learning activities developed by elementary teachers are described, including "Creating a Classroom Constitution" and "Debatable Dilemmas— Case Studies for Young Children." Each is responsive to the developmental and classroom climate guidelines given in this chapter.

CONCLUSION

Good citizens are informed, skillful participants in democratic processes. Their participation is undergirded by a disciplined commitment to democratic values, like justice and equality, and shaped by three points of view: global, pluralist, and critical. Cultivating these democratic citizens is the central goal of the social studies. This is no easy task, but it is an important one, and it requires potent citizenship learning experiences every day in every grade.

The four areas of research reviewed suggest that a formal citizenship curriculum should be active and interactive and contain discussions of controversial issues and moral dilemmas. Meanwhile, the informal citizenship curriculum— the climate—should encourage equitable participation, the expression (and comprehension) of a wide range of viewpoints, and opportunities to include students in decision making about classroom and school life.

NOTES

[1]See Greene (1983) on the "American Dream" and Giroux (1984) for an eloquent critique of the new public philosophy, which is undermining that dream in favor of a mundane, economic privatism.

[2]A review of attempts to apply Piaget's model in educational settings can be found in Kuhn (1979).

[3]Another important development in the study of moral judgment was James Rest's Defining Issues Test. See Moon (1985) and Thoma (1985) for reviews of studies using this measure.

[4]Probing discussions of the "hidden curriculum" can be found in Jackson (1968), Apple (1975), and Giroux and Penna (1979).

[5]See Beyer (1976) for guidelines on conducting moral discussions. See Berkowitz (1981), Fraenkel (1976), Gilligan (1982), and Noddings (1984) for critiques of the Kohlberg approach to moral development. Also, Cherryholmes's (1982) discussion of critical classroom discourse probes the ideological underpinnings of classroom interaction.

[6]Implementing a democratic classroom climate is difficult. VanSickle (1983) offers counsel, Raywid (1979) critiques student participation in school governance, and Cummins (1986) is explicit about how the school climate can empower or disable minority students.

REFERENCES

Abraham, K. G. (1983). Political thinking in the elementary years: An empirical study. *Elementary School Journal, 84,* 221–231.

Adelson, J., Green, B., & O'Neil, R. (1969). Growth of the idea of law in adolescence. *Developmental Psychology, 1,* 327–332.

Anderson, C. C. (1980). Promoting responsible citizenship through elementary law-related education. *Social Education, 44,* 383–386.

Anyon, J. (1979). Ideology and U.S. history textbooks. *Harvard Educational Review, 43,* 361–385.

Apple, M. W. (1975). The hidden curriculum and the nature of conflict. In W. Pinar (Ed.), *Curriculum theorizing: The reconceptualists* (pp. 95–119). Berkeley: McCutchan.

Apple, M. W. (1982). *Education and power.* Boston: Routledge & Kegan Paul.

Barr, R. D., Barth, J. L., & Shermis, S. S. (1977) *Defining the social studies* (Bulletin No. 51). Arlington, VA: National Council for the Social Studies.

Berkowitz, M. W. (1981). A critical appraisal of the educational and psychological perspectives on moral discussion. *The Journal of Educational Thought, 15,* 20–33.

Berkowitz, M. W. (1984). *Process analysis and the future of moral education.* Paper presented at the annual meeting of the American Educational Research Association, New Orleans.

Berkowitz, M. W., & Gibbs, J. C. (1983). Measuring the developmental features of moral discussion. *Merrill-Palmer Quarterly, 29,* 339–410.

Beyer, B. K. (1976). Conducting moral discussions in the classroom. *Social Education, 40,* 194–202.

Blatt, M. M., & Kohlberg, L. (1975). The effects of classroom moral discussion upon children's level of moral judgment. *Journal of Moral Education, 4,* 129–161.

Bourdieu, P., & Passeron, J. C. (1977). *Reproduction in education, society, and culture.* London: Sage.

Butts, R. F. (1979). The revival of civic learning. *Social Education, 43,* 359–363.

Cherryholmes, C. H. (1982). Discourse and criticism in the social studies classroom. *Theory and Research in Social Education, 9,* 57–73.

Cummins, J. (1986). Empowering minority students: A framework for intervention. *Harvard Educational Review, 56,* 18–36.

Damon, W. (1980). Structural-development theory and the study of moral development. In M. Windmiller, N. Lamberg, & E. Turiel (Eds.), *Moral development and socialization.* Boston: Allyn & Bacon.

Dawson, R. E., Prewitt, K., & Dawson, K. S. (1969). *Political socialization* (2nd ed.). Boston: Little, Brown.

Ehman, L. H. (1980). The American school in the political socialization process. *Review of Educational Research, 50,* 99–119.

Enright, R. D., Lapsley, K. D., Harris, D. J., & Shawver, D. J. (1983). Moral development interventions in early adolescence. *Theory Into Practice, 22,* 134–144.

Fenton, E. (1976). Moral education: The research findings. *Social Education, 40,* 188–193.

Frankel, J. R. (1976). The Kohlberg bandwagon: Some reservations. *Social Education, 40,* 216–222.

Gillespie, J., & Lazarus, S. (1976). Teaching political participation skills. *Social Education, 40,* 373–378.

Gilligan, C. (1982) *In a different voice.* Cambridge: Harvard University Press.

Giroux, H. A. (1984). Public philosophy and the crisis in education. *Harvard Educational Review, 54,* 186–194.

Giroux, H. A., & Penna, A. N. (1979). Social education in the classroom: The dynamics of the hidden curriculum. *Theory and Research in Social Education, 7,* 21–42.

Greene, M. (1983). On the American dream: Equality, ambiguity, and the persistence of rage. *Curriculum Inquiry, 13,* 179–193.

Greenstein, F. I. (1969). *Children and politics* (rev. ed.). New Haven: Yale University Press.

Hawley, W. D., & Eyler, J. (1983). *Teacher behavior and interest in the ideas of others: A demonstration of the influence of teachers on students' democratic values* (preliminary report). Paper presented at the annual meeting of the American Educational Research Association, Montreal.

Hess, R. D., & Torney, J. V. (1967). *The development of political attitudes in children.* Chicago: Aldine.

Jackson, P. W. (1968). *Life in classrooms.* New York: Holt, Rinehart and Winston.

Jacobson, M. G., & Palonsky, S. B. (1981). Effects of a law-related education program. *Elementary School Journal, 82,* 49–57.

Kohlberg, L. (1958). *The development of modes of moral thinking and choice in the years ten to sixteen.* Unpublished doctoral dissertation, University of Chicago.

Kohlberg, L. (1969). Stage and sequence: the cognitive developmental approach to socialization. In D. A. Goslin (Ed.), *Handbook of socialization theory and research* (pp. 347–480). Chicago: Rand McNally.

Kohlberg, L. (1973). Moral development and the new social studies. *Social Education, 37,* 369–375.

Kohlberg, L. (1976). This special section in perspective. *Social Education, 40,* 213–215.

Kuhn, D. (1979). The application of Piaget's theory of cognitive development to education. *Harvard Educational Review, 49,* 340–360.

LaRaus, R., & Remy, R. C. (1978). *Citizenship decision making: Skill activities and materials, grades 4–9.* Reading, MA: Addison-Wesley.

Moon, Y. (1985). *A review of cross-cultural studies on moral judgment development using the Defining Issues Test.* Paper presented at the annual meeting of the American Educational Research Association, Chicago.

Noddings, N. (1981). Caring. *Journal of Curriculum Theorizing, 3*(3), 139–148.

Noddings, N. (1984). *Caring: A feminine approach to ethics and moral education.* Berkeley: University of California Press.

Nucci, L. (1982). Conceptual development in the moral and conventional domains: Implications for values education. *Review of Educational Research, 52,* 93–122.

Nucci, L. (1984). *Piagetian stage and development in the societal domain.* Paper presented at the annual meeting of the American Educational Research Association, New Orleans.

Parker, W. C., & Jarolimek, J. (1984). *Citizenship and the critical role of the social studies* (Bulletin No. 72). Washington, D.C.: National Council for the Social Studies, ERIC Clearinghouse for Social Science/Social Studies Education, and the Social Science Education Consortium.

Piaget, J. (1928). *Judgment and reasoning in the child.* London: Routledge & Kegan Paul.

Raywid, M. A. (1979). The democratic classroom: Mistake or misnomer? *Theory Into Practice, 15,* 37–46.

Rest, J. (1974). Developmental psychology as a guide to values education: A review of "Kohlbergian" programs. *Review of Educational Research,* 241–259.

Shaheen, J. (1980). Cottage Lane: A student government program that works. *Social Education, 44,* 387–390.

Shaver, J. P. (Ed.). (1977). *Building rationales for citizenship education* (Bulletin No. 52). Arlington, VA: National Council for the Social Studies.

Siegel, L. S. (1977). Children's and adolescents' reactions to the assassination of Martin Luther King: A study of political socialization. *Developmental Psychology, 13,* 284–285.

Tapp, J. L., & Kohlberg, L. (1971). Developing senses of law and legal justice. *Journal of Social Issues, 27,* 65–91.

Thoma, S. J. (1985). *Do moral education programs promote moral judgment development? A statistical review of intervention studies using the Defining Issues Text.* Paper presented at the annual meeting of the American Educational Research Association, Chicago.

Torney, J. V., Oppenheim, A. N., & Farnen, R. F. (1975). *Civic education in ten countries.* New York: John Wiley & Sons.

Turiel, E. (1978). The development of concepts of social structures: Social convention. In J. Glick & A. Clarke-Stewart (Eds.), *The development of social understanding* (pp. 347–480). New York: Gardner Press.

Turiel, E. (1983). *The development of social knowledge: Morality and convention.* New Rochelle: Cambridge University Press.

VanSickle, R. L. (1983). Practicing what we teach: Promoting democratic experience in the classroom. In M. A. Hepburn (Ed.), *Democratic education in schools and classrooms* (Bulletin No. 70). Washington, D.C.: National Council for the Social Studies, 49–66.

Willis, P. (1977). *Learning to labour.* Westmead, England: Saxon House.

CHAPTER 3

INTERCULTURAL AND MULTICULTURAL EDUCATION

Lynda Stone

This chapter reviews recent research in two curricular domains of elementary practice—international and multicultural education.[1] It seems natural to attempt to synthesize research from both fields because a relationship can be thought to exist between them; that is, international education may be viewed as an extension of multicultural learning. Multicultural education is commonly conceived as students' learning about the various racial, ethnic, gender and class groups that comprise the population of the United States. International education extends learning to incorporate peoples and places outside the United States and aims to understand the universal elements of human experience.[2]

A research synthesis of the international and multicultural educational fields is problematic for at least two reasons: the lack of precise definitions (Spaulding, Colucci, & Flint, 1982; Vasquez & Ingle, 1982) and the lack of a clear focus in the research. Both fields have been identified as "emergent," which means that as developing research bodies they have not yet reached a stage when a central direction for inquiry has been established. Only the vaguest of trends in research direction can be noted. Research in international education has looked at student outcomes—the content and composition of knowledge and attitude development. In contrast, multicultural inquiry has been concerned with student learning processes rather than learning outcomes. Of this latter work, Vasquez and Ingle report that little has found its way into the general literature of multicultural education, and the influence of cognitive styles on curriculum has not been researched (Vasquez & Ingle, 1982). Finally, inquiry in these emergent fields spans a wide array of topics, with almost limitless possibility for relevant research. At this stage of investigation, it is important to keep the content of this variety in mind. From within the diversity of subtopics, many possibilities exist for future central directions for each field and for a synthesis of them.

Despite the problematic nature of summarizing and synthesizing research in the two developing fields, a critical review representative of available research is offered. Given the fluid conditions of both fields, no attempt is made to prescribe practice. This chapter is organized into four sections: reviews of research for international education; reviews of research on multicultural education; an overview of additional references and findings; and directions for

research and summary implications. Although the reader is counseled against taking direct prescriptions for practice from this chapter, it is hoped that its contents can serve two purposes. First, its research ideas can serve as catalysts for useful reflection on the part of practitioners. Second, it can serve as a source of references for further study of specific interests and problems.

RESEARCH ON INTERNATIONAL EDUCATION[3]

In recent years, several useful research reviews have documented work relevant to international education (Anderson, 1981; Kobus, 1982; Remy, Nathan, Becker, & Torney, 1975; Spaulding, Colucci, & Flint, 1982; Willett, 1982). What is reported in this section of the chapter draws heavily on the work of Torney-Purta (1982a, 1982b). She has synthesized significant contributions from the subfields of research on political socialization, cognitive development and second-language learning—all as they contribute to students' learning about other peoples and places. One central theme is students' conceptions of other peoples and places. Various studies dating as far back as the late fifties describe dimensions of "others" as students see them. Results indicate that young people perceive similarities and differences among persons based on physical characteristics, clothing, language and political orientation. Among findings is the point that certain areas of the world are conceived of as "most different" by children of the United States; these are Asia, Africa, and the Soviet Union (the "Communist" country). Several interesting investigations substantiate a developmental-stage theory of students' ideas of other countries. For instance, about grade 2, children recognize difference but have little emotional reaction to it. As they age, they understand greater difference, and this change is accompanied by greater feelings of rejection of others. Rejection is most pronounced at early puberty; but this is not the entire story. For several crucial years, students appear to have an expanded tolerance for difference. It has been documented that 4th graders are far more interested than 8th graders in studying and visiting foreign countries. One additional facet of research in this first topic concerns student stereotypic attitudes, which, the research indicates, begin to develop about grade 7.

A second area of research concerns students' knowledge of, and attitudes toward, global issues. Most of this research has been directed toward high school and college-age students, but two aspects are significant for the elementary educator. While experts point out what topics secondary students are supposed to know, research results show that high school and college-level students actually know very little about global topics. Torney-Purta (1982a) summarizes that students are unable to see the United States in a global context. Further, they tend to magnify both the accomplishments and the problems of their own country. Studies on the global issue of "war" are particularly interesting. It has been shown that young people are acutely aware of war by the age of six, and many believe that it is "inevitable, necessary and likely" (Torney-Purta, 1982a, p. 12). Of particular concern is the demonstrated increase in interest in war by students in grades 5 and 6. This finding, coupled with the idea that these same pupils also show more tolerance for other people, makes for an interesting combination of attitudes on the part of intermediate-age students, and suggests an interesting research question.

A third area of inquiry concerns the domain of international human rights education. Studies show that children hold deep beliefs about the rights that people are entitled to just because they are people. Research indicates, for instance, that more tolerance is expressed for differences in beliefs about race and religion than for beliefs about gender. In addition, equity issues have a particularly interesting twist: there is a tendency on the part of young people to blame the victim; that is, "good people have rights and bad people do not." However, students also seem willing to give up equity in certain matters, and to reward people who are most like themselves. Not surprisingly, this tendency increases in adolescence (Torney-Purta, 1982b).

A final area of research in international education looks at political socialization. In this domain several researchers (e.g., Ehman, 1980; Jones, 1980) have found differentiated roles for school and other socializing institutions. Most knowledge learned comes from school-based influences, while most attitudes are formed from nonschool sources (although international attitudes, rather than national values, are significantly more subject to school influences). Research documents that two important factors of school influence are curriculum exposure and teacher attitude. This means that depth of exposure to ideas and information is a key component along with the teacher's attitude toward the material. Finally, studies have indicated that nontraditional teaching techniques have been important to attitude formation. Using attitude development in human rights studies as an illustration, Torney-Purta (1982b) elaborates on this last point.

It is clear that a teacher trained to facilitate cooperative learning, to value student opinion, to present a role model of one who respects the rights and opinions of others, to encourage students to reflect upon their experience and play with new ideas, and to give students some responsibility for control over the learning process may facilitate many of the learning outcomes which are important in human rights education. (p. 45)

In sum, within international education, four significant subtopics of research that focus on student outcomes have been identified and described. It is important to note that actual studies have come from a wide range of disciplines and foci of research. It is to the credit of previous reviewers that the relevant topics have been identified.

The chapter now turns to research for multicultural learning. The status of research in this second field is even more developmental than in international education. Few attempts at review have been made. What one quickly sees, however, is a general trend for research about how students learn, rather than what they learn and believe.

In reading the next section of the review, the reader will note more detailed attention to particular studies from multicultural education than from the international realm. There are several reasons for this emphasis. First, it appears to this reviewer that more summaries and analyses of international education have been available to elementary educators. Second, this reviewer concurs with Vasquez and Ingle (1982) that important research on cognitive and learning styles has not found its way into the multicultural literature. Michael Cole (1985) makes the significant point that multicultural educators must be concerned with the learning diversity of their students: "It is important to note that culture-sensitive does not mean a focus on the traditional arts, foods and folklore of a group" (p. 243). Logically, learning about cultural diversity can only be accomplished if each child has cognitive access to what is to be learned and if each child's learning style is recognized and valued.

MULTICULTURAL RESEARCH

In multicultural education, relevant research has come from qualitative inquiries[4] in psychology and anthropology. In the first discipline, investigations have looked at student cognitive styles and learning strategies. In the second social science field, research foci have expanded to include the context in which student learning takes place. Most multicultural research has concentrated on learning by particular ethnic groups in multicultural educational settings. The overall impression from psychological research is that the learning preferences of children are culturally determined, and, furthermore, that children benefit from varying instructional approaches. One method is not satisfactory for all (Laosa, 1977). Research indicates that a relationship of cognitive and learning style not only exists for particular groups in verbal learning but that it is found in nonverbal learning as well. Recent studies of everyday classroom interaction, as well as more traditional experimental inquiries, support this conclusion. Variables such as income, student achievement and selection of friends have all been related in various ways to cognitive and learning style preferences.

In this area, work done by Cohen (1976) is particularly interesting for multicultural educators. She reports on varying degrees of dissonance and conflict between student learning styles and teacher instructional styles, and documents the particular difficulty that many minority students have with the analytic mode of learning that dominates elementary instruction (Cohen, 1976). Understanding styles of cognition and learning relates directly to the need for matching effective teaching strategies. An examination of this research indicates that the match of cognitive style and learning strategy is particularly important for bicultural children who must be able to switch repertoires as they switch cultures (Laosa, 1977).

Various studies from psycholinguistics have also contributed insight into language acquisition and development, important components of multicultural life. Research has looked at student dialect use, linguistic style, and language purpose. All three dimensions, according to Moses, Daniels, and Gundlach (1977), are related to cultural inheritance. Different cultures have various rules for the learning of language structures and language utility. For multicultural educators, the aim is to "create a school setting which stimulates each child to use all the language he has" (Moses, Daniels, & Gundlach, 1977). Research findings support an environment where all dialects are respected, where a great deal of talking goes on, and where a variety of language styles are operating.

In contrast to work in psychology, traditional research in anthropology was seldom relevant to multicultural education; however, a shift in research emphasis has occurred that brings a much closer tie between the discipline and the multicultural instructional domain. Traditional inquiry looked at broad notions of enculturation in exotic settings; recent research has focused on domestic sites and more narrow definitions of education. A general thrust in research has been to seek understanding of pluralistic classroom cultures and to describe components of their effective operation. Research has indentified a variety of classroom cultures built on diverse belief systems, participant values, operative cognitive structures and engendered meanings (C. S. Anderson, 1982.)[5]

Within anthropology, various subfields have developed that are making contributions to multicultural understanding (Johnson, 1977; Burton, 1978).[6] One of these is the area of microethnography. This is a new methodology where traditional time spent in the field is cut drastically, research is done domestically, and an interdisciplinary emphasis is added—with ties to and contributions from psychology, sociology and linguistics. Much microethnographic research has looked at multiethnic classroooms as they are embedded in cultural contexts. Many studies have focused on particular ethnic groups. In this subfield one research review is particularly helpful for introductory purposes. This is a synthesis of microethnographic studies by Trueba and Wright (1980–81).

Trueba and Wright identified four themes based on 15 microethnographic studies. These are (1) teaching styles/cultural congruences; (2) sociocultural roles of interaction within schooling structures; (3) children's social competence; and (4) language use and communication misconceptions. Subjects of the studies reviewed by Trueba and Wright represented children from a cross section of U.S. ethnic groups. They were Hawaiian and Samoan, Black, Anglo/

Italian, Native American, and Hispanic, including Puerto Rican. The children lived in nine different regions of the United States.

Results summarizing each of the four themes will be presented. This will be followed by a more detailed exploration of five studies documenting research about each of the representative ethnic groups (see Trueba & Wright, 1980–81, pp. 40–51).

The first group of studies looked at communication styles for the purpose of instruction of Hawaiian, Samoan, Alaskan Indian, continental Indian and Hispanic children. In most cases, ethnic minority children had Caucasian teachers. The importance of cultural congruence in teaching and learning styles was highlighted, and the need for teacher awareness and adaptation was emphasized. While teacher-student interactions were only contributing variables in the first group of studies, they became the central concern in the second set. Various social situations were investigated, including the setting-up of classroom procedures. The general conclusion was that norms for classroom practices must be congruent with community norms if effective student interaction is to occur. In the third group of studies, the focus shifts to measures of student social competence. This competence occurs in noninstructional situations; game-playing, tutoring and free time were explored. Results indicated the need for teachers to be aware of the competence students show in these situations, and also to be aware that judgments of student skills and abilities should be based on instructional as well as noninstructional activities. The final set of investigations looked at successful student communication. Language selection was studied in student-adult communication and in student-student language interactions in peer tutoring and interviews. Factors for effective communication were revealed for each particular ethnic group in each specific language situation.

A closer look at five studies (four from the Trueba and Wright review) elaborates on the content of the microethnographies and demonstrates their utility for multicultural education. Van Ness (1981) reported on procedures used by Alaskan Indian children in a kindergarten classroom as students "get ready" to read. These Indian children, he demonstrated, culturally defined the event and acted accordingly. Their definitions and actions, furthermore, differed from those of other cultural groups. Van Ness chronicled the actions of a caring teacher who learned *not* to single out Indian children for attention, either as a way to demonstrate her authority or to teach them. Avoiding the spotlight is an important norm of the Alaskan Indian community, and the teacher learned to employ this cultural standard for beneficial instruction.

Reading by Hawaiian children was the subject of work done by Au and Jordan (1981). A reading program using a Hawaiian communication form, the talk story, was developed and assessed. According to Au and Jordan, learning to read is effective if it "capitalizes on the pre-existing cognitive and linguistic abilities of children" (p. 140). The study revealed also that successful reading occurred for Hawaiian children when they were taught by a teacher who was socially relevant to them, who instructed in a manner with which the children were familiar, and who emphasized general completion of a task rather than the rules governing its operation.

Mexican-American students were the subjects of the third illustrative study (Carrasco, 1981), which reported on the interaction of one female student and the teacher who had "written her off because she could not make it" (p. 154). The researcher worked closely with the teacher with some positive results. The teacher learned that she had determined the student's ability based on premature first observations, pretests, and background knowledge of the child's family. Through expanded awareness of her own preconceptions, the teacher learned to look at positive social qualities the child had with peers as well as informal communication skills, those outside teacher-student interactions. From this awareness, the teacher's expectations for the pupil were raised and appropriate instruction was initiated.

The fourth example concerns language styles of black and white students in teacher-student interactions. While the subjects of the work by Ludwig (1981) were junior-high age, the study may have import for elementary practitioners. Ludwig found that the two groups of students employed different language strategies when trying to work through their failure to understand teacher expectations. Most commonly, black students in the study stepped back from the problem and assessed it among themselves, going over what had occurred in the interaction with the teacher. In contrast, white students responded to the problem directly and rehearsed possible future actions.

In the final illustration, incidents of miscommunication between Puerto Rican pupils and their teachers were investigated (McDermott & Gospodinoff, 1981). This study differed from other communication inquiries because difference in communication codes of whites and Puerto Ricans was accepted, but political relations of the two cultures was an added variable. The research showed that these minority children had to "catch up" right from the time they entered school. White children came to school with reading skills already functioning, and Puerto Rican children did not. As a result of a community norm, a well-meaning teacher organized differentiated reading instruction for the two groups. However, in an attempt to help the minority children, she inadvertently perpetuated their reading problems.

It is obvious that the microethnographic studies presented do not deal directly with multicultural education as it was defined at the outset of this chapter. There the field was conceived as students' learnings about the various racial, ethnic, gender and class groups that comprise the peoples of the United States. In the research review, the focus of inquiry was slightly different; studies were more concerned with the learning processes of various ethnic groups. It is the opinion of this reviewer that the microethnographic research is significant for both definitions of the field. One could argue that how various peoples learn constitutes an important aspect of their ethnicity or other cultural identity. The studies are further informative because they are vivid portrayals of life in elementary school classrooms that are multicultural—a condition that is increasingly common in all regions of the United States. From the studies, elementary educators can come to understand much about the students with whom they work. In the future, such information will be vitally important for curriculum development as well as instruction. These studies are part of the variety and vivacity that characterize the emerging research field of multicultural education.

ADDITIONAL REFERENCES AND FINDINGS

Diversity of research interests is a normal quality of developing research fields such as international and multicultural education. However, the categorizations of each area presented in the last two sections may not fully capture the diversity that characterizes the research. The purpose of this part of the chapter is to portray this variety through presentation of a chart (Table 1) summarizing 30 recent studies. These are directly related to or seem to impinge upon multicultural and international learning. It is important to note that no claim is made that the chart exhausts all available research, nor is its organization meant to imply research trends. It does, however, offer a fair sampling of pertinent research. Comments on each study serve to identify the subjects and topics of inquiry, and findings are mentioned in greatly abbreviated form. Each study is referenced at the end of the chapter, and readers are invited to seek more detailed information by reading particular works.

Some interpretative comments about the research seem warranted on the basis of what is and is not found in the summary chart. Goodlad's (1984) national study is included because it is one of the few recent national research efforts that includes attention to elementary education. Further, it is one of the few studies to look at multicultural and international learning. The reader will note that no national classroom-based summaries have been undertaken in either domain, and only a few single-program evaluations have been conducted. Laudable examples of program evaluations are those by Skeel and Mitsakos and their colleagues found on the chart (1978, 1980). This reviewer believes that a national evaluation of both international and multicultural classroom-based programs is called for.

The chart also illustrates that reports continue to become available on textbook bias. A general impression is that texts are treating minorities and foreigners more appropriately than in years past, but subtle biases persist. Finally, studies of students' and teachers' attitudes in both international and multicultural education continue to be conducted. In much of the survey research, however, little attention is paid to elementary-age students. Two studies from the chart, Allen (1979) and Washington (1982), contain large enough sample sizes for significant survey analyses. A caution, however: self-reports about what someone believes, and even might do, do not necessitate future actions. Attitude surveys are important if they indicate actions that can be subsequently researched. It is this reviewer's opinion that research on students' and teachers' school-based actions, rather than on their attitudes, holds the most promise for multicultural and international education.

DIRECTIONS FOR RESEARCH, AND SUMMARY IMPLICATIONS

The point just made is a simple one: actions of students and teachers can tell us if people have learned to be multicultural and international. Thus, research

TOPIC OF STUDY	AUTHOR (YEAR)	COMMENTS
Text Analysis	McAulay, 1978 Butterfield et al., 1979 Garcia & Woodrick, 1979 Grant & Grant, 1981	Four studies looked at treatment of minorities, gender discrimination and representation of "politically sensitive places." Found attempts to balance treatment, but oversimplification of persons and issues. Warnings against subtle bias.
National Classroom Study A Place Called School	Goodlad, 1984	Included in national study. Emphasis on enculturation goal, learning about one's culture, not others. Self-responsibility, no mutuality. Some attention to other countries in expanding social studies curriculum not very "global."
Program Evaluation Family of Man Program	Mitsakos, 1978	Third grade study shows favorable development of student attitudes, positive view of learning about others.
Tennessee State Global Education Project	Pickel, Lipman, Smith, & Skeel, 1980	Demonstrated need for protracted teacher inservice training and time for curriculum development.
National Association of Elementary School Principals	Skeel, Dudley, & Mitsakos, 1980	Three-year inservice program, Washington, DC. Participant response favorable to program to develop materials. Looked at program outcomes of student learning of international concepts; six-nation area study.

TABLE 1
References and Findings of
International and Multicultural Research

TOPIC OF STUDY	AUTHOR (YEAR)	COMMENTS
Multiethnic program	Pate & Garcia, 1981	Survey of 150 social studies supervisors. Multicultural curriculum "confusing, lacking in purpose and direction." No typical program.
Goodlad's Mankind Curriculum Follow-up	Klein, Novotney, & Burkett, 1981	Creation evaluation instrument. Pilot test, multicultural first grade. Indicates social mixing, little student freedom, lack of problem solving and spontaneity, minimum student-teacher interaction.
Studies of Student Attitudes		
"International" Attitude survey, Canada, Australia, US	Allen, 1979	Over 1000 children, grades 1, 3, 6. Indicates drop in egocentrism over grades. Greater attention to differences than to similarities; few evaluation comments overall. Views of own countries similar across settings.
Impact of children's literature on attitudes toward Mexican-Americans	Koeller, 1977	Over 200 Denver 6th graders. Indicates positive effect of story on boys', but not girls', attitudes.
Survey of student "world" views	Millard, 1981	Attitude survey shows elementary children found world "changing, confusing, active and violent." Indicates impact of media.
Student views of teachers	Cangemi, 1979 Sizemore, 1981	Two studies of minority student attitudes. Elementary gifted preferences and older (Black/White students). Significant variables suggested; some indication of "individual" preferences.

TABLE 1
(Continued)

TOPIC OF STUDY	AUTHOR (YEAR)	COMMENTS	
Teacher Attitudes/ Perceptions			
Sex-role stereotyping	Motta & Vane, 1976 Prawat & Jarvis, 1980	First:	Girls more creative, achievement-oriented and dependent; boys more aggressive; grade and IQ not factors; little change in perceptions in 20 years.
		Second:	Boys' aggressiveness upheld; no gender preferences in IQ.
Student physical attractiveness and home climate	Adams, 1976	Prediction of school success relates to positive ideas of physical attractiveness and positive home image.	
Permissive use of black dialects in school	Pietras & Lamb, 1978	Male teachers more permissive, as are all the more educated; age and experience of teachers not factors. Demonstrates need for inservice, rather than preservice.	
Inservice education influence on racism/ multicultural attitudes	Washington, 1981	Findings show no impact of inservice education; most positive attitudes from experienced black teachers of poor students.	
Attitudes toward Mexican-American students and their education	deKanter & Frankiewicz, 1981	Three studies of undergraduates, graduates, and teachers. Documents need for positive school policy, impact of positive teacher attitude, support for ethnic pride and desire for equal opportunity. Some negative impact of ethnicity on educational achievement possibilities.	

TABLE 1
(Continued)

TOPIC OF STUDY	AUTHOR (YEAR)	COMMENTS
Attitudes toward multicultural education	Washington, 1982	Survey of more than 3000 elementary teachers. Neutral attitudes toward desegregation. Positive beliefs about multicultural education. Demonstrates need for materials, testing and counseling, and for experiential inservice.
Personal multicultural attitudes	Giles & Sherman, 1982	300 teacher trainees. Perceptions of personal and professional life. To achieve NCATE standards— factors identified: well adjusted, decisive, flexible, sociable, enthusiastic to achieve professionally.
Quality of multicultural education	Grant, 1981	Small sample preservice teachers. Demonstrates student awareness but little initiative for promoting multicultural education during "survival" or apprenticeship stage of training. Comfort with discussion of issues. One course not sufficient for multiculturality. Suggests field-based experience.
Student Groupings		
Immigrant adaptation to school	Nguyen & Henkin, 1980	Fourth year in school for 100 Indo-Chinese students. Enculturation difficulties continue, especially in culture-bound subjects. Self-perception of acceptance important. Suggests strategies and programs.

TABLE 1
(Continued)

TOPIC OF STUDY	AUTHOR (YEAR)	COMMENTS
Cross-sex friendships	Cohen, 1980	5th graders in U.S. and Sweden, middle class. Preferences on personal and school matters. U.S. boys most willing on school, not on personal friendship. U.S. girls unwilling on either.
Classroom behavior by race and gender	Sagar, Schofield, & Snyder, 1983	Urban desegregated 6th graders. Indicates gender as most important grouping variable. Most interaction same race and sex; boys cross racial lines more than do girls; blacks cross racial lines more than whites; blacks cross gender lines more than whites.
Informal social organization in desegregated school	Clement & Harding, 1978	Two-year study, southern public elementary schools. Shows informal segregation continues, impact of no out-of-school contact, attempts often at friendships, which may fail because of different behavioral styles, promotion of interactions underdeveloped.
Cross-color play	Polgar, 1978	6th grade free play, boys teams; single color and mixed color games, single color and mixed color teams. Mixed color teams least stable patterns and interaction but most positive long-range possibilities.
Tracking and peer relationships	Schwartz, 1981	Large study include 3rd and 4th graders, inner-city. Demonstrates institutional effects on individual relationships. High achievers form positive peer groups for mutual success in system; low-achievers form non-positive groupings for social or academic purposes.

TABLE 1
(Continued)

needs to focus on school and classroom events where such learning can be demonstrated. Such a call, however, does not mean that past research has not been informative and beneficial. We have learned much about what constitutes multicultural and international beliefs. We have some idea, further, about appropriate school and classroom settings that foster the development of beliefs and actions. Finally, we have indications of types of knowledge that can foster appropriate learning.

What do we know? Certain kinds of knowledge help in understanding similiarities and differences which characterize multicultural and international understanding. Thus far, educational efforts have focused on two forms of intellectual knowledge: knowing about and knowing how to. For example, the idea has been that students form attitudes about people when they learn to read and comprehend a pie or circle graph that shows something like worldwide resource distribution. Although it is believed that worthwhile actions can result from such intellectual understandings, this reviewer contends that we have had no way to detemine the carry-over of fact and attitude formation into acts that are multicultural and international.

What is missing is the development of interpersonal knowing as a way to evaluate multicultural and international understandings and as a way to see beliefs transformed into actions. The necessity for interpersonal knowing has escaped the attention of researchers; it has, however, received some note from theorists in the international and multicultural fields. For example, Hanvey (1976) suggested the need to learn two elements of interpersonal knowing: perspective-taking and transspection. The first is the ability to take on the view of others toward the world, and the second is the ability to see oneself from the viewpoint of others. Anderson, Anderson and Winston (n.d.) called for respect for others as a needed global skill. Both Hahn (1983) and Johns (1979) recognized the need for personal commitment on the part of internationally able people. Reminiscent of Blum (1980), Hahn advocated the need for compassion as part of interpersonal knowing, and Johns called for a form of responsibility called "man-in-dialogue." The latter is the idea that self-responsibility means that others must be considered in the international context in which we live. Finally, in the multicultural literature, Hoopes (1979) suggested a continuum of multicultural skills that includes awareness of and respect for others.

Although contributions from each of these influential scholars are important, this reviewer argues that collectively they failed to understand interpersonal knowing in its fullest dimension. Built on the conception of relation developed by Martin Buber (1965, 1970), Nel Noddings contended that we need to educate persons to care for each other. Noddings (1984) suggested that genuine caring comes from the desire to enter and the actuality of entering into relation with the other and of acting on the other's behalf. In schools and classrooms, such caring can be seen in the actions that teachers and students take toward each other and, particularly, in the actions of friends. One could argue that multicultural and international learning has taken place if students willingly cross ethnic lines to form genuine friendship groups, or if students respond to distant others as if they were friends (or potential friends).[7]

While friendship, as a crucial dimension of international/multicultural education, has not been widely suggested previously, a relevant research base already exists that supports interpersonal knowing. Areas of research that come to mind include student grouping practices, cooperative learning processes, peer tutoring mechanisms, and the general area of school climate research. Several of these relevant research fields have been suggested previously as aspects of multicultural and international education (see Anderson, 1981). However, unfortunately, none has yet become part of the mainstream dialogue in either field.

Research in student groupings (see Table 1) provides a useful illustration. Two studies, Cohen (1980) and Sagar, Schofield, and Snyder (1983), are representative. Results of both of these studies showed an unwillingness on the part of white preadolescent females to cross gender and racial lines to form friendships. These findings are particularly significant given the work of Gilligan (1982), which demonstrated the importance of caring relationships in the development of female persons. Still other research from the same general area can provide insight into possible solutions to this problem. For example, in Polgar (1978) and Schwartz (1981), structural features from inside and outside of classrooms are described which can enhance formation of friendships.

Research on small group cooperative learning is also relevant for the addition of an interpersonal dimension to multicultural/international education. This research is closely tied to the previously reported research on cognitive and communication styles of particular ethnic groups. Valentine (1976) suggested that small-group cooperative learning provides more active student involvement in less threatening learning situations than did the conventionally teacher-centered learning. Students get a chance to know each other well as they work together to achieve common goals. Research reviewed by Webb (1982) further suggests that the most significant form of cooperative activity incorporates children helping each other (see, also, Schuncke & Bloom, 1979; Ryan & Wheeler, 1977; Cohen, D'Heurle, & Widmark-Petersson, 1980). Friendships, genuine instantiations of relations of caring, develop as students learn while mutually helping each other.

Examples of helping activities include multi-ability task group projects and peer tutoring programs. In the former, curriculum projects are designed in which a variety of skills are needed to produce a successful common product. Equal value is given for all contributions. In such programs,[8] at first students' natural talents and previously acquired skills are utilized; then gradually students shift places within the project structure and acquire new skills as well. Research has demonstrated that such projects are particularly effective in multicultural classrooms. In the second area, peer tutoring, a large research base has been developed. Of interest here, Larsen & Ehly (1976) suggested that perhaps the greatest benefits from peer tutoring programs are not academic, but possibly are the emotional and psychological experiences of participants. However, little of the available research on peer tutoring (Devin-Sheehan, Feldman, & Allen, 1979; Paolitto, 1976; Bowermaster, 1978; Lindsey & Watts, 1979) has looked at cross-racial or cross-ethnic tutorial experiences. This particular focus requires further research attention.

School climate research (C. C. Anderson, 1982; C. S. Anderson, 1982; Johnson, 1980; Pickney & Esporito, 1976; Simpson, 1981; Weinstein, 1979) is the final area of inquiry that this reviewer identified as relevant for "personalized" multicultural and international education. Researchers such as Damico, Bell-Nathaniel, and Green (1981) recognized the possible contributions from understanding elements of schooling and classroom structures:

> Before a friendship can evolve, individuals . . . [must] have an opportunity to . . . discover those things they share in common . . . . The structure of the school can provide the opportunity for students of different racial and cultural groups to come together, interact, and develop friendships. (p. 391)

Research has identified many significant "climate" variables that can contribute to caring relations and friendship formation. Among these are size of classes, staff stability (i.e., residence longevity at a school site), schoolwide communication channels, and relevant instructional goals that are clearly understood by all school participants.

The final section of this research review has offered a new conception for international and multicultural education in the form of an interpersonal element. Such an idea is, perhaps, one that can provide practical as well as theoretical and research synthesis for the two fields. In support of the development of such an idea—the creation of caring relations among students on the multicultural as well as international levels—comments on several areas of relevant research have been presented.

CONCLUSION

Concluding remarks are now in order. At the beginning of this chapter, it was asserted that summarizing and synthesizing research in multicultural or international education was problematic. However, it is hoped that the point has been made that the problem is not one of poor research, but that it exists as a natural condition of emerging research fields. Each area of research is currently characterized by a wide diversity of investigative foci.

This review has attempted to locate general trends of inquiry amidst the research variety. Initially, several significant themes of international and multicultural research in past reviews were identified. In international education, the tendency has been for research to concentrate on the content of student knowledge and attitudes, with some consideration of the conditions necessary for such learning. In multicultural education, research has focused on how particular groups of students learn. These findings can likely contribute significantly to various instructional tasks and to curriculum development. Next, diversity of research was demonstrated in Table 1, which summarized 30 recent studies. Two points have been made as suggestions for future and conceptual development of the two fields. First, multiculturality and internationality of students are best demonstrated in actions among people. Research needs to focus on school and classroom life. Second, in school and classroom research, we might do well to look at student friendship practices as a manifestation of multicultural and international learning, and we might focus on research that assists in the development of friendship and caring.

In sum, at several points readers have been cautioned against forming definitive judgments based on research findings. This reviewer maintains that drawing major implications from most research is problematic, particularly if fields are just developing. However, just because multicultural and international research is emerging does not mean that elementary educators cannot learn something from the reported studies. Indeed, generalized ideas for reflection, and for future verification from practice, are all that research can hope to provide. In doing so, it can contribute in many ways to our understanding of effective educational practice.

A final word: The reader may have noticed that the title of this chapter reads "intercultural" and not "international" education. The last term is more commonly used by education practitioners. However, given the point of this chapter, a title of intercultural education is highly appropriate. By moving to a level of interpersonal understanding, as in friendship, students can realize for themselves the meaningful connections inherent in intercultural and multicultural education.

NOTES

I wish to thank Judith Torney-Purta, Carole Hahn, and Michael S. Katz for reading drafts of this chapter and offering valuable advice. Several other individuals deserve mention for providing resources on research: Nicholas Appleton, Beatriz Arias, Susan Duggan, Shirley Brice Heath, Sheila Shannon, and Jerri Willett.

Since this chapter was written in 1983, my own consciousness and that of many others has grown greatly concerning the matter of gender bias in schooling and society. This development supports increased attention to the feminine side of our lives. It justifies advocacy of the conceptual synthesis of multicultural and international education around the development of genuine friendship. Such friendship must arise from an ethic of caring and is *fundamentally* feminine.

[1] This research review was completed in the spring of 1983 and includes representative studies to that date. Readers may look at recent issues of social studies and other journals cited in this review for the latest research reports. This reviewer has no reason to suspect that trends within international or multicultural research have changed since the review was conducted.

[2] In the chapter, the term "international education" is synonymous with both cross-cultural and global education. Likewise, subsumed under the title "multicultural education" are studies in multiethnic and ethnic studies. Some reference is made to gender studies in the review, although other reviewers might not include this area of research in either multicultural or international education.

[3] Because this is an introductory overview of research, reviews done well by others have been cited whenever possible. Readers can refer to individual reviews and to studies reported therein for a closer examination of findings.

[4] Qualitative research is generally conducted through lengthy observation of actual educational situations and through intensive interviews. Particular events are described, and less emphasis is placed on generalizing from findings than is done in more traditional quantitative investigation.

[5] Anderson subsumed these four dimensions under the rubric of "school climate." Her review is an excellent place to begin the study of contextual factors that influence international as well as multicultural education.

[6] See the entire issue of *Anthropology and Education Quarterly*, 8(4) 1976, (formerly *The Council on Anthropology and Education Quarterly*), for some of the first theoretical pieces that tied anthropological research to multicultural education.

[7] This reviewer notes the connection made between selection of friend and cognitive and learning style preferences mentioned previously in the discussion of research in multicultural education.

[8]For information about instructional programs based on multi-ability task grouping, write to Dr. Elizabeth Cohen, School of Education, Stanford, CA 94305.

REFERENCES

Adams, G. R. (1976). Characteristics of children and teacher expectancy: An extension to the child's social and family life. *The Journal of Educational Research, 70*(2), 87–90.

Allen, D. I. (1976). Children's association with their own and other countries. *Theory and Research in Social Education, 4*(2), 80–92.

Anderson, C. S. (1982). The search for school climate: A review of research. *Review of Educational Research, 52*(3), 368–420.

Anderson, C. C. (1982, May). *Ecological issues of curricular conception as they relate to global education.* Paper presented at the Conference on Priorities in Global Education, Easton, MD.

Anderson, L. F. (1981). *Research in teaching issues in international education.* Paper prepared for the National Institute of Education. Washington, D.C.: U.S. Department of Health, Education and Welfare.

Anderson, L., Anderson, C., & Winston, B. (n.d.). *The basic question: What should social studies do for children?* Palo Alto, CA: Houghton Mifflin.

Au, K. H., & Jordan, C. (1981). Teaching reading to Hawaiian children: finding a culturally appropriate solution. In H. Trueba, G. Guthrie & K. Au (Eds.), *Culture and the bilingual classroom.* Rowley, MA: Newbury House.

Blum, L. (1980). *Friendship, altruism and morality.* London: Routledge and Kegan Paul.

Bowermaster, M. (1978). Peer tutoring. *The Clearing House, 52*(2), 59–60.

Buber, M. (1965). *Between man and man.* New York: Macmillan.

Buber, M. (1970). *I and thou.* New York: Charles Scribner's Sons.

Burton, A. (1978). Anthropology of the young. *Anthropology and Education Quarterly, 9*, 54–70.

Butterfield, R. A., Demos, E. S., Grant, G. W., Moy, P. S., & Perez, A. L. (1979). A multicultural analysis of a popular basal reading series in the International Year of the Child. *Journal of Negro Education, 48*(3), 382–389.

Cangemi, J. P. (1979). How culturally different, gifted and creative students perceive their teachers. *The Clearing House, 52*, 419–420.

Carrasco, R. L. (1981). Expanded awareness of student performance: A case study in applied ethnographic monitoring in a bilingual classroom. In H. Trueba, G. Guthrie, & K. Au (Eds.), *Culture and the bilingual classroom.* Rowley, MA: Newbury House Publishers, Inc.

Clement, D. C., & Harding, J. R. (1978). Social distinctions and emergent student groups in a desegregated school. *Anthropology and Education Quarterly, 7*, 272–282.

Cohen, J. J., D'Heurle, A., & Widmark-Petersson, V. (1980). Cross-sex friendships in children: Gender patterns and cultural perspectives. *Psychology in the Schools, 17*, 523–529.

Cohen, R. A. (1976). Conceptual styles, culture conflict and non-verbal tests of intelligence. In J. Roberts & S. Akinsanya (Eds.), *Schooling in the cultural context* (pp. 290–322). New York: David McKay.

Cole, M. (1985). Mind as a cultural achievement: Implications for IQ testing. In E. Eisner (Ed.), *Learning and teaching the ways of knowing* (pp. 218–249). Chicago: University of Chicago Press.

Damico, S. B., Bell-Nathaniel, A., & Green, C. (1981). Effects of school organizational structure in interracial friendships in middle schools. *Journal of Educational Research, 74*, 388–393.

DeKanter, E., & Frankiewicz, R. (1981). Measuring teachers' attitudes toward Mexican American students. *Journal of the National Association for Bilingual Education, 6*(1), 77–92.

Devin-Sheehan, L., Feldman, R. S., & Allen, V. L. (1976). Research on children tutoring children: A critical review. *Review of Educational Research, 46*, 335–385.

Ehman, L. H. (1980). The American school in the political socialization process. *Review of Educational Research, 50*, 99–119.

Garcia, J., & Woodrick, C. S. (1979). The treatment of white and non-white women in U.S. textbooks. *The Clearing House, 53*, 17–22.

Giles, M. B., & Sherman, T. M. (1982). Measurement of multicultural attitudes of teacher trainees. *Journal of Educational Research, 75*, 204–209.

Gilligan, C. (1982). *In a different voice.* Cambridge: Harvard University Press.

Goodlad, J. I. (1984). *A place called school.* New York: McGraw-Hill.

Grant, C. A. (1981). Education that is multicultural and teacher preparation: An examination from the perspectives of preservice students. *Journal of Educational Research, 75*, 95–101.

Grant, C. A., & Grant, G. W. (1981). The multicultural evaluation of some second and third grade textbook readers—A survey analysis. *Journal of Negro Education, 50*(1), 63–74.

Hahn, C. L. (1983, November). *Promise and paradox: Challenges to global citizenship.* Presidential address delivered at the sixty-third annual meeting of the National Council for the Social Studies, San Francisco, CA.

Hanvey, R. G. (1976). *An attainable global perspective.* New York: Global Perspectives in Education.

Hoopes, D. S. (1979). Intercultural communication concepts and the psychology of intercultural experience. In M. Pusch (Ed.), *Multicultural education, a cross-cultural training approach* (pp. 9–38). Chicago: Intercultural Press.

Johns, R. W. (1978). Man-in-dialogue: An image for global-minded citizenship. *Theory and Research in Social Education, 6*(2), 1–25.

Johnson, N. B. (1977). On the relationship of anthropology to multicultural teaching and learning. *Journal of Teacher Education, 28*(3), 10–15.

Jones, R. S. (1980). National vs. international learning: Political knowledge and interest in the USA. *International Journal of Political Education, 3*(1), 33–47.

Klein, F. M., Novotney, J. M., & Burkett, D. (1981). *An investigation into the characteristics of a mankind classroom* (Research report to Educational Inquiry). New York: Global Perspectives in Education.

Kobus, D. K. (1982). *The developing field of global education: A review of the literature.* Unpublished manuscript. The University of the Pacific, Stockton, CA.

Koeller, S. (1977). The effects of listening to excerpts from children's stories about Mexican Americans on the attitudes of sixth graders. *The Journal of Educational Research, 70*, 329–334.

Laosa, L. M. (1977). Multi-cultural education—How psychology can contribute. *Journal of Teacher Education, 28*(3), 26–30.

Lindsey, J. D., & Watts, E. H. (1979). Cross-age (exceptionality) peer tutoring programs: Have you tried one? *The Clearing House, 52*, 366–368.

Ludwig, M. (1981). Structuring classroom participation: The use of metaphrasing by black and white eighth grade students. In H. Trueba, D. Guthrie, & K. Au (Eds.), *Culture and the bilingual classroom*. Rowley, MA: Newbury House.

McAulay, J. D. (1978). Evaluation of textbook content on Southeast Asia. *The Clearing House, 52,* 105–106.

McDermott, R. P., & Gospodinoff, K. (1981). Social contexts for ethnic borders and school failure. In H. Trueba, G. Guthrie, & K. Au (Eds.), *Culture and the bilingual classroom*. Rowley, MA: Newbury House Publishers, Inc.

Millard, J. E. (1981). As the world changes. *The Clearing House, 54,* 281–283.

Mitsakos, C. I. (1978). A global education program can make a difference. *Theory and Research in Social Education, 6*(1), 1–15.

Moses, R., Daniels, H., & Gundlach, R. (1977). Children's language and the multicultural classroom. In D. Cross, G. Baker, & L. Stiles (Eds.), *Teaching in a Multicultural Society* (pp. 82–96). New York: The Free Press, Macmillan.

Motta, R. W., & Vane, J. R. (1976). An investigation of teacher perceptions of sex-typed behaviors. *Journal of Educational Research, 63,* 363–368.

Nguyen, L. T., & Henkin, A. B. (1980). Reconciling differences: Indochinese refugee students in American schools. *The Clearing House, 54,* 105–108.

Noddings, N. (1984). *Caring: A feminine approach to ethics and moral education.* Berkeley: University of California Press.

Paolitto, D. P. (1976). The effects of cross-age tutoring on adolescence: An inquiry into theoretical assumptions. *Review of Educational Research, 46,* 215–237.

Pate, G. S., & Garcia, J. (1981). Multi-ethnic multicultural education: A review or program. *The Clearing House, 55,* 132–135.

Pickle, C., Lipman, S., Smith, D. L., & Skeel, D. (1980, November). *Global Education in Memphis.* Paper presented at the annual meeting of the National Council for the Social Studies, New Orleans, LA.

Pickney, H. B., & Esposito, J. P. (1976). Organizational climate of desegregated elementary schools: Black and white teachers' perceptions. *Journal of Educational Research, 69,* 226–231.

Pietras, T., & Lamb, R. (1978). Attitudes of selected elementary teachers toward nonstandard Black dialects. *Journal of Educational Research, 71,* 292–297.

Polgar, S. K. (1978). Modeling social relations in cross-color play. *Anthropology and Education Quarterly, 9*(6), 283–289.

Prawat, R. S., & Jarvis, R. (1980). Gender difference as a factor in teachers' perceptions of students. *Journal of Educational Psychology, 72,* 743–749.

Remy, R. C., Nathan, J. A., Becker, J. M., & Torney, J. V. (1975). *International learning and international education in a global age.* Washington, D.C.: National Council for the Social Studies.

Ryan, F., & Wheeler, R. (1977). The effects of cooperative and competitive background experiences of students on the play of a simulation game. *Journal of Educational Research, 70,* 295–299.

Sagar, H. A., Schofield, J. W., & Snyder, H. N. (1983). Race and gender barriers: preadolescent peer behavior in academic classrooms. *Child Development, 54,* 1032–1040.

Schuncke, G. M. (1978). Social effects of classroom organization. *Journal of Educational Research, 71,* 303–307.

Schuncke, G. M., & Bloom, J. R. (1979). Cooperation as a goal and a tool in the classroom. *The Clearing House, 53,* 117–122.

Schwartz, F. (1981). Supporting or subverting learning: Peer group patterns in four tracked schools. *Anthropology and Education Quarterly, 7,* 99–121.

Simpson, C. (1981). Classroom organization and the gap between minority and non-minority student performance levels. *Educational Research Quarterly, 6*(3), 43–53.

Sizemore, R. W. (1981). Do black and white students look for the same characteristics in teachers? *Journal of Negro Education, 50*(1), 48–53.

Skeel, D. J., Dudley, D., & Mitsakos, C. I. (1980, November). *Children and the world, a global education project for the elementary school.* Paper presented at the annual meeting of the National Council for the Social Studies. New Orleans, LA.

Spaulding, S., Colucci, J., & Flint, J. (1982). International Education. In H. E. Mitzel (Ed.), *The encyclopedia of educational research* (5th ed.) (pp. 945–956). New York: The Free Press, Macmillan.

Torney, J. V. (1979). Psychological and institutional obstacles to the global perspective in education. In J. Becker (Ed.), *Schooling for a global age* (p. 59–93). New York: McGraw-Hill.

Torney-Purta, J. (1982a). *Research and evaluation in global education: The state of the art and priorities for the future.* Paper presented at the Conference on Priorities in Global Education, Easton, MD.

Torney-Purta, J. (1982b). Socialization and human rights research: Implications for teachers. In M. Branson & J. Torney-Purta (Eds.), *International human rights, society and the schools* (pp. 35–47). Washington, D.C.: National Council for the Social Studies.

Trueba, H. T., Gutherie, G. P., & Au, K. H. (Eds.). (1981). *Culture and the bilingual classroom, studies in classroom ethnography.* Rowley, MA: Newbury House.

Trueba, H. T., & Wright, P. G. (1980–81). On ethnographic studies and multicu'tural education. *Journal of the National Association for Bilingual Education, 5*(2), 29–56.

Valentine, C. A. (1976). Using small group methods for social education. *The Clearing House, 50,* 115–117.

Van Ness, H. (1981). Social control and social organization in an Alaskan Athabaskan classroom: A microethnography of "getting ready" to read. In H. Trueba, G. Guthrie, & K. Au (Eds.), *Culture and the bilingual classroom.* Rowley, MA: Newbury House.

Vasquez, A. G., & Ingle, H. T. (1982). Multicultural and minority education. In H. E. Mitzell (Ed.), *The encyclopedia of educational research* (pp. 1267–1268). New York: The Free Press, Macmillan.

Washington, V. (1981). Impact of antiracism multicultural training on elementary teachers' attitudes and classroom behavior. *The Elementary School Journal, 81*(3), 186–192.

Washington, V. (1982). Implementing multicultural education: Elementary teachers' attitudes and professional practices. *Peabody Journal of Education, 59*(3), 190–200.

Webb, N. M. (1982). Student interaction and learning in small groups. *Review of Educational Research, 52,* 421–445.

Weinstein, C. S. (1979). The physical environment of the school: A review of the research. *Review of Educational Research, 49,* 577–610.

Willett, J. (1982). *A bibliographic essay on global education.* Unpublished manuscript, Stanford University, Stanford, CA.

CHAPTER 4

GEOGRAPHIC LEARNING

JoAnne Buggey and James Kracht

What is geography? What is geography's role in the elementary classroom? How and when should geographic principles be included in the elementary curriculum? Educators are seeking answers to these puzzling questions.

A good working definition of geography establishes the foundation for what geographic education should be in the elementary classroom. One such definition follows:

> "Geography" is one way of selecting things to observe in the world around us, assembling the observations and thinking about them. Its observations are descriptive of the physical and cultural features of human settlements and their natural settings. . . . The discipline considers data in terms of geographic patterns and changes in pattern. In order to guide its thinking, it asks questions about human settlements and seeks answers. . . . Geography studies human settlements at the scales and levels of generalization at which map, map symbols, and legends are necessary for understanding. (Borchert, 1983)

There seems to be general agreement that geographic education is a fundamental part of the elementary curriculum. Advocates include the National Council for the Social Studies (NCSS), the National Council for Geographic Education (NCGE) and State Boards of Education. NCSS (1984) lists geography as one of the areas of knowledge to be considered when selecting information goals for social studies; the Council also suggests a sequence for teaching map and globe skills at the elementary level (Figure 1).

State Boards of Education are requiring instruction in geographic concepts in all grades, K–12 in Texas and Minnesota, for example. Test construction, nationally and locally, includes questions related to geographic education. NCGE (1983) has developed a test for use in the intermediate grades in response to demand for valid assessment. The 75 multiple-choice items are organized into three categories: geographic skills, physical geography, and human geography.

Textbook developers, responding to demands for increased geographic competence, include detailed scope and sequence charts in 1983–86 elementary social studies series. Several companies—such as MECC (1984) and Nystrom (1984)—have developed geographic materials to supplement textbook lessons. For example, computer software offers drill and practice in map skills. Elementary social studies methods courses also emphasize the importance of geographic education, making it necessary for methods texts (Ellis, 1986; Jaroli-

mek, 1986) to address the role of geographic education in the elementary classroom.

Students, teachers, and parents are also interested in geographic education as a part of the curriculum. In one recent study (Schug, Todd, & Beery, 1984), only a small percentage of 6th graders chose social studies as their favorite subject. However, in another study (Buggey, 1984), when elementary students were asked to identify from a list of specific units and activities those parts of the school day they liked best, 72 percent identified one or more aspects of geographic education in their top five choices. Similar results occurred when elementary teachers were asked to select those areas they liked to teach; 69 percent identified one or more aspects of geographic education in their top five choices. Buggey also found that parents wanted geographic education included in their children's curriculum. Of those surveyed, 78 percent identified some aspect of geographic education in their top five choices of subjects to be included in their child's schooling.

Although support exists for geographic education in the elementary schools, there does not seem to be agreement about how and when geographic concepts should be included. What does current research reveal on this important question?

RESEARCH AND GEOGRAPHIC LEARNING

In an effort to determine what research reveals on this question, two approaches will be utilized: first, there will be a summary of two major reviews (Rush-

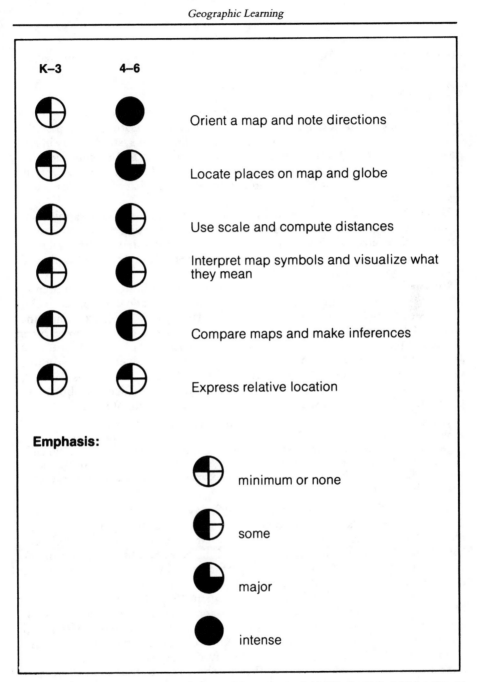

K–3   4–6

Orient a map and note directions

Locate places on map and globe

Use scale and compute distances

Interpret map symbols and visualize what they mean

Compare maps and make inferences

Express relative location

Emphasis:

minimum or none

some

major

intense

NOTES: From NCSS "In Search of a Scope and Sequence for Social Studies." *Social Education,* 48 (April 1984): 260.

FIGURE 1
Map and Globe Reading Skills Sequence

doony, 1968; Rice & Cobb, 1978). Then, these findings will be augmented by more recent research findings.

Research Reviews

Two significant reviews of research relating to geographic education have been conducted. Rushdoony (1968) reviewed research relating to map skills. He found that studies were generally not longitudinal, not systematically investigated, and involved only a small number of students. Rushdoony reported that prior to 1960 most map skill research consisted of status studies. Only in the later years of his study did he find concern about what children learn as a result of systematic instruction.

When Rice and Cobb (1978) reviewed research relating to geographic education, they expected to find a wide range of research relating to the geographic concepts children could learn. However, they found that few studies had been done. As a result, the review focused on studies relating to map skills and children's conceptual and analytic processes.

Rice and Cobb reported a number of studies that indicated that children in the primary grades could perform at a higher map skill and conceptual level if given proper instruction. For example, Crabtree (1968, 1974) examined the effects of systematic instruction of geographic skills and concepts on learners in grades 1–3. She devised two experimental curricula to teach about areal association. The presentations took 16 weeks and involved 12 classrooms. Following instruction, students in all grades made significant gains "at each cognitive level and across levels of symbolic abstraction" (Rice & Cobb, 1978, p. 75). Crabtree's second study investigated the sequencing of skills.

> To a greater extent than any other research identified, these two investigations . . . provide systematic, valid evidence of young children's potential for learning geographic concepts, map interpretation skills, and analytic processes. . . . When young children are active participants in a highly structured and sequential series of geographic inquiries, they can learn complex analytic processes and concepts of geography. (Rice & Cobb, p. 76)

Other studies (Hart, 1971; Imperatore, 1968; Savage & Bacon, 1969; Stoltman & Goolsby, 1973) also found evidence that systematic map activities improved map skills of primary grade students. In their study of first grade children, Savage and Bacon found that when map skills were taught using two methods—concrete and abstract—students performed equally well. However, the abstract treatment took only half as long.

Another group of studies (Balchin & Coleman, 1973; Klett & Alpaugh, 1976; Neperud, 1977) provided conflicting views about the order of presentation of map skills. Some supported Piaget's developmental stages, and others found there was no definite progression in graphic presentation and spatial development. Cox (1977) also attempted to identify the sequence in which students learn map skills in order to verify Piaget's theories. He found some areas of support but not conclusive evidence. He recommended that the best direction for map research was to examine the effect of instruction on performance. Cox, like Rushdoony, made recommendations about an appropriate map skills sequence (reported in Rice & Cobb, 1978, Appendix A and B, pp. 101–106).

Although they did not agree on the sequence, they did agree that planned instruction was crucial.

A number of studies investigated the age at which students are able to learn geographic skills and concepts. A group of studies by Blaut, McCleary, and Blaut (1970) in the Place Perception Project at Clark University found evidence to indicate that 1st graders of varied backgrounds can read some maps. Blaut and Stea (1974) discovered that children as young as three have some ability to deal with maps. Lanegran, Snowfield, and Laurent (1970) found that children can learn cardinal directions as early as kindergarten. However, Bettis and Manson (1975), developers of the Michigan Elementary Geography Test (MEGT) for 5th graders, concluded that "if geographic literacy is the goal for elementary education, substantial evidence exists which indicates that the goal is not being attained" (p. 24).

Rice and Cobb (1978) also reviewed a series of studies related to vocabulary development. Eskridge (1939) specified six variable factors that he believed were related to growth in understanding: (1) the amount of experience, (2) kind of experience, (3) level of geographic attainment, (4) ways in which meanings are verbalized, (5) mental age and (6) sex (Rice & Cobb, p. 59). Eskridge's findings also stressed the importance of interpretation of student responses and how different people interpret the same data differently. Milburn (1972) found that children often misunderstand words that adults take for granted. Attempts at remediation based on his findings indicated positive results with young learners. He stressed the importance of systematic development of vocabulary.

Finally, a number of studies (Huck, 1955; Kaltsounis, 1961; Lowry, 1963; Mugge, 1968; Newgard, 1962; Sheridan, 1968) emphasized the importance of measuring knowledge before instruction. Most of the researchers felt that their studies also supported the idea that young children can learn more content.

Rice and Cobb's (1978) review of the research indicated that children can learn what well-prepared teachers teach, and that it is not necessary to wait until the intermediate grades to introduce systematic instruction in geography. They did, however, include certain qualifications. Research in geographic education had not been systematic; the studies were not conclusive but suggested directions for further studies. Longitudinal studies were rarely undertaken. Quality of instruction was not a major concern. And studies dealing with geographic education had been restricted to a few topics, and did not reflect the total picture. Rice and Cobb also emphasized that, for learning in geographic education to take place, teachers must be convinced that children can learn more, even in the primary grades. Teachers must be prepared to teach geographic education to assure that learning objectives will be met.

Additional Research

Since the report of Rice and Cobb (1978) the number of research studies in elementary school geography has again been limited. Several, however, do add to the findings of the works summarized above.

A recent study by Atkin (1981) is based on Piaget's theory that children go through stages of understanding. Twenty-two preschool children, 4.4 to 5.4

years of age, were left in two intact groups. The experimental and control groups showed no significant difference on a pretest. They were instructed daily for a month in map and globe skills. Lessons focused on the child's environment and included ideas about the shape of the earth, the globe as model of the earth, directions, orienting a map, distance and scale, symbols-location, earth–sun relationship, and abstract location. Except for abstract location, the experimental group did significantly better on all parts of the posttest. A follow-up test was given a year later, and again the experimental group performed significantly better. The study was replicated with another group of preschool children with the same results. The researcher concluded that, if presented in a clearly structured manner, many map and globe skills can be understood by young children.

Buggey (1971) examined the relationship between classroom questions and map skill achievement of second grade children. Two teaching techniques were evaluated: one used 70 percent knowledge-level questions and 30 percent higher-level questions; the other used 30 percent knowledge-level questions and 70 percent higher-level questions (Bloom, 1956). A total of 108 students were randomly assigned to three groups. There was no significant difference between groups on a pretest.

The control group received no instruction. The two treatment groups received instruction daily for three weeks. The teachers followed eight-lesson sequences, which contained questions relating to visual materials that presented the concept of location. On the posttest, students who received instruction based on pre-dominantly higher-level questions outperformed those instructed using pre-dominantly knowledge-level questions. Both groups significantly outper-formed the control group. A parallel study (Tyler, 1971) also found that 2nd graders could demonstrate a significantly higher level of achievement when presented with systematic instruction.

Miller, in an effort to examine what should be included on maps for students in intermediate grades, first investigated the effective use of color on maps (1973) and later focused his research on overall design and layout (1982). By interview-testing 96 randomly selected 4th–6th grade students, he examined the merits of four experimental maps. Students were asked questions at the application level or higher (Bloom, 1956). Six categories were investigated: political features, physical features, interpretation of symbols, compass direc-tions, distance measurements, and longitude and latitude. Miller concluded that:

- No more than three or four different sizes of type should be used.
- City symbols should be differentiated.
- A compass rose should be included with at least three of the cardinal direc-tions named.
- A latitude-longitude grid system with lines and degree labels should be used.
- Information on symbols, colors, and measurements should be combined into an attractive and prominent legend.
- National boundaries should be marked with bold lines.
- Names of countries, cities, and other political units, and most physical features, should be set in a compact horizontal format. Miller also suggested

that better maps be designed and that some way be found to help teachers and students use maps more effectively.

With the launching of Landsat satellites and the resultant images of the earth's surface, a new map skill was added to the elementary curriculum. A series of studies by Kirman (1977) examined the use of Landsat maps. He found that children as young as in the 3rd grade could use infrared false color Landsat images. In 1981, Kirman further investigated to see whether children could use black and white Landsat images. His results with 70 3rd–5th graders were not conclusive but showed promise. Another study (Kirman, 1984) was limited to 3rd graders. Eighteen hours of instruction were provided to a class of 29 students. They were able to demonstrate on an achievement test that they were capable of interpreting "Band 5" black and white Landsat images. The researcher concluded that if 3rd grade students can understand Landsat maps, probably older students can also. Qualifications regarding the above conclusion included the importance of the teacher being well prepared in the use of materials, a clear sequence of presentation, and allowance of sufficient time.

The Place Vocabulary Research Project has been examining place vocabulary development since 1976 (Saveland, 1983). As a result, the World Basic Place Vocabulary Test was developed. The 50-item test includes a meridian map on an oval projection. Five oceans and seas, 32 countries (with population in excess of four million and area in excess of 50,000 square miles), and 13 major cities were included. The test was administered to 12,500 13-year-olds in 13 countries. General results indicated that most 13-year-olds tested had limited place vocabulary knowledge; and that if teachers and curriculum materials ignore place vocabulary, students are not likely to learn place names independently.

Although his was not an empirical study, Herman (1983) identified social studies content, including map and globe skills, and appropriate grade level placement. In the study, begun in 1979, 25 areas were selected, including geography. Five academicians—Philip Bacon, George Carey, Robert Gabler, Clyde Kohn, and John W. Morris—were selected to identify the geography content. Social studies educators were then asked to identify the grade level where the content should be taught (Figure 2). The findings indicate that students should not be introduced to geographic concepts earlier than they have in the past.

We can summarize this section now by stating that, although geographic education has been a part of the elementary school curriculum during the last century, there is inconclusive evidence as to the best time to introduce students to geographic concepts and skills. While all studies do not suggest the early introduction of geographic concepts and skills, most experimental studies indicate that when materials are carefully sequenced and teachers are well prepared, students in the elementary classroom can learn geographic concepts and skills at a younger age than would have been expected.

THE TEACHER AND GEOGRAPHIC LEARNING

The teacher is the key! What little agreement there is in the research seems to indicate that students can learn what well prepared teachers systematically

GEOGRAPHY	K–3	4–6
1. Describes and appreciates the relationship between the physical and cultural worlds (human-land relationships, including environmentalism and conservation).	2	51
2. Explains with examples the interdependence of nations (economic and social).	0	35
3. Explains how people and places (regions) differ from one another at various scales—local, national, world; describes area differentiation.	6	63
4. Identifies problems resulting from physical and economic factors, including population distribution and density.	2	11
5. Applies geographic concepts and principles to contemporary social, economic, and political problems; uses skills of observation, mapping, analysis.	0	4

SOURCE: W. L. Herman, Jr., "What Should Be Taught Where?" *Social Education* 47 (February 1983): 96.

FIGURE 2
Percent of Educators Identifying Appropriate Grade Level for Each Geographic Statement

teach. Research is not conclusive about the optimum grade level to introduce concepts and skills, but it suggests that whenever introduced, it is the presentation of the materials and preparation of the teacher that are crucial elements. With this in mind, a group of 30 elementary teachers met to identify sample lesson sequences, three of which follow. All were implemented successfully with students at varied grade levels from kindergarten through 6th grade.

Suggested Geographic Lessons

Aerial Perspective. Before learners can understand a map, they must understand that a "map view" is "looking at the world from a bird's eye view." This idea can be introduced in a meaningful way by using something as simple as a paper cup. Begin by showing the students the side view of the cup. Then have them look at the cup placed on the floor, so that they are looking down at it from the top. Have them draw each view and label it (Figure 3).

Repeat this exercise with other items that can be easily drawn; for example, doll furniture. Follow the drawing activity with a discussion of where they can most easily see their classroom as it would appear on a map. Students should visualize sitting on a clear plastic ceiling, so they could look down on the room as they did on the cup. Students can then be introduced to two pictures of the same place, one showing the side view and the other showing a "map view."

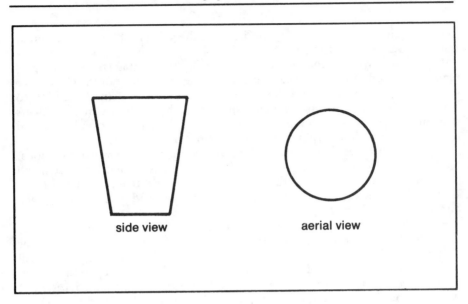

FIGURE 3
Aerial Perspective

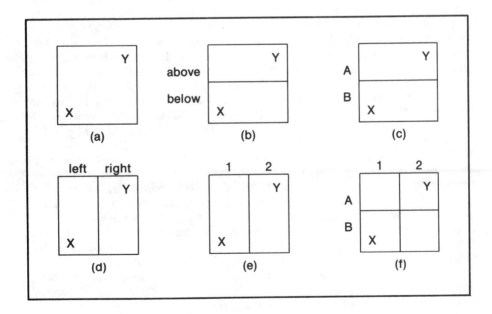

FIGURE 4
Using a Grid To Develop the Concept of Location

Once students, of any age, are familiar with the side and "map view," maps can be increased in complexity.

Direction. Introduce the cardinal directions by first asking students to "pretend" north and south. Have two students come to the front of the class. Give one a card labeled north and the other south, and have them stand back to back. Explain that north and south are opposites. Then have two more students come up to represent east and west. Give them cards labeled east and west, and orient them correctly. Repeat this activity with other students.

Once students are familiar with the relationship of the cardinal directions, introduce true north. Use a globe to help students understand that true north is toward the North Pole and that true south is toward the South Pole. Have students label the cardinal directions in the classroom and practice facing each direction as it is named.

After students are familiar with classroom directions, they are ready to be introduced to the compass rose. Introduction of the intermediate directions follows naturally using the same procedure with labeled cards. Age level will indicate how much practice is needed in order to master each step in the lesson.

Location. Introduce a grid by having students try to identify the location of X and Y in a large rectangle on the board (Figure 4a). Add a line across the middle of the rectangle and print "above" and "below" on the board (Figure 4b). Again locate X and Y. Erase "above" and "below" and substitute A and B at the side of the rectangle (Figure 4c). Have the students locate X and Y using A and B. Talk about how both the line and the A and B make it easier to locate X and Y. Remove the horizontal line and replace it with a vertical line (Figure 4d). Print "left" and "right" on the board. Again locate X and Y. Erase "left" and "right" and substitute 1 and 2 at the top of the rectangle (Figure 4e). Have the students locate the X and Y using 1 and 2. Talk about how both the line and the 1 and 2 make it easier to locate X and Y. Return the horizontal line to the rectangle and relabel A and B (Figure 4f). Explain that this is a grid. Have the students locate X and Y using A and B, and 1 and 2. Explain to the students that they name the letter first and the number second; it is written "A-1," and, when read aloud, the dash is silent. Talk about how the grid made it easier for them to locate X and Y.

Activities such as making a grid in the classroom and playing tic-tac-toe with a grid provide practice needed for successful use of a grid on a map. The size of the grid and the complexity of the map can be increased depending upon the ability of the students. Longitude and latitude, and time zones, are easily introduced once students are thoroughly familiar with the use of grids.

Research has not indicated the key geographic concepts or skills, or the one right grade level sequence, but has only suggested that there be carefully planned lessons. This chapter has presented only three samples of conceptually focused map skill sequences. Other planned lessons are included in all elementary social studies programs. Journals such as *Social Education* and the *Journal of Geography* frequently provide other suggestions.

Parents can also encourage geographic learning in their young geographers. Opportunities for parent-student workshops can provide parents with the skills necessary to carry on the learning process at home. Travel presents an excellent time for them to reinforce geographic concepts and skills, and local neighbor-hoods provide unlimited opportunities every day.

CONCLUSION

Geographic education is an important part of the elementary school curric-ulum. Research is inconclusive as to how and when to include geographic concepts and skills in the curriculum, but it indicates that students can learn geographic concepts and skills when well-prepared teachers present carefully sequenced lessons. This is only a beginning, however. Further research in geographic education is sorely needed.

REFERENCES

Atkins, C. L. (1981). Introducing basic map and globe concepts to young children. *Journal of Geography, 80*, 228–233.

Balchin, W. G. V., & Coleman, A. M. (1973). Progress in graphicacy. *Times Educational Supplement, 44*, 3024.

Bettis, N. C., & Manson, G. A. (1975). An assessment of the geographic learning of fifth grade students in Michigan. *Journal of Geography, 74*, 229–245.

Blaut, J. M., McCleary Jr., G. S., & Blaut, A. S. (1970). Environmental mapping in young children. *Environment and Behavior, 2*, 335–349.

Blaut, J. M., & Stea, D. (1974). Mapping at the age of three. *Journal of Geography, 73*, 5–9.

Bloom, B. S. (Ed.). (1956). *Taxonomy of educational objectives, handbook I: Cognitive domain.* New York: David McKay Company.

Borchert, J. R. (1983). Questions students ask. *Journal of Geography, 82*, 43.

Buggey, L. J. (1971). *A study of the relationship of classroom questions and social studies achievement of second-grade students.* Unpublished doctoral dissertation, University of Washington, Seattle.

Buggey, L. J. (1984). *What teachers, students, and parents really like.* Unpublished manuscript, University of Minnesota.

Cox, W. (1977). *Children's map reading abilities with large scale urban maps.* Doctoral dissertation, University of Wisconsin at Madison. Duplicated as Publication No. 78-4, Geography Curriculum Project, University of Georgia, 1978.

Crabtree, C. (1968). *Teaching geography in grades one through three: Effects of instruc-tion in the core concept of geographic theory* (Project no. 5-1037). Washington, D.C.: Department of Health, Education, and Welfare, Office of Education.

Crabtree, C. (1974). *Children's thinking in the social studies. Part 1: Some factors of sequence and transfer in learning the skills of geographic analysis.* Los Angeles: University of California.

Discovery. (1984). Chicago: Nystrom.

Ellis, K. E. (1986) *Teaching and Learning Elementary Social Studies.* Newton, Ma.: Allyn & Bacon, 3rd ed. 55–60.

Eskridge, R. J., Jr. (1939). *Growth in understanding of terms in grades 4 to 6.* Durham, N.C.: Duke University Press.

Hart, R. A. (1971). *Aerial geography: An experiment in elementary geography.* Master's thesis, Clark University. Duplicated for distribution by Environmental Research Group, Chicago, Peace Perception Report No. 6.

Herman, W. L., Jr. (1983). What should be taught where? *Social Education, 47,* 94–100.

Huck, C. (1955). Children learn from their culture. *Educational Leardership, 13,* 171–175.

Imperatore, W. A. (1968). *Earth, man's home: A beginning geography unit.* Athens, Ga.: Geography Curriculum Project.

Jarolimek, J. (1986) *Social Studies in Elementary Education:* New York, Macmillan, 7th ed. 137–145.

Kaltsounis, T. (1961). *A study concerning third graders' knowledge of social studies content prior to instruction.* Unpublished doctoral dissertation, University of Illinois.

Kirman, J. (1984). A new elementary level map skill: Landsat "band 5" satellite images. *Social Education, 48,* 191–195.

Kirman, J. (1977). The use of infrared color satellite images by grades 3, 4, and 5 pupils and teachers. *The Alberta Journal of Educational Research, 23,* 52–64.

Kirman, J. (1981). Use of "band 5" black-and-white Landsat images in the elementary grades. *Journal of Geography, 80,* 224–228.

Klett, F. R., & Alpaugh, D. (1976). Environmental learning and large-scale environments. In G. T. Moore and R. G. Colledge (Eds.), *Environmental Knowing: Theories, research, and methods.* Stroudsburg, Pa.: Dowden, Hutchinson and Ross.

Lanegran, D. A., Snowfield, J. G., & Laurent, A. (1970). Retarded children and the concepts of distance and direction. *Journal of Geography, 69,* 157–160.

Lowry, B. L., (1963). *A survey of the knowledge of social studies concepts possessed by second grade children previous to the time these concepts are taught in the social studies lessons.* Unpublished doctoral dissertation, State University of Iowa.

MECC. (1984). *MECC educational computing catalog.* St. Paul: MECC.

Milburn, D. (1972). Children's vocabulary. In N. Graves (Ed.), *New movements in the study and teaching of geography.* London: Temple Smith.

Miller, J. W. (1973). Comparisons of conventional "subdued" to vivid "highly contrasting" color schemes for elementary school maps: Report of an experiment. *Journal of Geography, 72,* 41–45.

Miller, J. W. (1982). Improving the design of classroom maps: Experimental comparison of alternative formats. *Journal of Geography, 81,* 51–55.

Mugge, D. J. (1968). Are young children ready to study the social sciences? *Elementary School Journal, 68,* 232–240.

National Council for Geographic Education. (1983). *Intermediate-level geography test.* Macomb, IL: NCGE.

National Council for the Social Studies. (1984). In search of a scope and sequence for social studies. *Social Education, 48,* 249–262.

Neperud, R. W. (1977). The development of children's graphic representations for the large-scale environment. *Journal of Environmental Education, 8,* 57–65.

Newgard, C. S. (1962). *A survey of selected social studies and science understandings as evidenced by first-grade children.* Unpublished master's thesis, University of Washington, Seattle.

Primary social studies skills. (1984). Chicago: Nystrom.

Rice, M. J., & Cobb, R. L. (1978). *What can children learn in geography?: A review of the research.* Boulder: SSEC.

Rushdoony, H. A. (1968). A child's ability to read maps: Summary of the research. *Journal of Geography, 67,* 213–222.

Savage, T. S., Jr., & Bacon, P. (1969). Teaching symbolic map skills with primary-grade children. *Journal of Geography, 68*, 326–332.

Saveland, R. A. (1983). Map skills around the world. *Social Education, 47*, 206–210.

Schug, R., Todd, R., & Berry, R. (1984). Why kids don't like social studies. *Social Education, 48*, 382–387.

Sheridan, J. M. (1968). Children's awareness of physical geography. *Journal of Geography, 67*, 82–87.

Stoltman, J. P., & Goolsby, T. N. (1973). Developing map skills through reading instruction. *Journal of Geography, 72*, 32–36.

Tyler, J. F. (1971). *A study of the relationship of two methods of question presentation, sex, and school location to the social studies achievement of second-grade children.* Unpublished doctoral dissertation, University of Washington, Seattle.

CHAPTER 5

TEACHING HISTORY: A DEFINITIONAL AND DEVELOPMENTAL DILEMMA

Linda S. Levstik

Despite the dominance of history in the elementary social studies curriculum, research has very little to say about the teaching of history at the elementary level. Instead, scholars concentrate on the adolescent learner, and leave elementary educators to draw what implications they can from such work. The result is considerable debate over what aspects of history should be taught, how they should be taught, and even if any history at all is appropriate before adolescence.

This debate and the small body of research on history at the elementary school level provide the focus for this chapter. Before a discussion of these issues, however, a brief section will outline the historical background of history as a school subject. The chapter will also present a discussion of the implications of current research and theory for classroom practice, as well as specific examples of history in action.

HISTORY AS A SCHOOL SUBJECT

History, especially United States history, has been a feature of public and private education in this country since shortly after the colonies became independent. The move to require United States history began early in the 19th century. It was rooted in an emerging nation's desire to create a past separate from its European, and especially British, history. Advocates of U.S. history sought to build national pride and citizenship through an emphasis on a heroic, if brief, past (Kownslar, 1974; Hansen, 1923, p. 15).

Teaching U.S. history gained additional support as a method of Americanizing immigrants from non-English speaking countries. As immigration increased, some "old" Americans worried that the perceived laxity of immigration and citizenship requirements would result in the loss of a distinctive American culture. Schools were charged with the task of Americanizing immigrant children:

> Let us take their children, then, and educate them in the same schools with our own, and thus amalgamate them with our schools. (Mansfield, 1835, as cited in Hansen, 1923)

In 1827, Massachusetts made U.S. history a required course of study, thus providing a model for other states. Later support by the American Historical Association and the National Education Association helped establish the pattern of U.S. history in grades 5, 8 and 11 throughout most of the nation. History, as taught in the schools, was a linear, chronological arrangement of information, emphasizing government and "great men" for the purpose of producing good citizens (Knownslar, 1974).

Reform movements in the 20th century advocated a more interdisciplinary social studies. Yet emphasis on process, reflective inquiry and the structure of the disciplines resulted in a negligible change in actual classroom practice. History and geography remain prominent features of the social studies curriculum, with little change in either the definition of history or in strategies of instruction (Hertzberg, 1985; Clegg, 1977; Gross, 1977).

Research also reflects this traditional view of history. Most often, historical thinking is investigated in terms of the development of time and space concepts. Secondarily, researchers study the development of analytic ability using the professional historian as a model. More recently, two theoretical and research perspectives can be seen in conflict. The first looks to Piagetian stage theory for a model describing historical thinking. The second concentrates on the patterns of children's responses to historical material. Each of these perspectives and its supporting research will be discussed in turn.

THE PIAGET-PEEL-HALLAM MODEL

In the 1960s, British scholars applied Piagetian stage theory to learning history. Their studies indicate that historical thinking develops slowly, requires a level of formal operations not attainable in the early years of schooling, and is only rarely obtained even at the secondary level. Subsequently, some writers have suggested postponing the study of history until the collegiate level (Elton, 1974). Others recommend that curriculum during the preadolescent years be modified to emphasize concrete experiences and strong analogies to areas of significance to the child (Lello, 1980). This school of thought and the supporting research have been labeled the "Piaget-Peel-Hallam" or "empiricist-Progressivism" model (Zaccaria, 1978; Watts, 1972).

E. A. Peel (1967) and Roy Hallam (1972, 1974, 1975) used Piaget's theory of development as the criterion against which to measure historical thinking. Similar studies on the development of logical thinking in science and mathematics provided a model for Peel's theoretical conclusions and Hallam's empirical studies. Initially, Hallam selected three historical passages to elicit student response. One hundred students aged 11 to 16 responded to 10 questions for each passage; responses were then categorized as representing pre-operational, concrete operational and formal operational stages. When categorized in this manner, children's answers indicated that formal operational thinking appeared much later in history than in science and mathematics. Hallam (1972) calculated the appearance of formal thought at between 16.2 and 16.6 years of age, with concrete operations appearing during the 12th year. By implication, elementary children, in the pre-operational stage, would be incapable of understanding history in any meaningful way. Such conclusions provide ammunition for those who suggest that history is unsuited to any but formal operations (see discussion in Laville & Rosenzweig, 1982). There are, however, more moderate positions.

Researchers in the Peel-Hallam tradition in Australia (Kennedy, 1983; Jurd, 1973), England (Collis & Biggs, 1979), and the United States (Sleeper, 1975; Poster, 1973) have questioned the assumptions underlying previous developmentalistic work. They suggest that logical structures in science and mathematics may not have analogies in history. Jurd (1973), for example, argues that the search for evidence out of which to construct laws in science and mathematics is not characteristic of history. Instead, evidence in history is particularistic. Interpretation, too, is dependent on the historian's perspective. Jurd suggests, then, that historical understanding be seen, at least in part, as the development of personal interpretation, rather than the ability to establish through logical analysis what is "true." Along with Collis and Biggs (1979), Jurd distinguishes the "open" nature of historical thinking from the "closed" structure of science and mathematics. He suggests that stages of development reflect an emphasis on personal interpretation, similar to Kohlberg's stages of moral development, rather than the exercise of evidence-testing behaviors described by Hallam. Neither Jurd nor Collis and Biggs argue with Hallam's conclusion that historical thinking can be explained developmentally, or that it is a slow process. They believe that history requries a systematic reasoning beyond many children, and they argue only that the usual interpretation of systematic thinking commonly applied in the sciences does not fit history.

The Piaget-Peel-Hallam model assumes a definition of history congruent with history as it is taught in most schools: that history is essentially non-observable and learned through the abstractions of language, and that it is inextricably bound to chronology and the concept of time. The strength of the assumption that historical incident must be fixed in time and space can be seen in such comments as "since an understanding of history depends upon the development of a mature consciousness of time and chronology . . ." (Zaccaria, 1978, p. 328) or "History requires . . . a sense of time" (Lello, 1980, p. 341). But, what kind of time sense is required? Gustav Jahoda suggests that children develop a sense of "temporality, of things in flux and change with a gradual reaching out into future and past" (Zaccaria, 1978, p. 328). He argues that time is defined contextually, dependent on the prevailing social and intellectual climate. In some societies time is perceived as linear, in others as parallel strands, or recyclings. John Poster (1973) postulates that there are different times within a single cultural context. There is social time, literary time, personal or interior time, physical or clock time and historical time—"the time excised and refashioned out of the otherwise dead past by historians. . . . History . . . is a mirror held up to the present, and historical time, far from being constant, is transformed by change in the mentality of the society it reflects" (p. 588).

The time sense most often studied is physical, not historical, time. Piaget, for example, regards time in terms of duration, order, succession and velocity. He defined the development of a sense of the past in terms of a child's ability to extend conceptions of measurement and antecedent/consequent relationships backwards (Poster, 1973). Other writers have described time concepts in terms of clock and calendar, and the ability of children to comprehend time words. Similarly, William Joyce's study of the ability of 5th graders to comprehend time words led him to conclude that a knowledge of chronology and sequence, together with an ability to make generalizations based on "definite" and "indefinite" time, constitute time sense (Poster, 1973, p. 589). In these studies, time concepts are seen as slowly acquired achievements, defined in terms of a linear time scale and a Western conception of the nature of time (Lello, 1980).

If an understanding of history requires a mature conception of time, and if Piagetian stage theory is the most likely explanation of how children think about historical material, then there are serious problems with teaching history at the elementary level. There are, however, scholars who suggest that there may be cognitive processes that fall outside this model. As D. G. Watts (1972) notes in *The Learning of History,* "It is possible to construct an alternative model of thinking and learning about [history] in which Piaget's work is only part of the evidence, but which is nevertheless based on serious work and sound sources" (p. 18). Is history, for instance, a process of fixing people and events in time? Does the study of history inevitably require formal operational thinking?

John B. Poster (1973) presents a model that considers the relationship between time and history. He suggests that physical time is not the form most relevant to historical thinking. Rather, a sense of history involves more than clock time; it requires "a sense of existing in the past as well as the present, a feeling of being in history rather than standing apart from it" (p. 589). Poster further suggests that a sense of historical time is only partly developmental. A sense of the past might also be explained in terms of reinforcement:

If children in western society have little sense of the past and develop whatever conception of it they are likely to achieve considerably past the age at which they master other ideas and perspectives, might not the delay in the onset of historicality be explained solely in terms of the psychological concept of reinforcement? In traditional societies the past provides guidance for the future, making age and wisdom familiar bedfellows. Moreover, the stability of basic individual and social patterns of living may contribute to cyclical rather than purely sequential conception of time. The study of the past is thus rewarded by increased efficacy in coping with the present. (Poster, 1973, p. 594)

In societies where history has little perceived utility, a sense of history is slowly, if ever, developed. Because Poster identifies western society as having little use for the past, one is left to conclude that Poster has dealt a double blow to history teaching. Not only do physical time concepts develop slowly, but the more important historical time concept is hampered by cultural disinterest and a concomitant lack of reinforcement.

Watts (1972) presents a more optimistic view of chronology as it relates to history. Few of us, he argues, have more than an imperfect conception of time and chronology. Even professional historians use time phrases such as "rapid rise," "sudden collapse," or "speedy recovery" rather loosely. Watts suggests that instead of limiting history to chronology, we recognize that a "historical response" is possible "as soon as children can conceive of an event having occurred in the past" (p. 87).

Watts concludes that children are capable of seeing patterns and sequence in real events, though the patterns are general and imprecise: "cave men," "the old days," and "nowadays." New information can be fitted into and used to refine these general categories, or "chunks." Watts agrees that the process is slow, but does not accept that a mature time sense is a prerequisite to thinking historically. Rather he defines history in different terms, and with reference to a different psychological model.

I propose . . . a definition in terms of response: to say that history is that to which people respond historically, and that historical response is an emotional or intellectual reaction to the knowledge, or the belief that certain things happened in the past. Such a response is . . . "a sense of the past. . . ." (Watts, 1972, p. 43)

Such a definition allows Watts to describe the development of historical thinking as a gradual progression from history of low validity to history of high validity, with the one a necessary precursor to the other. Children's lack of mature time concepts or formal operational thinking is not then an impediment to historical response. Instead, the rudimentary "chunking" of time and the often stereotypical explanations of historical persons or events characteristic of young children are interpreted as historical thinking—a beginning that must be nurtured by experience and reflection. Watts does not believe that experience in history must be concrete in quite the same manner as Piagetians describe the term. Using Vygotsky's theories regarding language and thinking, Watts suggests that verbal instruction must be an important part of experience in subjects such as history. He also argues that historical response is more than logical thinking; it carries an expressive component that leads children toward conceptualization. "There is a manifest symbolic or iconic content in the concept,

and the work-symbol is then readily matched to the icon, and 'understood' "
(p. 31). These concepts, Watts explains, lack the richness of personal experience,
but they can be expanded by schoolwork and reading.

More recently, Kerry J. Kennedy (1983) proposed a third description of
historical thinking, linking information processing capacity and level of historical understanding. In Kennedy's research, 139 children in grades 7, 8, 9 and
10 from two suburban Sydney schools were measured according to developmental level, information-processing capacity, and historical understanding.
Historical understanding was assumed to be a formal operation in Piagetian
terms. Kennedy's results showed weak, though significant, correlations between
developmental levels and historical understanding. He concluded that historical
understanding might not be a developmental construct in the usual sense. "That
is to say, the measure of developmental level and the measures of historical
understanding were measuring different constructs" (Kennedy, 1983, p. 17).
Other studies by Piagetian researchers have explained low correlation between
tasks assumed to be measuring the same construct by reference to "decalage"—
a child's failure to use a logical structure used successfully on one task to solve
another. Kennedy suggested otherwise, positing a definition of historical understanding as

> a process that transforms historical data into a means of understanding past realities
> and their relationships to the present and future. The process is defined by at least
> three factors: the amount of data confronted at any one time, the manner of its
> presentation, and the processing strategies available to and used by readers and
> listeners. (p. 18)

Kennedy's work suggests that children can understand history when methodology includes attention to information processing capacity.

Research that tests Kennedy's thesis with elementary children remains to be
done. His work does, however, provide an alternative within the developmentalist tradition. How this alternative might affect classroom practice also remains
to be worked out.

RESPONSE AS A FUNCTION OF HISTORICAL UNDERSTANDING

In contrast to the Piaget-Peel-Hallam model, some researchers are analyzing
children's response to historical material. This line of inquiry proceeds from
studies of children's developing sense of story and response to literature. If
historical thinking is more closely related to thinking in literature than in science
and mathematics, then what has been learned through research on reader
response could be significant in the teaching of history.

Consider the development of skilled readers. Good readers usually grow up
with books. They are read to; they are given books long before they can
"decode" the text. The stories they hear are not necessarily about the near and
familiar. Rather, *Mother Goose,* nonsense verse, talking bears, fairy tales and
fantasy adventures are shared. During the years when social studies emphasizes
the "here and now," children's literary interests involve the distant and fantastic

(Applebee, 1978). Children enjoy enchanting literary adventures, while at the same time social studies curriculum withholds historical adventures assuming that history must be a creature of logic and analysis, even for the young. Studies of response suggest rethinking this stance, and observing children's patterns of development in historical thinking.

Research in the developmentalist model assumes that historical understanding requires logical analysis, but the research designs also require students to use and understand a particular form of discourse not necessarily familiar to younger children (cf. Wishart & Smith, 1983). James Moffat (cited in Meek, Warlow, & Barton, 1978, p. 18) suggests that children do not differentiate their thoughts into categories of discourse available to most adults. Instead, Moffat suggests, they begin by using a narrative framework to explain themselves and to understand others. Narrative remains a powerful form of discourse through preadolescence. Research also indicates the importance of context in aiding comprehension (French & Nelson, 1982; White & Gagné, 1976). This is the point at which Hallam begins his research, using a type of discourse relatively new to many of his subjects.

The failure of current practice to aid historical understanding may, then, be less a function of cognitive development than a faulty understanding of how children come to understand history. Moffat's work suggests attending to forms of discourse; James Britton (cited in Meek et al., 1978, p. 10) goes a step further, arguing that children's historical understanding proceeds from a subjective involvement in stories of individual lives to a later, more mature level of historical objectivity. Failing to introduce children to history in an appropriate context could limit later understanding. Rather than eliminate history, Britton suggests following the children's inclinations by providing opportunities for children to encounter history in a subjective context—narrative—that engages their emotions as well as their intellects. Curriculum could provide a variety of opportunities for children to respond to history in increasingly analytical ways. For example, children could use historical fiction and biography to explore a variety of perspectives on an issue. They could then use nonliterary sources to verify their perceptions. In this way, narrative and personal response could nurture inquiry (Levstik, 1981; Levstik, 1986).

NARRATIVE AS AN AID TO HISTORICAL UNDERSTANDING

This approach to historical understanding links emotion to reflective thinking. As Louis Rosenblatt (1934) maintained in *Literature as Exploration,* the process of reflective thinking begins with conflict or discomfort, or—as Piaget would have it—disequilibrium. Although problems, whether literary or historical, may be more easily considered without reference to emotion, they are also less real. Narrative, the mode of discourse most comfortable, combines historical incident with emotion and conflict. In narrative, children come close to a participant's view of history. They will not "understand" all the historical information they encounter, anymore than they fully understand all they encounter in literature (Meek et al., 1978; Rosenblatt, 1934). Their subjective response is seen, instead, as a prerequisite to more mature historical understanding.

One of the most fully developed explications of this approach can be found in the work of Kieran Egan (1979, 1980, 1982, 1983a, 1983b). Over the past decade, Egan has been developing a theoretical framework in opposition to the developmentalist model. Egan's model provides an alternative description of historical thinking in children.

Egan questions the use of Piagetian stage theory in setting educational objectives. He argues that available research leaves the theory open to considerable debate. For instance, if Piaget's operatory structures exist, then possession of one structure should transfer to a corresponding logical form, and a child lacking a particular structure should be incapable of learning forms requiring that structure. Instead, attempts at demonstrating these connections have proved inconclusive (Donaldson, 1978; Smedslund, 1977; Ashton, 1975; Brainerd, 1973; Brison, 1966). Successful performance of a particular task turns out to be a weak predictor of success in corresponding forms. According to Egan, reference to decalage does not adequately explain the phenomenon of lack of transfer. With Kerry Kennedy (1983), Egan believes that the lack of transfer indicates that some thinking may not be a developmental construct in the Piagetian sense.

Egan also cites a series of training studies by Brainerd (1977, 1978a, 1978b) in which children demonstrated concept attainment after instruction despite having demonstrated the lack of the assumed prerequisite operation. The Piagetian response that true learning did not occur, cannot, according to Egan, be supported by current research. He concludes that there is insufficient reason to assume that Piagetian theory is correct in postulating a natural psychological-developmental process that constrains learning (Egan, 1980, p. 265).

Unlike Laville and Rosenzweig (1980) and Kennedy (1983), Egan does not go on to define history as a process. He argues instead that emphasizing process is often done at the expense of content, and that content does matter. He sees process as inextricably linked with content in any intellectual endeavor. Emphasizing one over the other would not further the development of historical understanding (Egan, 1983). As an alternative, Egan offers this definition of historical thinking:

> We may see in historical understanding a range of different skills. . . . We recognize a form of imagination as an important component; ability to empathize with others; a sense of causality as it operates both in stories and in logical inference; the ability to reflect philosophically on general historical processes; moral sensitivity; the making of romantic associations with heroes and heroines or ideas; the excitement of seeing ideals and ideas being worked out through events; hobby-like fascination with particulars, whether costume through the ages or the design and building of pyramids or castles or what supplies were carried on voyages of discovery on and on and on. These are all parts of the engagement with history. They do not all develop together in some regular sequence; some . . . seem prominent at one time and then fade later. Yet each of these, or some aspect of each, persists in sophisticated historical understanding. The question for the educator is how the very different pieces, skills, concepts, modes of making sense of things, do or

should accumulate along with accumulating historical knowledge toward a sophisticated historical understanding. (Egan, 1983, p. 70)

In Egan's (1983) model, curriculum is planned to capitalize on student interests and to contribute particular aspects of "sophisticated historical understanding" (p. 72). He outlines four stages, or paradigms, as guides for instructional planning. Each paradigm, though prerequisite to the succeeding stages, is also distinct in its contribution to historical understanding. Mature historical understanding has access to all levels. The stages applicable to elementary children are:

1. The Mythic Stage (up to approximately seven years of age)

The mythic stage is organized around children's interests in stories with clear conflicts between opposites: good and evil, fear and security, big and little. Children draw meaning from these stories by an affective association with both positive and negative features of the content. In addition, they begin to understand causality in the story format. These structures, Egan suggests, allow children access to "the fantastic and exotic" (1983, p. 75). Such an approach reverses the traditional expanding horizons curriculum by arguing that what is familiar or "known" has more to do with emotional than physical distance.

At this stage Egan suggests that history be organized around dramatic struggles between good and evil—knowledge, freedom, and courage against ignorance, slavery, and fear. Instead of listening to an accounting of facts, or memorizing the functions of "community helpers," children would be engaged by history as dramatic story.

2. The Romantic Stage (approximately 8 to 13 years of age)

The bounds of reality become important to children in the romantic stage. Fantasy must be embedded in reality to ensure believability. People who struggle courageously with real problems appeal to children at this stage, as do superheroes and heroines. Egan believes the history curriculum should be based on an empathetic encounter with courageous people. He asserts the importance of setting their struggle in a narrative framework, both for the narrative's motivational power and its ability to transmit a notion of causation.

As long as the story is "real," and the situation is an encounter with human struggle, the content need not be immediately familiar to children. Stories of Sojourner Truth or Anne Frank are relevant to children during the romantic stage because they tell children what they want to know about human behavior in the face of great odds.

Egan sees the mythic and romantic stages as constituent parts of mature historical understanding. The emphasis in each of narrative causality and narrative discourse can also be supported by research on response discussed previously. The effects of such an approach on children's ability to understand history remain largely untested. Egan has described possible curricular arrangements based on his model, but he has not indicated the results of any field-testing.

METHODOLOGY

The lack of research on how children learn history is matched by the dearth of studies investigating methodology. The literature contains suggestions for teaching techniques and scope and sequence plans, but these are rarely research-based. Many refer to a developmentalist or expanding horizons interpretation, emphasizing personal, family and local history (cf. Burns, 1983; Sunal, 1981; Elkind, 1981). In part, this also reflects a shift in historiography towards social history, with family and local histories serving as microcosms of national and international patterns.

Kathy Thornburg (1983) reports one of the few empirical studies in this area. She investigated primary-aged children's ability to understand familial relationships, and her findings indicate that her subjects had difficulty comprehending these relationships. Thornburg concludes that children would be even less able to comprehend things distant in time or space. Whether this conclusion can be supported remains to be researched. Possibly, family relationships are more complex for children than are other aspects of history.

If familial concepts do precede those related to history beyond the family, the present expanding horizons approach may be appropriate. If, on the other hand, historical understanding develops as Watts and Egan suppose, radical restructuring of curriculum would be necessary. In order to plan effectively, though, there must be research on how elementary children come to understand history; research that does not now exist. Research on secondary students will not suffice. In the meantime, eliminating history from the curriculum cannot be justified.

IMPLICATIONS

What, then, can be concluded about teaching and learning history in the elementary years?

1. Current practice appears to be unsuccessful in developing historical understanding as defined by any of the models reviewed.

2. Social studies educators might make more use of research from children's response to literature than is currently the case, applying the techniques of response research to history. Britton, Moffat and Egan provide valuable insights into the nature of children's thinking. Their work suggests redefining history, not just as a process of inquiry, but as a complex discipline constructed of myth and romanticism as well as logic and analysis. Encouraging an initial personal response to history and designing a curriculum that provides for increasingly sophisticated encounters with historical material may be the place to start in history instruction.

3. Researchers need to investigate the power of narrative as it relates to history. Topics in history that interest children should be studied. There should also be analyses of the difference between children who demonstrate interest in historical topics and those for whom history is uninteresting.

A useful approach might be documenting the development of interest, and the ways in which concepts of time and space are used by children in refining historical understanding. Researchers might then investigate how understanding is inhibited or enhanced. Classroom teachers could play a crucial role in this process.

TWO APPROACHES TO A NARRATIVE-BASED ELEMENTARY CURRICULUM

We have discussed alternative ways to approach history at the elementary level. If a classroom teacher elected to implement a curriculum with reference to narrative-based history, how might such an approach look in practice? The following classroom experiences are examples.

Fourth graders working with Kentucky studies visited historic sites in their community, including the homes of Mary Todd Lincoln and John Hunt Morgan. In addition, guest speakers were invited to school to talk about the role of women in 19th-century Kentucky. The speakers brought artifacts representative of women's everyday life, including period costumes, hoops and bustles, old picture albums, kitchen utensils, letters, diaries and slave narratives. Children speculated on the uses of the artifacts, and discussed the work involved in managing daily life in the 19th century.

Students were asked to respond in writing to their experiences. Writing samples indicate areas of interest, and the personal nature of their response:

> They spoke to us
>   on Kentucky women.
> It seemed like they
>   were probably there.
> Ghosts, spirits,
>   came through a time machine.
> They knew everything
>   that happened in the
>   late 1800's. . . .
> And I'm glad I live in the
>   late, late
>   20th century!
> > *Stan Rosenbaum*

> No electricity,
> just candles. . . .
> Hard work,
> gathering firewood,
> fighting Indians
> Corsets pulled tighter,
> no gas,
> just a fire. . . .
> We fought,
> we got jobs,
> we got the vote. . . .
> We fought,
> and succeeded.
> > *Kate McAllister*

So many clothes
So many clothes
I don't know what
    to do!
When it is 92° outside
I'm dressed like
it's 22° outside!
So many clothes,
So many clothes.
    Janie Douglass

When I see things about old times, I like to pretend I am Laura Ingalls. I like to pretend that I have to make tea with mint and hot water. I like it much better the way we have it now.

My mother has my great, great, great, grandmother's shoes, but she doesn't wear them. They are the ugliest things I have ever seen! I am glad I wear loafers.
    Alexandra Gariepy

These 4th graders demonstrated an ability to compare their lives with a historical past long before they could be expected to reach historical understanding as defined by Hallam. They imagined themselves in the past, and identified with historical individuals and causes. They demonstrated a grasp of historical details from the past and they revealed that they enjoyed this approach to history:

I like to hear about the Civil War and how slavery was prohibited. The masters didn't want the slaves to learn to read because they could leave them.
It's neat how people save all those things like corsets, hoops and bustles.
I see how it would be fun to be a historian . . . have fun and be able to learn things too!

    Aaron Bird[1]

Sixth graders in another school began their study of history by reading historical fiction and biography. In the time that was allotted to language arts, a program of individualized reading, formal and informal group discussion, and opportunities to write was planned to precede research on historical topics. A broad selection of books, emphasizing biography, history, and historical fiction, was selected from the public library and the teacher's personal collection. Children selected books, were encouraged to finish them, but were allowed to switch if they did not like a book. Children averaged seven books each, and approximately 1,600 pages. They reported that they loved the opportunity to choose their own books, explore topics in depth, and work independently. They talked about being moved, inspired and sometimes angered by what they read, and frequently added that they had learned something they labeled "the truth." Their responses provide some insight into the ways in which the children became interested in history and attempted to make sense of it.

The frequency with which children commented on their need to know about various topics in history is remarkable. The teacher deserved part of the credit.

She had worked to build an environment in which both knowing and asking were valued. In another sense, her arrangement freed children to do what several writers suggest is the task of the beginning adolescent—the exploration of possible adult roles (Meel et al., 1978). A clear example of this behavior can be seen in the readings of one informal group of girls. Each girl read a biography of a woman with an unusual life story. In interviews, the girls were explicit in describing their reasons for selecting the books. They wanted, they said, to read about successful women. As one of them explained, in regard to her admiration for Amelia Earhart, "She did what she wanted to do." Another said, "I know now that I will be a doctor no matter what. I can do that [struggle as Elizabeth Blackwell had done], too." Using biography as a reference point, they discussed possible adult roles, debated the relative merits of careers in medicine, physics and computer science, and compared their futures to those of women from history.

Students also demonstrated a willingness to read difficult texts if the result was knowing something of importance to them. One boy struggled through a psychological biography of Adolf Hitler because it told him "the truth." Children were generally fascinated by the Nazi era. The search for truth, or at least understanding, may explain some of the fascination with the holocaust. The exploration of the border areas of human experience may also account for the strong response, for the children were both fascinated and repelled. They talked about the anger they felt at Hitler, about their realization of the horrors of that period, and their gratitude for their own more peaceful lives.

In small group discussions, children identified with holocaust victims, and some of the Hitler Youth.

"I would have run away! Why didn't they run away?"

"I would have been terrified!"

"I've been fascinated by Hitler. . . . He got to be so powerful. And why did he kill those people? He was prejudiced. The way he was raised, he just didn't like some people. There was this scene in the book. He's at a meeting and they're saying to join Austria, Germany and another country. And he jumps up and says thats impossible. It'll never happen. He really wanted power and he would do anything to get it. At the end he knew he was going to lose and so he killed himself. The book says he bit down on a poison capsule and shot himself in the head. I could not devote myself to killing and war like he could. He had a messed up mind. He was very confused."

The selection of books with themes of human suffering was noticeable in this class. Stories appeared to help children safely explore the "unwished for worst" (Hardy, 1978), as well as the heroic best, and to test themselves and their own potential for good or evil. They did not look for historical information in the traditional chronological sense. Instead, they sought for emotional truth and the possibilities that other human experiences might hold for their lives. They willingly read challenging books and forcefully participated in discussions. They constantly compared literary characters to themselves, and to choices that they might have made under similar circumstances. They empathized with characters in books, whether those characters were near or distant in time and space. Physical distance was not a problem; emotional distance and the need to understand human behavior determined whether a book was read or a historical era stirred interest.

As children read, and formal and informal groups formed and reformed, the teacher encouraged children to select topics for history projects. Selections included "Elizabeth Blackwell and the Admission of Women to Medicine," "The Battle of Hastings," "Pearl Harbor," and "Soldiers Look at World War II," a project reflecting British, American, German and Russian fears and feelings as troops faced each other in battle.

Reports written for each project demonstrate the power of the literary introduction. Instead of paraphrases of encyclopedia entries, they reflect how the children felt about their subjects. The paper on Elizabeth Blackwell included this description of Blackwell's medical training:

> When she arrived she was greeted cordially, but soon all the fun went away. The students were friendly but some of the professors were obnoxious. When studying childbirth she was asked to leave the room, on one occasion they took a corpse apart and she was asked to leave, but instead of leaving she sat in her seat. The professor grew red and angry, but to everyone's surprise at the end of the class she had taken apart and labeled every organ correctly (and didn't get sick!). The semesters went by and soon it was time to graduate. Elizabeth graduated at the top of her class with honors.[2]

Reports incorporated details that particularized a subject, especially if the detail emphasized the magnitude of a character's triumph or problem. The emotional impact of literature led one child to explain: "I loved this book because it sees through the eyes of this person. I never knew how hard people had it. This book is so real. I find this period especially interesting for some reason that I don't know about."

CONCLUSION

The variety of topics investigated by the 6th graders and the literary responses of the 4th graders are only two examples of history-in-action. The literature abounds with other suggestions. Many are imaginative and most would interest children. A classroom teacher faced with implementing a history-based curriculum would certainly be well advised to refer to these suggestions to enliven social studies. What is not available, however, represents a significant lack. First, there is no clear consensus regarding the objectives of history instruction. Second, there is almost no research indicating how children learn history, no matter how history is defined. Teachers are left with a definitional and developmental dilemma.

Considering the prevalence of history in most social studies curricula, this state of affairs is disturbing. There is evidence that current practice is inadequate, but insufficient research to suggest alternatives. This is a particularly serious problem for elementary teachers who are expected to deal with all curricular areas and may not have extensive background in the social studies. They need theory supported by research and translated into practical classroom suggestions. As a field, social studies needs to attend more to elementary curriculum, particularly in researching prominent features of the elementary program such as history.

In the meantime, good classroom teachers must do what they have always done: use available resources to interest and challenge children, experiment with method and content, and carefully observe their students' responses for evidence of historical understanding. We might also ask that they invite researchers to join them in studying how children come to understand history.

NOTES

[1]Material provided by Mark Scarr and Jennifer Stith, The Lexington School. Children's work used by permission.

[2]Material gathered during a research project at Millcreek Elementary School, Lexington, Kentucky; Lois Daniel, teacher.

REFERENCES

Applebee, A. N. (1978). *The child's concept of story: Ages two to seventeen.* Chicago: The University of Chicago Press.

Ashton, P. T. (1975). Cross-cultural Piagetian research: An experimental perspective. *Harvard Educational Review, 45,* 475–506.

Booth, M. B. (1984). Skills, concepts and attitudes: The development of adolescent children's historical thinking. In *History and theory: Studies in the philosophy of history* (pp. 101–117). Belkeft 22: Wesleyan University Press.

Brainerd, C. J. (1977). Cognitive development and concept learning: An interpretive review. *Psychological Bulletin, 84,* 919–939.

Brainerd, C. J. (1978a). Learning research and Piagetian theory. In L. S. Siegal & C. J. Brainerd (Eds.), *Alternative to Piaget: Critical essays on the theory.* N.Y.: Academic Press.

Brainerd, C. J. (1978b). The stage question in cognitive-developmental theory. *Behavioral and brain sciences,* 173–213.

Brison, D. W. (1966). Acceleration of conservation of substance, *Journal of Genetic Psychology, 109,* 311–322.

Burns, B. (1983). History for the elementary school child. *Social Studies, 74,* (1), 16–17.

Clegg, Ambrose (1977). Three midwest cities: The status of social studies education. *Social Education, 41* (7), 585–587.

Collis, K. F., & Biggs, J. B. (1979). *The structure of learning outcomes in history.* Unpublished paper, University of Newcastle.

Commager, H. S., & Muessig, R. H. (1980). *The study and teaching of history.* Columbus, Ohio: Charles E. Merrill.

Donaldson, M. (1978). *Children's minds.* London: Croom Helm.

Downey, M. (Ed.) (1985). *History in the schools* (Bulletin 74). Washington, D.C.: National Council for the Social Studies.

Egan, K. (1983). Accumulating history. *History and theory: Studies in the philosophy of history* (pp. 66–80). Belkeft 22: Wesleyan University Press.

Egan, K. (1982). What does Piaget's theory describe? *Teachers' College Record, 84* (2), 454–475.

Egan, K. (1980). On Piaget and education. *Harvard Educational Review, 50,* 263–269.

Egan, K. (1979). What children know best. *Social Education, 43* (2), 130–139.

Elkind, D. (1981). Child development and the social science curriculum of the elementary school, *Social Education, 45* (6), 435–437.

Elton, G. R. (1974). What sort of history should we teach? In M. Ballard (Ed.), *New movements in the study and teaching of history* (pp. 221–230). Bloomington, Indiana: Indiana University Press.

French, L., & Nelson, K. (1982). Taking away the supportive context: Preschoolers talk about "then & there." *The Quarterly Newsletter of the Laboratory of Comparative Human Cognition, 4* (1), 1–6.

Gross, R. (1977). The status of social studies in the public schools of the U.S.: Facts and impressions of a national survey. *Social Education, 41* (3), 194–200.

Hallam, R. N. (1975). *A study of the effect of teaching method on the growth of logical thought with special reference to the teaching of history.* Unpublished doctoral dissertation, Leeds University, Leeds.

Hallam, R. N. (1974). Piaget and thinking in history. In M. Ballard (Ed.), *New movements in the study and teaching of history* (pp. 162–178). Bloomington, Indiana: University of Indiana Press.

Hallam, R. N. (1972). Thinking and learning in history. *Teaching History, 2,* 337–346.

Hansen, O. A. (1923). *Early educational leadership in the Ohio Valley.* Bloomington, Indiana: Public School Publishing Co.

Hardy, B. (1978). Narrative as a primary act of mind. In M. Meek, A. Warlow, & G. Barton (Eds.), *The cool web* (pp. 12–26). New York: Atheneum.

Hertzberg, H. (1985). Students, methods and materials of instruction. In M. Downey (Ed.), *History in the schools* (Bulletin 74) (pp. 25–40). Washington, D.C.: National Council for the Social Studies.

Jurd, M. (1972). Adolescent thinking in history-type material. *The Australian Journal of Education, 17,* 2–17.

Kennedy, K. J. (1983). Assessing the relationship between information processing capacity and historical understanding. *Theory and Research in Social Education, 11,* 1–22.

Kownslar, A. O. (Ed.). (1974). *Teaching American history: The quest for relevancy (NCSS 44th yearbook).* Washington, D.C.: National Council for the Social Studies.

Laville, C., & Rosenzweig, L. (1982). Teaching and learning history. In L. Rosenzweig (Ed.), *Developmental perspectives on the social studies* (Bulletin 66) (pp. 54–66). Washington, D.C.: National Council for the Social Studies.

Lello, J. (1980). The concept of time, the teaching of history, and school organization. *History Teacher, 13,* 341–350.

Levstik, L. (1981). Using adolescent fiction as a guide to inquiry. *Theory into Practice, 20* (3), 174–178.

Levstik, L. (1986). The relationship between historical response and narrative in a sixth grade classroom. *Theory and Research in Social Education.*

Meek, M., Warlow, A., & Barton, G. (Eds.), (1978). *The cool web.* New York: Atheneum.

Peel, E. A. (1967). Some problems in the psychology of history teaching. In W. H. Burston and D. Thompson (Eds.) *Studies in the Nature and History of Teaching* (pp. 159–190). New York: Humanities Press.

Poster, J. B. (1973). The birth of the past: Children's perception of historical time. *History Teacher, 6,* 587–598.

Rosenblatt, L. (1938). *Literature as exploration.* New York: Noble (rev. ed., Champaign, Illinois: National Council of Teachers of English, 1976).

Rosenzweig, L. (1983). *Developmental perspectives on the social studies* (Bulletin 66). Washington, D.C.: National Council for the Social Studies.

Sleeper, M. E. (1975). A developmental framework for history education in adolescence. *School Review, 84,* 91–107.

Smedslund, J. (1961). The acquisition of conservation of substance and weight in children, II, external reinforcement of conservation of weight and operations of addition and subtraction. *Scandinavian Journal of Psychology, 2,* 71–84.

Smith, R. N., & Tomlinson, P. (1977). The development of children's construction of historical duration: A new approach and some findings. *Educational Research, 19* (3), 163–170.

Sunal, C. (1981). The child and the concept of change. *Social Education, 45* (6), 438–441.

Thornburg, K. (1983). Young children's understanding of familial concepts with implications for social studies units. *Social Education, 47* (2), 138–140.

Watts, D. G. (1972). *The learning of history.* London: Routledge and Kegan Publishers.

White, R. T., & Gagné, R. M. (1976). Retention of related and unrelated sentences. *Journal of Educational Psychology, 68,* 843–852.

Wishart, E., & Smith, J. L. (1983). Understanding logical connections in history. *Australian Journal of Reading, 6* (1), 19–29.

Zaccaria, M. A. (1978). The development of historical thinking: Implications for the teaching of history. *History Teacher, 11,* 323–339.

CHAPTER 6

LEARNING ABOUT THE ECONOMIC WORLD

Beverly J. Armento
Assisted by Sharon Flores

Young children "spontaneously" develop notions about their own economic worlds of work, exchange, production, and consumption, aside from any formal process particularly aimed at having them learn or master these concepts (Vygotsky, 1962). Part of the role of social studies programs during elementary school years is to use children's informal learning as a basis for formal development of critical thinking skills and for the construction of useful and powerful economic knowledge.

What economic pseudo-concepts do children bring to school, and what do we know in general about the cognitive development of children ages 5–13? The first section of this chapter explores these questions. In the second section, the discussion turns to the nature of economic education and its relevance to elementary school children. Finally, the focus shifts to one of the major components of economic education, that of conceptual development and the implications for instruction that derive from research on learning and teaching for cognitive outcomes.

RESEARCH ON DEVELOPMENT OF ECONOMIC KNOWLEDGE

During the last 30 years, only a few researchers have specifically addressed the content and processes of children's economic thought. Rather, most child development researchers have pursued Piaget's interest in the child's development of concepts of the natural world. But Piaget was as concerned with social and moral learning (1963, 1965, 1970) as he was with that of the natural world; and his work in this area, along with that of his student Hans Furth (1970, 1980) and that of the Soviet psychologist Vygotsky (1962, 1978), has strongly influenced the direction and interpretation of the content of research on the evolution of social thought. More precisely, the paradigm of the stages or levels of complexity of social cognition, framed by Piaget in 1952 and elaborated by Furth in 1970, has provided the theoretical dimension to help explain the results of the sometimes untheoretically based research into economic thought conducted since 1955.

Danziger (1958), for example, after he interviewed 41 Australian children ages 5–8, postulated four stages in the development of economic thought. At

the earliest levels of awareness, Danziger discovered, children demonstrated little or no understanding of the economic ideas of money, exchange, or poverty. More mature students offered functional, ritualistic, or moralistic explanations for exchange and for the use of money. Gradually, children verbalized reciprocal relationships between people and saw money more as a medium of exchange than as part of the ritual of trade. The most mature students easily comprehended and verbalized a system of relationships among the various concepts and could offer reasonable explanations for the specified economic ideas.

Four years later, Sutton (1962) interviewed 85 children, ages 6–13, and found that they generally had more verbal facility with economic concepts with which they had some experience. Thus, children knew more about exchange than about production. Sutton wondered whether there were enough naturally occurring environmental events in the lives of children to enable them to develop a range of economic pre-concepts.

The response of Burris (1976), Fox (1978), Furth (1980), and Strauss (1952) to Sutton's query would probably be that young children are surrounded by and actively involved in numerous "economic" experiences daily. The cognitive processing skills of children, however, influence and often limit the meanings they attach to these situations. Each of these four researchers discovered this fact when examining children's understanding of money. They found that the youngest children had little or no understanding of the reciprocal nature of transactions between buyers and sellers in stores; rather, the children saw money as part of a ritual occurring in stores. Some thought that the buyer gave money because it was the law or right thing to do. Many children thought that stores were sources of money—that is, that "change" was money you received by going to the store. In all cases, the youngest children focused on the money itself rather than on the transactions of buying and selling. Thus, the economic experience in and of itself most likely does not result in direct and predictable learning by a given child. The meanings constructed by a child are more probably a function of the child's cognitive capabilities at the moment, of the value and motivational orientation of the child, of the nature of the experience, and of the child's prior knowledge (Feldman, 1981; Levin & Allen, 1976; Piaget, 1970; Wittrock, 1974, 1977, 1978).

Similar patterns of economic thought surfaced in studies by Armento (1982), Schug (1981, 1983), and Schug and Birkey (1985). Schug (1983) and Schug and Birkey (1985) interviewed preschool, 1st and 3rd grade children on the economic concepts of scarcity, choice, opportunity cost, and monetary value. They categorized students' responses as representative of *unreflective reasoning* or *emerging reasoning*. The unreflective responses typically made by the younger children were concrete, tautological, or moralistic; children at this level were unable to see relationships between ideas or even to articulate supporting explanations for a particular economic example. Children who demonstrated emerging reasoning were able to describe ways in which economic phenomena were related and were more flexible in their thinking. Emerging reasoning tended to be demonstrated at earlier ages for concepts with which children had many experiences.

In Armento's study of 355 children ages 3–16, a conceptual shift occurred between ages five and seven in handling micro-economic concepts. For concepts such as work, wants, and decision making with one's own money, children younger than five years of age tended to respond by naming specific concrete examples; by giving tautological responses (for example, "Yes, people have everything they want because they always do"); by viewing the situation only from their own perspectives; and by giving inaccurate and moralistic responses (for example, "No, people do not have everything they want, because Jesus don't want them to"). But between the ages of five and seven, the responses changed and became more sophisticated. By age seven, children had formulated fairly accurate conceptions of work, wants, and scarcity and had developed a method for making decisions.

When Armento's children were questioned about such topics as taxes and international trade, however, a different age-related pattern emerged. The shift from naive to informed responses generally occurred between the ages of 10 and 12. Perhaps the experiences of a child under the age of 10, which might lead to an understanding of such macro-economic concepts as taxes and international trade, are neither focused nor frequent enough to serve as adequate data for the child's spontaneous concept generation. For example, the direct experiences children under 10 have with taxes (what taxes are, who pays taxes, what taxes are used for) are probably quite limited. Even though they have had experiences paying sales tax on items they have purchased and have undoubtedly heard parents discussing taxes, this information apparently is not sorted out by young children as being relevant and important.

Although significant age-related conceptual responses were found in the Armento study (1982), it is important also to recognize the presence of developmental inversion. Some very young children offered very sophisticated responses, even to questions concerning macro-economic concepts, while some of the oldest children indicated very little comprehension of the economic world.

After interviewing 195 children ages 5–11 from southern England on both economic and other societal topics, Furth (1980), Piaget's student, proposed a model to explain the development of all social understanding. Furth's research led him to believe, as Danziger's earlier work in economic thought had led him, that there are four basic stages, or ways of thinking about the social world. Furth gave these experiential stages of development the following names:

Stage I: Personalistic Elaborations and Absence of Interpretive System
Stage II: Understanding of First-Order Societal Functions
Stage III: Part-Systems in Conflict
Stage IV: A Concrete-Systematic Framework

Furth found that the youngest children (ages 5–6), in Stage I, represented their social worlds in terms of their own personal views and desires. They were highly imaginative and playful in their elaborations. Generally, these children were able neither to distinguish between personal and societal roles nor to see beyond the superficial aspects of particular events. For instance, they saw stores as producers of both goods and money, and they viewed the change given to a customer as a primary source of money for that person.

But children demonstrating Stage II-thought, Furth observed, understood the basic function of money as a means of exchange. They were not, however, able to see beyond the surface, or what Furth called the "First-Order Societal Function." Although they could see the role of money in exchange, they still did not understand what happened next with it. What the store owner did with the money remained a mystery to the child, or, more likely, was not at all thought of by the child. Children at this second stage of thought (approximately ages 6–8), Furth determined, were still playful with their images of society and were happy with the pictures and storylines they were creating.

However, as children began to see that reality did not coincide with their descriptions of events, this playful imagery of early childhood began to give way to a search for logical consistency. Children approximately ages 8–10 (Stage III) were able to go beyond the surface explanation of economic phenomena but were still only able to develop "part-systems." They were able neither to coordinate multiple reasons or causes for events nor to assess causes and effects adequately.

The oldest children in Furth's study (1980), ages 9–11 (Stage IV), were the most reflective and logical in their descriptions and interpretations of social events; yet, their explanations of these events remained highly concrete and their ideas were limited by their experiences. Children in this fourth stage, Furth observed, fully understood the role of money in exchange and the idea of production costs and of profit, but still had little understanding of the role of government in the economy or of the economy in the aggregate sense.

The theoretical model of the four stages of societal understanding proposed by Furth in 1980 could well serve researchers of economic thought both in conducting future research and in interpreting previously conducted research. Findings, reported in this chapter, of empirical research on the spontaneous development of concepts of the economic world appear to be generally consonant with Furth's paradigm.

Researchers' understanding of research findings of the last 30 years, however, has too often lacked the theoretical dimension provided by Furth, which, in revealing relationships among results, adds to and clarifies the meaning of this work as a whole. Though his is a comprehensive model for the development of social understanding in general, Furth's paradigm has the potential to elucidate the development of economic cognition. Furth's model seems to provide the theoretical perspective from which researchers in economic thought can more clearly see the past and thus more ably build the future.

To summarize, a number of researchers have explored the nature of the ideas children spontaneously develop about the economic world. The focus of these studies is on the concepts that children develop mainly through their own mental efforts, rather than through formal instruction. In all cases, age-related patterns of thought were identified. These concept response patterns tend, in general, to progress from egocentric to objective; from tautological, literal, and rule-oriented to generalizable; from concrete to abstract; and from inconsistent and narrow to consistent, flexible, and accurate. Furth's empirically derived model for stages of societal understanding provides a sound framework for both past and future work in this area.

The research on spontaneous concept development attempts to capture child constructions independent of formal instruction. Thus, these studies focus on what is, not on what could be or should be, in terms of economic conceptual development. To examine what *could be,* we need to refer to research on nonspontaneous concepts, or on those concepts developed through formal instruction. However, issues surrounding the *should be* questions are more difficult to answer empirically. For example, should instruction be used to "speed up" development (Rohwer, 1973)? What economic concepts should be taught to children at various levels of development? What should be the goals of economic education for young children? These questions pose issues too complex to be thoroughly addressed in this chapter. These are, however, the questions that researchers and economic educators must ask when trying to define the subject of the discussion to follow: the nature of economic education.

NATURE OF ECONOMIC EDUCATION

The aim of economic education is to improve our understanding of the worlds in which we live. . . . Comprehension of the economic realities of one's world enhances self-confidence and self-esteem. Accordingly, both intellectual and emotional barriers are lowered for the making of rational individual decisions, in the light of one's values, in both personal and social matters. (Horton & Weidenaar, 1975, p. 41)

Since this rather open statement gained the consensus acceptance of the more than 200 social scientists, economists, social studies educators, and businesspersons polled by Horton and Weidenaar in 1973–74, one might have expected a range of ideas on the best instructional plan for achieving such a goal to be forthcoming (Ellis, 1979; McKenzie, 1977; Yates, 1978). However, today, as in the past, educators are uncertain about what a "developmentally appropriate" economic education program for elementary school children would look like. Economic education, like most of the social studies curricula, has traditionally been conceptualized from an adult perspective of the social world. Complicating matters further, economic education has been strongly influenced both by Bruner's often quoted and now questioned notion that any concept can be taught to any child in some kind of intellectually honest manner (1960) and by a narrow interpretation of the social science discipline movement in social education (Popkewitz, 1977). The dominant approach to economic education created from this condition involves primarily the teaching of basic concepts of economics to children at all grade levels, K–12 (Saunders et al., 1984).

Conceptual knowledge is indeed fundamental to the development of higher order cognitive processes of principle formation and decision making. Understanding key economic ideas of the adult world does enable the learner to communicate more effectively, to participate more fully, and to solve problems more efficiently than would be the case otherwise. However, economic educators must still ask what knowledge of the social world should be taught learners, in what form, and when.

Because individual minds construct the knowledge they have of the social world, various explanations of economic reality exist. This fact complicates the search for a way to identify the knowledge component in economic education curriculums. Social science knowledge is not a closed set of immutable rules and generalizations. Rather, it is a body of tentative, yet vital, theories (Popkewitz, 1972). The knowledge we have should be viewed and taught as an open construction of reality, to which the spirit of social inquiry is an indispensable aid. Most elementary school students may not be able to exercise the full measure of hypothetical and deductive reasoning necessary for social inquiry, but the groundwork for their learning should be set during these years. Young children are able to learn better methods of forming and criticizing opinions and beliefs and are able to extend their spontaneous concept generation to more formal constructions of the economic world. Children should thus be encouraged in their curiosity of the social environment and in the active generation and analysis of economic knowledge.

As we have seen, one of the major tasks of teachers and curriculum developers is to identify the aspects of the economic world which will serve as the focus of inquiry for children of various ages. However, given the complexity and the variety of conceptual economic knowledge, how can we determine what concepts should be taught and when should we teach them? What criteria can we use to assess the importance of alternative economic conceptual knowledge and the difficulty levels of various concepts? (Klausmeier, 1976a, 1976b; Klausmeier, Ghatala, & Frayer, 1974).

The concepts most commonly used to describe and evaluate economic phenomena in a society should be part of any formal instruction in economic education and should provide the basis for the causal, relational, and hierarchical thinking that is essential to logical thinking and, therefore, to problem solving (Voss, Tyler, & Yengo, 1984). One can also apply the criteria of power or importance, usability, and validity to knowledge alternatives. The "power" of a concept has to do with how essential the idea is to the learning of other ideas. For example, key economic concepts, such as scarcity, serve as organizing ideas around which other superordinate and subordinate concepts and examples revolve. One concept is more "usable" than another if it can be used to explain more examples. Thus, "supply" and "demand" are highly usable concepts while "monopoly" is much less so. The last criteria, the "validity" of a concept, refers to the accuracy of the concept definition in terms of generally agreed-upon definitions; but, clearly, there may be different philosophical perspectives on certain ideas, and a consensus view may be difficult to find. Given the wealth of data one could emphasize in economic education and the competing pressures for alternative curricular choices, the question of identifying the most important areas for inquiry becomes critical.

Assessing the difficulty levels of economic concepts can be done by analyzing their structure, instance perceptibility, instance numerousness, and their degree of generality (Klausmeier, 1976; Klausmeier, Ghatala, & Frayer, 1974). The ease with which children learn economic concepts has to do with the nature of the knowledge itself, the child's prior knowledge, and his or her developmental competence and level of motivation for learning particular ideas. Laboratory and classroom research (Clark, 1971) conducted on children's capacity to learn concepts provides many clues about the difficulty levels of conceptual knowledge which, in addition to the analysis of the economic knowledge itself, should inform our decisions about sequencing instruction.

We know, for example, that concepts having straightforward definitions (or structures) and observable and clear illustrations are less difficult to learn than those concepts having "if-then" or relational structures (Clark, 1971). Concepts such as goods, services, producers, and consumers are simpler to learn than concepts such as price, scarcity, and comparative advantage, precisely because definitions of the former, unlike those of the latter group, are not dependent upon "if-then" relationships. The structure of a concept like price, for instance, is complex primarily because its meaning is a function of pre-existing relationships between other concepts (Armento, 1978). Relational concepts are generally the most difficult type of concepts to learn. However, if a relational concept has numerous concrete examples, the difficulty level is not as high. Scarcity and supply and demand are good examples of economic relational concepts that can be illustrated easily and clearly to elementary school children.

The degree of generality, or the hierarchical arrangement of a concept, also influences the difficulty level of concepts. Subordinate and coordinate concepts are easier for younger children to grasp than more general superordinate ideas. As children develop multiple classification skills, they become better able to see how clusters of ideas relate to one another. For example, natural, human, and capital resources are kinds of productive resources around which many specific, illustrative examples can be clustered. Seeing how these and other idea-clusters "go together" is an important aspect of economic education and can be facilitated as children practice classifying concepts and examples of concepts.

Curriculum developers can make general predictions about the difficulty level of economic knowledge by applying the criteria discussed here. The anticipated difficulty level assessment of economic conceptual knowledge is an essential step in the identification of a developmentally appropriate scope and sequence statement for economic education for the elementary school years. But gaining and applying this information is only part of the total problem. We must also consider formal learning and teaching of economic knowledge. In the next section, we will draw on effective learning and teaching literature to discover what is known about formal conceptual development and, from this knowledge, derive implications for economic education for young children.

ECONOMIC EDUCATION: CONCEPT LEARNING

Research on the development of spontaneous economic ideas reported in the first section of this chapter gives a good description of the knowledge children generally possess at various ages. Yet, this developmental knowledge, however useful it may be, is nonetheless only descriptive and is but one component of the data needed to create a theory of instruction in economic education for children. To develop a sound theory, we must also refer to the body of literature on different kinds of learning, as well as to literature on the best ways of promoting the desired educational outcomes.

Concept learning is an important outcome of economics programs in elementary schools, for it is fundamental to acquiring and building problem-solving and decision-making skills. Although it is not the only kind of economic learning young children undertake, it is clearly an important one because a considerable amount of young children's formal and informal learning time is engaged in processing experiences and reorganizing ideas of the economic world. A large body of theoretical and empirical work exists on concept learning and concept instruction; such research can be of assistance to economic education. We will now concentrate on concept learning by drawing on the general literature, as well as on the literature concerned specifically with learning social/economic concepts. We turn first to a discussion of the general principles describing concept learning and next to an analysis of the cognitive processes underlying concept learning at various levels. Selected research on the teaching of economic concepts on the various concept attainment levels, and the implications of this research for instruction in economic education, will then be discussed.

Based on theoretical and empirical work in the area, Klausmeier (1976a) proposed five principles of general concept learning:

1. The attainment level of any given concept varies among children of the same age.
2. Various concepts are attained by individual children at individual rates.
3. Concepts learned at successively higher levels are used more effectively for the three functions that concepts serve in understanding supraordinate-subordinate relationships, in understanding principles, and in solving problems.
4. Knowing their names and knowing their attributes facilitate both the attainment of concepts at the various levels and the three functions that concepts serve (see #3).
5. Concepts are attained at four successively higher levels in an invariant sequence (Klausmeier, 1976a, pp. 15–23).

According to Klausmeier's model, children attain a given concept at four successively higher levels: concrete, identity, classificatory, and formal. Success at each level is related to a child's ability to perform the necessary mental operations of the level and also to the kind of concept instruction provided. The key to effective teaching for concept attainment lies in the capacity of the instructional method to engage learners in the relevant psychological processes demanded by concept learning at that particular level (Klausmeier, 1976; Rohwer, 1973; Snelbecker, 1974; Tobias, 1982; Wittrock, 1974, 1977, 1978).

What psychological processes are involved in concept attainment? At the concrete level, the child observes an object, distinguishes it from others, mentally represents the object as an image, then recalls it as the image or idea of the object. At the identity level, the learner is able to recognize the idea or concept when presented in a new context and is also able to generalize the essence of the concept in its various forms. Students at the classificatory level begin to understand that examples of the concept belong to the same category and thus become capable of differentiating non-examples from examples. The formal level of concept learning is achieved when the learner can define the concept, name its attributes and consciously apply them to the identification of new examples (Klausmeier, 1976a). Thus, numerous psychological processes are involved: observing (or focusing attention upon an object), distinguishing or separating (the object from other things), image-making, recalling, comparing and contrasting, classifying, inferring, generalizing, and, finally, using written and spoken language to convey information about the object.

Although the cognitive processes involved mature with experience and age, there is nevertheless a great deal of variation within age groups. At any particular age level, a teacher is apt to find a combination of students who possess only those skills necessary for concept learning at an identity level and those who are capable of operating at a formal level. Moreover, individual children will learn different concepts at their own individual rates; they will, in general, learn concepts having few or no perceptible examples much later than those for which clear examples exist (Clark, 1971; Klausmeier, 1976a). These are facts certain to complicate the search for a scope and sequence statement that can identify selected economic concepts to be introduced at particular grade levels.

However, conceptualizing the sequencing of concept instruction in economic education can be accomplished by organizing learning tasks according to the psychological processes being refined at each concept learning level. The development of Chart 1, Concept Construction Phases, was based on theoretical and empirical work conducted on concept learning (Armento, 1978; Case, 1975; Chandler, 1977; Clark, 1971; Farley, 1981; Feldman, 1981; Klausmeier, 1976a, 1976b; Klausmeier et al., 1974; Luria, 1976; Siegler, 1978; Vygotsky, 1962, 1978). Effective instruction at each phase on the chart requires learners to engage in thinking processes associated with that level of learning. The section to follow considers the psychological processes, the instructional techniques, and the research in economic concept learning applicable to each of the phases.

Early Childhood Phase

Language development, Vygotsky has noted (1978), lags behind conceptual development. Or, stated another way, a child's capacity to describe events is preceded by the development of the ability to act out the meanings of events. Thus, it is through the child's actions that meanings are eventually developed and through the child's emerging language capacities that labels become attached to experience. Instruction should focus on helping children to describe more accurately these events and the types of interdependencies and interactions which occur. We know that young children are perception bound, or unable to create, remember, and use images of events not observable at the moment. It is mainly through playing that young children best explore their economic environment, learning to describe the obvious and to discern the hidden aspects of economic situations and events.

The economic content emphasized during these early years should be that contained in the ordinary transactions, relationships, and events in the child's life and community. Children therefore should examine buying, selling, and

Informal, Early Childhood Phase

As young children engage in economic experiences, they can indicate their understanding by:

- role-playing or enacting the main ideas of the experience;
- drawing pictures and describing the ideas in their own words;
- grouping experiences together and giving the groupings names or labels;
- identifying examples of particular ideas.

Formal, Concept Introduction Phase

When an economic concept is first formally introduced to learners in an instructional setting, the learners can indicate their understanding by:

- describing the concept in their own words;
- indicating recognition of the concept when presented in another context;
- distinguishing examples from non-examples of the concept;
- using labels (names; synonymous, developmentally appropriate words) for particular concepts. For example, young children might use the term "trade-offs" as opposed to the term "opportunity cost."

Formal, Concept Development Phase

A concept is developed as students examine a range of examples which illustrate the core idea. As these examples become more sophisticated in depth and breadth, students should be able to demonstrate their understanding by:

- distinguishing between closely-related concepts;
- grouping concepts to illustrate their hierarchical arrangement (superordinate, subordinate, coordinate organization);
- comparing and contrasting examples;
- identifying new examples of the concept;
- explaining new situations by applying concept.

Formal Concept Refinement Phase

As students examine examples illustrating the breadth, depth, and scope of conceptual knowledge, they continue to reorganize and refine their knowledge. Students should be able to engage in the following constructive behaviors at this stage of learning:

- defining the concept and evaluating examples in terms of their correspondence with the concept definition;
- classifying concepts to illustrate relations, causal and hierarchical patterns;
- predicting cause-effect relationships in new examples;
- analyzing situations by applying conceptual knowledge;
- synthesizing knowledge through the development of a new mode of expression (play, essay, paper, etc.)
- applying knowledge to the assessment of problems and social issues;
- evaluating knowledge and the uses one makes of that knowledge.

CHART 1
Concept Construction Phases

trading transactions; the process of making goods and services; and the origin of materials and products in their everyday lives. Common events such as going shopping, eating a hamburger, and making choices with their allowances are full of potential economic "links and chains." To illustrate how much so, ask a child to "trace" a commonplace item—a hamburger, for example—from his or her environment. Ask the child where the hamburger came from, what (simply) the steps of its production are, what people worked at which jobs along the way, how much the hamburger costs, where the money went, what other choices there were (when the child bought the hamburger), and why the child chose the hamburger. In responding, the child will begin to see beneath the surface of daily economic events; he or she will begin to recognize ways in which seemingly isolated occurrences may be related to group phenomena, and to build language skills capable of describing these events. When appropriate, concept labels can be used with young children as synonymous terms. The important factor is having children put ideas in their own words, rather than merely parroting terms or formal definitions.

A popular economics program for young children, the Kinder-Economy (Kourilsky, 1977), follows these basic principles. In this program, young children develop an awareness of certain micro-economic concepts by enacting lifelike economic situations. The program stresses action, simulation, and participation, introducing each concept through experience and practicing and reinforcing the idea through the use of games, learning centers, and discussions. In one study of the effectiveness of Kinder-Economy, Kourilsky found that kindergarten children were able to comprehend the micro-economic concepts of scarcity, decision making, production, distribution, consumption and savings, demand and supply, business organization, and money and barter. The most difficult concept for them to grasp, she discovered, was specialization, an interesting finding which supports the literature (Clark, 1971) that suggests that disjunctive concepts, such as specialization, are more difficult to learn than conjunctive ones, such as production and consumption. Specialization, of course, can refer to a number of things, from an assembly-line form of product preparation to the focusing of a region on the production of particular goods or services. It is most likely the case that kindergarten children are simply unable to coordinate the multiple meanings and examples of this concept.

There is considerable evidence that teachers and parents can maximize children's learning by "concretizing" for them—as the Kinder-Economy program does—the subject of instruction: by having children simulate real-life economic events and by using materials and methods that capitalize on children's prior experience and knowledge. Children should be called upon to construct meanings from these experiences and to describe their ideas through both actions and words, pictures, or other symbols. Using pictures as an instructional tool is a valuable way of helping young children develop and remember images and conceptual examples. A much more powerful teaching tool than words alone (Chandler, 1977; Clark, 1971; Levin, 1976), pictures and other concretizing tools can greatly benefit children with learning disabilities and those who have not enjoyed a broad variety of experience.

Concept Introduction Phase

Economic concepts can be formally and purposefully introduced to young children (ages 6–8) or to older elementary school students who have had no prior formal economic education. The general goal of this instruction is to provide experiences that illustrate economic concepts and thereby to help students question and organize their spontaneously generated experiences. When economic concepts are formally introduced, students should be encouraged to describe the essence of the concept in their own words, to recognize it when it appears in another context, and to identify and distinguish its examples from non-examples.

Opportunities to encourage the child to actively construct meanings and mental images should occur often, even for older students. The visual images and the symbols the child has created will facilitate retention of the concept (Wittrock, 1974). Children should be increasingly encouraged to develop their maturing cognitive capacities for using multiple classifications and for identifying subtleties in the environment.

The Mini-Society instructional program (Cassuto, 1980; Kourilsky, 1977) emphasizes these cognitive processes as children in grades 4–6 conceptualize their classroom as a society. Students develop their own economic and political systems, create their own currency, and establish their own productive enterprises. Their active manipulation of economic phenomena and their discussions and writings on these experiences enable them to develop conceptual ideas in a painless manner. The instructional plan of the Mini-Society stresses the *Example > Rule* model of concept learning by which students develop concept definitions only after having experiences with several of the concept's examples. Most simulations (see Armento, 1980) are based on the eliciting of conceptual ideas from students. Since most elementary school children will be unable to generate conceptual meanings from the experience alone, the keys to successful instruction with this approach lie in the selection of well-constructed and clear concept examples and in the teacher's perceptive questioning skills.

The important role of the teacher in economic concept learning is emphasized in a study by Walstad (1980), who examined the effectiveness of teacher training in economics on the teacher's ability to implement *Trade-Offs*. *Trade-Offs* is a 15-lesson film series for grades 4–6, and it features children who encounter a variety of economic problems. *Trade-Offs* is a form of visual instruction based upon both experience and sound principles of concept instruction. It introduces, and in some cases develops, micro-economic concepts and encourages active student involvement with the conceptual examples by presenting concepts in a number of different contexts. Students are asked to identify new examples of the concept and to distinguish these from the non-examples. The experiences used in the series are familiar to children and thus can help them build upon spontaneously developed economic ideas.

Walstad found that the contribution of teacher training represented a 93 percent increase in economic achievement by trained teachers' students over students who were exposed to *Trade-Offs* by teachers not trained in economic content. This significant finding supports the idea that strong instructional materials cannot stand independently of strong and knowledgeable teachers who understand the content well enough to help children develop conceptual systems.

Concept Development and Refinement Phases

Once children begin to organize conceptual ideas into hierarchical systems of interrelationships, they become aware, for the first time, of the concept itself. It is the act of placing concepts within systems of relationships of generality, Vygotsky (1962) postulated, that transforms the child's ways of spontaneously generating ideas about reality. That is, instruction prompts the learning of systems of concepts; these organizational patterns and the processes of classification are then transferred to the child's generation of everyday concepts.

At the concept development phase, the learner can apply his or her conceptual understanding to describing and explaining new examples and problems. The scope and complexity of these new examples and problems should depend on the students' interests and abilities, although for elementary school children, the examples and concepts most easily understood will be those from microeconomic content. For example, younger children can apply their notions of opportunity cost to the classroom problem of how to deal with limited supplies of red construction paper, while older students can discuss the dilemma their communities face concerning the construction of a road or the preservation of a park. Students can follow through with their decision making by actually applying their decisions or, at the least, by communicating them in some way to others involved with the problem. Students operating at a concept refinement level should be able to evaluate the adequacy of the conceptual and factual knowledge they applied to the problem.

In an investigation of teacher behavior during the introduction and development of the economic concept of specialization, Armento (1977) found that students in grades 3–5 performed better on a concept test when their teachers demonstrated certain instructional behaviors. Student achievement increased as teachers: (1) gave more concept definitions and more positive concept examples and reviewed the main ideas of the lesson; (2) used accurate economic conceptual and factual knowledge relevant to the objectives of the lesson; (3) included more of the relevant knowledge generalizations and more of the related concept labels; and (4) expressed more enthusiasm and interest in the content of the lesson.

The most productive concept learning during elementary school years occurs as part of a larger study of some phenomena, event, person, or institution in children's environment. The Mini-Society simulations and *Trade-Offs* vignettes illustrate this point well. In showing children how economic concepts can be used to explain real-world situations and to solve practical and social problems, they demonstrate how various ideas relate, how patterns and systems of thought emerge, and how an individual idea or concept fits into a higher system of ideas or concepts. They show children how to process or synthesize information and ideas by grouping, organizing, and classifying them. The practice of teaching a series of concept definitions to elementary school children does little to help children develop images of whole systems or to use this knowledge for higher levels of thought and problem solving. Only by facilitating the child's growth through the various levels of conceptual attainment can we hope to provide children with meaningful, dynamic and useful knowledge of the economic world.

SUMMARY

We know that young children actively construct meanings for economic phenomena in their lives and that, indeed, many occasions exist for this spontaneous idea generation. Elementary school years provide an exciting arena for the exercise of children's further inquiry into the social world, for building healthy attitudes for such investigation, and for constructing sound conceptual understandings of economic phenomena. The natural curiosity, energy and spontaneity of young children challenge economic education curriculum developers to provide interesting and developmentally appropriate instruction during the elementary years.

Further research can undoubtedly contribute to informed curriculum development and instruction. Particular attention, however, needs to be paid to the following areas and questions:

1. *Developmental Research.* A theoretical framework is needed to guide further inquiry into the spontaneous development of economic concepts. Furth's model (or similar alternative) should be applied to a research synthesis of past work in order to improve the explanatory power of isolated studies. Further work of this kind should be grounded in a theoretical framework.

2. *Developmental-Learning-Teaching Research.* What models of the economic world do children have prior to and after certain kinds of instruction in economic education? How do these models change as children become more cognitively sophisticated, and how do they change as a function of alternative instructional techniques?

3. *Learning-Developmental Research.* How difficult is it for children of various ages to learn various economic concepts? What factors contribute to a concept's degree of ease or difficulty in learning?

4. *Teaching Research.* What instructional strategies promote meaningful economic learning and retention for elementary school children? What teacher skills and knowledge are needed to facilitate learning outcomes?

REFERENCES

Armento, B. J. (1977). Teacher behaviors related to student achievement on a social science concept test. *Journal of Teacher Education, 28*(2), 46–52.

Armento, B. J. (1978). Conceptualizing: A basic process in economic education. *Educational Perspectives, 17,* 17–21.

Armento, B. J. (1980). Experiencing economic concepts: Formal and informal concept learning. *Peabody Journal of Education, 57,* 160–162.

Armento, B. J. (1982, March). *Awareness of economic knowledge: A developmental study.* Paper presented at annual meeting of the American Educational Research Association, New York.

Bruner, J. (1960). *The process of education.* Cambridge: Harvard University Press.

Burris, V. I. (1976). *The child's conception of economic relations: A genetic approach to the sociology of knowledge.* Unpublished doctoral dissertation, Princeton University.

Case, R. (1975). Gearing the demands of instruction to the developmental capacities of the learner. *Review of Educational Research, 45*(1), 59–87.

Cassuto, A. E. (1980). The effectiveness of the elementary school mini-society program. *The Journal of Economic Education, 11*(2), 59–61.

Chandler, M. (1977). Social cognition: A selective review of current research. In W. Overton & J. Gallagher (Eds.), *Knowledge and development.* New York: Plenum Press, p. 93–147

Clark, C. D. (1971). Teaching concepts in the classroom: A set of teaching prescriptions derived from experimental research [Monograph]. *Journal of Educational Psychology, 62,* 253–278.

Danziger, K. (1958). Children's earliest conceptions of economic relationships (Australia). *The Journal of Social Psychology, 47,* 231–240.

Ellis, M. (1979). The psychology of learning economics: A dissatisfied economist's view. *The Journal of Economic Education, 10*(2), 49–53.

Farley, F., & Gordon, N. J. (Eds.). (1981). *Psychology and education: The state of the union.* Berkeley, CA: McCutchan Publishing Co.

Feldman, H. (1981). Beyond universals: Toward a developmental psychology of education. *Educational Researcher, 10*(9), 21–32.

Fox, K. F. A. (1978). What children bring to school: The beginnings of economic education. *Social Education, 42*(6), 478–481.

Furth, H. G. (1970). *Piaget for teachers.* Englewood Cliffs, NJ: Prentice-Hall.

Furth, H. G. (1980). *The world of grown-ups: Children's conceptions of society.* New York: Elsevier North Holland.

Horton, R. V., & Weidenaar, D. J. (1975). Wherefore economic education? *The Journal of Economic Education, 7*(1), 40–44.

Klausmeier, H. J. (1976a). Conceptual development during the school years. In J. R. Levin & V. L. Allen (Eds.), *Cognitive learning in children: Theories and strategies.* New York: Academic Press.

Klausmeier, H. J. (1976b). Instructional design and the teaching of concepts. In J. R. Levin & V. L. Allen (Eds.), *Cognitive learning in children: Theories and strategies* (pp. 5–29). New York: Academic Press.

Klausmeier, H. J., Ghatala, E., & Frayer, D. (1974). *Conceptual learning and development: A cognitive view* (pp. 191–217). New York: Academic Press.

Kourilsky, M. (1977). The kinder-economy: A case study of kindergarten pupils' acquisition of economic concepts. *The Elementary School Journal, 77*(3), 182–191.

Levin, J. R. (1976). What have we learned about maximizing what children learn? In J. R. Levin & V. L. Allen (Eds.), *Cognitive learning in children: Theories and strategies* (pp. 105–134) New York: Academic Press.

Levin, J. R., & Allen, V. L. (1976). *Cognitive learning in children: Theories and strategies* (pp. 105–134). New York: Academic Press.

Luria, A. R. (1976). *Cognitive development: Its cultural and social foundations.* Cambridge, MA: Harvard University Press.

McKenzie, R. B. (1977). Where is the economics in economic education? *The Journal of Economic Education, 9*(1), 5–13.

Piaget, J. (1952). *The origins of intelligence in children.* New York: W. W. Norton & Co., Inc.

Piaget, J. (1963). *The child's conception of the world.* Paterson, NJ: Littlefield, Adams.

Piaget, J. (1965). *The moral judgment of the child.* New York: The Free Press.

Piaget, J. (1970). *Genetic epistemology.* New York: W. W. Norton.

Popkewitz, T. S. (1972). The craft of study, structure, and schooling. *Teachers College Record, 74*(2), 155–165.

Popkewitz, T. S. (1977). The latent values of the discipline-centered curriculum. *Theory and Research in Social Education, 5*(1), 41–60.

Rohwer, W. D. (1973). Children and adolescents: Should we teach them or let them learn? In M. Wittrock (Ed.), *Changing education: Alternatives from educational research* (pp. 103–123). Englewood Cliffs, NJ: Prentice-Hall.

Saunders, P., Bach, G. L., Calderwood, J., & Hansen, W. L. (Eds.). (1984). *A framework for teaching the basic concepts.* New York: Joint Council on Economic Education.

Schug, M. C. (1981). What educational research says about the development of economic thinking. *Theory and Research in Social Education, 9*(3), 25–36.

Schug, M. C. (1983). The development of economic thinking in children and adolescents. *Social Education, 47*(2), 141–145.

Schug, M. D., & Birkey, J. (1985). The development of children's economic reasoning. *Theory and Research in Social Education.*

Siegler, R. (1978). *Children's thinking: What develops?* Hillsdale, NJ: Lawrence Erlbaum Associates.

Snelbecker, G. E. (1974). *Learning theory, instructional theory and psycho-educational design.* New York: McGraw-Hill.

Strauss, A. L. (1952). The development and transformation of monetary meanings in the child. *American Sociological Review, 17,* 275–286.

Sutton, R. S. (1962). Behavior in the attainment of economic concepts. *The Journal of Psychology, 53,* 37–46.

Tobias, S. (1982). When do instructional methods make a difference? *Educational Researcher, 11*(4), 4–9.

Voss, J. F., Tyler, S. W., & Yengo, L. A. (1983). Individual differences in the solving of social science problems. In R. F. Dillon & R. R. Schmeck, *Individual differences in cognition* (pp. 205–232). New York: Academic Press.

Vygotsky, L. S. (1962). *Thought and language.* Cambridge, MA: Massachusetts Institute of Technology Press.

Vygotsky, L. S. (1978). *Mind in society: The development of higher psychological processes.* Cambridge, MA: Harvard University Press.

Walstad, W. B. (1980). The impact of "Trade-Offs" and teacher training on economic understanding and attitudes. *The Journal of Economic Education, 12*(1), 41–48.

Wittrock, M. (1974). Learning as a generative process. *Educational Psychologist, 11,* 37–95.

Wittrock, M. (Ed.). (1977). *The human brain.* Englewood Cliffs, NJ: Prentice-Hall.

Wittrock, M. (1978). The cognitive movement in instruction. *Educational Psychologist, 13,* 15–29.

Yates, J. (1978). Research in economic education: Are our horizons too narrow? *The Journal of Economic Education, 10*(1), 12–17.

CHAPTER 7

ANTHROPOLOGY AND SOCIOLOGY

Richard K. Jantz and Kenneth Klawitter

Teachers of elementary social studies make decisions about their instruction in three major areas. The first is content. Content decisions are also made by local education agencies when they adopt a particular social studies program for their school system, but content decisions for a group of children on any given day must still be made by the classroom teacher. The second area of decision making is the behavior of the learners. Curriculum guides provide guidance for classroom teachers, but again the specific objectives in terms of the learners' behavior must be decided by teachers for each group of students for a particular lesson or unit of study. The third area of decision making involves selecting teacher behaviors that will lead to efficient learning by students. Decisions in this area require that teachers have effective teaching skills to accomplish their objectives. These skills involve knowledge of the propositions from learning theory, particularly concept development, motivation, reinforcement, retention, and transfer. They also include knowledge of effective teaching strategies and their application to specific teaching situations.

The purpose of this chapter is to assist elementary classroom teachers in making decisions about the content of elementary social studies that involves the social science disciplines of anthropology and sociology. In addition, instructional strategies that research has demonstrated to be effective in aiding concept formation and comprehension monitoring will be applied to the content of these two social science disciplines. A brief overview of five major social studies projects which made extensive use of anthropology and/or sociology, will be followed by a more extensive review of research relevant to each of these disciplines.

OVERVIEW OF SELECTED PROJECTS

There is a very limited amount of empirical data available to assist elementary classroom teachers in making content decisions involving sociology and anthropology as components of the social studies program. The social studies curriculum projects of the 1960s and early 1970s provide the best evidence that content from these two social science disciplines can be successfully taught at the elementary school level. The major social studies projects from this period were reviewed and reported in the November, 1972 issue of *Social Education* (Haley, 1972). Reviewing the content chosen for these projects can be helpful to practitioners.

The University of Michigan Elementary Social Science Education Program developed seven social science laboratory units that strongly emphasized sociology. Units 5, 6, and 7, in particular, focused upon groups, group decision making, and different types of influences involving group roles. These materials were published by Science Research Associates for grades 4 to 6.

Another project from this period focused upon three questions: What is human about human beings? How did they get that way? How can they be made more so? The Education Development Center produced these project materials as *Man: A Course of Study* (MACOS). The materials, developed for 5th grade students, centered around the core discipline of anthropology. Simulations, role-playing, independent study, and class discussions, with emphases on comparing and contrasting, were the primary methodologies employed in this program.

The Anthropology Curriculum Project at the University of Georgia was designed to supplement existing elementary social studies programs. The project emphasized physical, cultural, archaeological, and linguistic anthropology. Field studies indicated that teachers did not need a background in anthropology in order for their students to learn from the materials. This program is available from Macmillan and Company.

The University of Minnesota Project Social Studies was developed as a K–12 program with an interdisciplinary focus centered around the concept of culture. The project relied heavily upon key concepts from anthropology and sociology and emphasized concept formation, categorization, and generalization. Family and community study kits were developed as part of this project. These were produced as the *Family of Man* kits and included such things as artifacts, filmstrips, study prints, books and clothing; and they covered such topics as an early New England family, a Japanese family, and an Ashanti family in Ghana.

The Taba Program in Social Science was developed in cooperation with the Contra Costa County, California school system and San Francisco State College. This program utilized content from the various social science disciplines including anthropology and sociology. It had a strong focus on the development of concepts and generalizations and the identification of key supporting factual statements.

Selecting important facts, concepts and generalizations, and translating these into meaningful terms for children involve some of the most important content decisions that classroom teachers will make in incorporating knowledge from anthropology and sociology into the elementary social studies curriculum. We will highlight this point as we proceed to analyze the educational potentialities of sociology and anthropology.

SOCIOLOGY

The study of human society and how individuals relate to or interact with each other and groups encompasses the social science discipline of sociology. Sociology is concerned with the study of people and their relationship to social groups. Concepts of self, social roles, group membership, and interdependence are areas of study within this discipline for the elementary school.

The prominence of sociology as a discipline of study in the elementary school has long been established. Ragan and McAulay (1973) cited a curriculum model that emphasized the study of humans and included defining the person and studying various roles, ages, and other differences. Major ideas to be developed included:

1. Why do different groups of people develop different ways of living in the same or similar environments?
2. How does urbanization alter people's relation to the natural environment?
3. What happens when different groups of people come in contact?
4. What happens when a new group enters an established society?
5. How do different groups of people interact with each other in the modern urban environment? (Ragan & McAulay, 1973, pp. 160–162)

More recently, a number of ideas involving the concepts and principles related to sociology have been identified by experts in the social science disciplines and the field of social studies (Herman, 1983). A scope and sequence scheme was developed to provide some guidance as to what should be taught at what level. Content experts first identified important ideas from their disciplines and then rated these ideas as to their appropriate grade level placement. The following list contains those principles that were given a first-choice rating by over 50 percent of the experts as appropriate for the elementary level:

1. Describes reasons why interdependency of human relation-   66 percent
   ships is vital for need and support.
2. Lists and appreciates similarities and differences of people.   92 percent

3. Lists and appreciates other people's contributions including   64 percent
those different from himself/herself, including the ethnic and
cultural groups and different nations to which others belong.

4. Improves self-identity, self-concept, and self-understandings;   82 percent
also applies attitudes to groups to which one belongs.

5. Identifies examples of sexism in their lives.   56 percent
(Herman, 1983, pp. 97–98)

Superka and Hawke wrote that the focus of social studies content and instruction should be the various roles that individuals participate in as members of society. Such a focus "can help young people understand, value, and function creatively and competently in these social roles—thereby helping them become effective individuals and effective participants in our society" (Superka & Hawke, 1982, p. 1).

This argument—that children, in order to become effective citizens, need to have knowledge about various social roles that they and others will assume—is worth further examination. The elementary child by nature is egocentric; yet he or she is forced to participate in various groups (age, male/female, racial, religious, ethnic, socioeconomic, recreational), each of which has its own role expectations. At times, these group role expectations may produce internal conflict in the individual. An instructional emphasis that focuses on social role demands may help alleviate this conflict and at the same time aid in the development of a productive and valued citizen (Superka & Hawke, 1982).

Family

The family is normally the first social group that children study in school. Understanding the roles of the various members is important to the development of the concept of family groups and to the individual's maintenance of a personal identity in relationships to others. These relationships are exemplified in a riddle on family groups taken from a 2nd grade social studies textbook:

Some are big, and some are small.
Some are young, and some are old.
Some have dads, some have moms, some have both.
Some have children in them, and some have none.
Into some, children are born; in others they are chosen.
What are they? (Schreiber, 1979, p. 110)

Thornburg (1983) used a photograph of four children and their parents to obtain familial task scores as an indication of children's knowledge of the roles associated with a family group. The kindergarten-age children answered about two-thirds of the questions relating to family label correctly, and the 8-year-old children were correct 88 percent of the time. Children also have some knowledge of family members other than parents and siblings within their own families. Individual interviews with 120 children from preschool to grade 6 revealed that almost 90 percent of the children could identify an elderly person within their family structure (Jantz et al., 1976). Only 5 percent of the preschool and kindergarten children, however, could identify an elderly person outside the family.

Moore (1977) reported that children's concept of family included not only relatedness and proximity, but also the role of domestic function. Powell and Thompson (1981) used pictures of family groupings in their study of preschool children. They reported that their subjects identified two parents, siblings, and grandparents as a family. The use of a questionnaire also revealed that domestic functions, family activities, physical contact, and material possessions had a positive effect on family identification.

Cataldo and Geismar (1983) studied 37 four- and five-year-olds to determine how they viewed family membership. Using interviewing, questioning, and drawing techniques, the authors reported results consistent with Powell and Thompson's (1981) findings. In addition, because "three-quarters of the children described positive and negative feelings in relation to family members and ways in which those feelings were resolved in the home" (Cataldo & Geismar, 1983, p. 11), the authors suggested that attention be focused on the affective nature of the family. Today's children appear to be knowledgeable concerning familial make-up, but would seem to require help in conflict resolution.

Superka and Hawke (1982) agree and suggested that a person's role in the family be studied as it changes through infancy, childhood, adolescence and adulthood. They wrote that a person's role in the family is often in conflict with other roles within and outside the family. Finally, the composition of families is unstable and changes due to birth, death, divorce, adoption, marriage and financial reasons. All of these factors compound to confuse the individual's understanding of what his or her role is in the family and what the family's role is.

Friendship

Another role understanding that is vital to the elementary child is that of friend. Peer relations, like families, both satisfy needs and arouse conflicts. Superka and Hawke (1982) have identified this role as one of the seven major roles for study.

Hartup (1983) reported that during their third and fourth years, children seek increased contact with their peers. Continued interaction with their peers has been shown to be influential in several areas of behavioral development. Hartup's research revealed that children's sexual attitudes and basic sexual repertoire are shaped primarily by their contacts with other children. Additionally, the quantity and quality of social interaction have a positive correlation with both children's moral development and emotional adjustment. Finally, "scattered evidence suggests that children master their aggressive impulses within the context of the peer culture rather than within the context of the family, the milieu of television, or the culture of the school" (Hartup, 1983, p. 222). Hartup concluded that children's social competencies can be modified, but that constructive interaction with a peer group was among the necessities of child development.

Rubin (1983) attempted to define the concept of friend and reported that it was developmental in nature. Children ages 3 to 5 believe that friends are people who are momentary physical playmates. They do not conceptualize the possibility of enduring relationships. By the ages of 11 or 12, however, friendship involves "intimate and mutual sharing" (Rubin, 1983, p. 250). Friendship at this level requires time to nurture the trust and support needed in the relationship. Rubin concluded that it is the developmentally determined mental structures that define friendship, and that this fact will have a major impact on the way that people interact.

Children must possess certain abilities to form friendships. At the preschool level, friendship was defined as social play. Garvey (1983) studied 36 children, ages 3½ to 5½, in play situations. He concluded that for play dyads to be successful both children must have three related abilities. First, both children must have a firm grasp of reality and be able to differentiate play and nonplay states. Second, both children must accept the rules of procedure, such as role playing or taking turns. Finally, both children must jointly construct the theme of the activity.

The concept of individual differences is believed to be one of the underlying elements in children's formation of friendships. Children between the ages of 6 and 14 readily see individual differences in such areas as material resources, physical health, school-related skills, special talents, social skills, and personality traits and states (Youniss, 1983, pp. 167–168).

Race and Gender

Children also identify sex and race differences in people at an early age. The beginnings of both race and gender categorizations appear by about age 3, and the concepts of boy, girl and skin color are formed by age 6. Racial attitudes tend to become more definite about 10 or 11, and there is some evidence that adolescence may be an important period for sex-role attitude formations (Katz, 1983). Self-identity and group awareness are other important concerns in looking at racial awareness. Semaj (1980) indicated that by about age 5, children could categorize by race, but they did not understand the basis for the classification. By about age 8 or 9, children could identify themselves in relationship to their own racial group.

Butzin (1981, p. 49) wrote that children are influenced by family, school, media and peers in innumerable ways. Teachers who want to promote sex equity in their classrooms must do so in countless ways as well. Everyday actions are more important for establishing equitable sex or race attitudes than a special unit taught once a year. Butzin suggested the use of bulletin boards, equal assignment of classroom jobs, changing gender of characters in books read, and complete participation of both sexes in all assignments, whether it be home economics or athletics. Scott (1982, p. 53) suggested that teachers "focus on the non-violent events and behaviors, especially of males," to give a more balanced view of society. Superka and Hawke (1982) believe that children who develop an understanding of sexual and racial differences will be able to add new dimensions to their individual and collective role functions. As with the family role, a conscious effort to educate children concerning role expectations and responsibilities will help promote harmony, resolve conflict and develop worthwhile citizenry.

Superka and Hawke's (1982) sociological focus on social role education has also been extended to other areas (citizen, consumer, worker) that were mentioned earlier. Space will not permit an exploration of how these concepts are related to the elementary child. It should be readily apparent, however, that they do not stand in isolation from the concepts presented above, and such interrelatedness should warrant further exploration of the sociological focus of teaching social studies.

ANTHROPOLOGY

Anthropology is the study of people and their works with the key concepts being culture and cultural change. Anthropology is closely related to sociology but includes content from the other social science disciplines, the biological sciences, and the humanities. It includes cross-cultural comparisons of present cultures and historical examinations of past cultures. The study of cultures may include those with a high level of technology or cultures with emerging technologies. In effect, the main ideas from anthropology are most often infused throughout the elementary school social studies curriculum.

In discussing the concept of culture, Rice (1972) indicated that "people in any and all cultures live in groups, rear families, socialize their children, make a living, worship, play and adjust to their environment" (p. 5). The constant adjusting to the environment results in cultural change. All cultures undergo change, but cultures differ in the rate at which they change. Change may occur in the fundamental ways in which the culture meets its needs, the ways in which it is organized, or the behavioral patterns that develop within the culture. Modification of such factors as technology, increased communication, new knowledge, population increases and the influences of other cultural groups can result in cultural change (California State Department of Education, 1975).

School systems have used the concepts of culture and cultural change in developing their curriculum (California State Department of Education, 1975; Fairfax County Schools, Virginia, 1970; New York City Board of Education, 1969). Questions such as "What culture has changed?" "How has it changed?" and "What factors have contributed to the change?" could serve as the major organizing ideas for the inclusion of anthropology in elementary school social studies.

Generalizations from anthropology identify the relationships between key concepts and may also serve as the main ideas for selecting and organizing content. Chase and John (1972) suggested the following generalizations from anthropology for elementary school social studies:
1. Human beings are more alike than different. They have similar physical characteristics and basic needs and wants.
2. People living in groups develop a culture. This includes their particular patterns of behavior and the resulting material products.
3. Culture is socially learned and serves as a potential guide for human behavior in any given society.
4. Human beings are in part a product of their culture.
5. Cultural change occurs continuously and at an accelerating rate (p. 34).

There is evidence that the ideas from anthropology can be learned by elementary school age children (Potterfield, 1966). The concepts associated with cultural variation, enculturation, and cultural dynamics from the Anthropology Curriculum Project were taught in the unit "Concept of Culture" to 4th, 5th, and 6th graders. Findings indicated that children could learn the vocabulary, concepts and the abstract reasoning required in the unit. In another study (Hunt, 1969), materials from grade 1 of this same project were adopted for use with kindergarten children. The key concepts taught were associated with cultural universals, enculturation, and cultural variation. The conclusions from this study were that children at this age level could learn the concepts as they were presented.

The program Man: A Course of Study (MACOS) was compared with a more traditional approach to teaching social studies (Peckham & Ware, 1973). In this study, 14 teachers from six different elementary schools in grades 4, 5 and 6 were randomly assigned to either the MACOS treatment group or to a traditional social studies control group. The MACOS teachers were trained, and the effectiveness of the program was examined after one year of implementation. Findings of the study favored the MACOS group in several areas. Results of the study indicated that:

1. The participants in the MACOS group learned material covered in this program to a significantly greater extent than those not in this program.
2. In the broader area of learning facts and concepts, there was some evidence favoring the MACOS group over the control group.
3. There were no differences between the two groups in their ability to make inferences and generalize.
4. Students in the MACOS program had a more positive view of themselves as students than did those students in the control group.
5. MACOS students felt that teachers viewed them more positively as social studies students than they did the students in the control group.
6. Teachers in the MACOS program had a more positive view of social studies than did other teachers in the study. They particularly felt that the program offered greater emphasis on the rights of people, more opportunities for intellectual development, increased ability to capitalize on individual student differences, and more attention to the transfer of knowledge.

In another study involving MACOS, children from three different schools ranked social studies as the least liked subject at the beginning of the school year (Herlihy, 1974). After one year of working with the program, the children rated social studies as either their first or second favorite school subject.

The effects of MACOS were intensively examined in a two-year longitudinal study involving 57 5th and 6th grade classes in 11 states across the country (Cort & Peskowitz, 1977). The average amount of instructional time was 40 minutes per day for 27 to 30 weeks. Students in the MACOS group learned the content of the program significantly better than did students in another social studies group. Both groups were given a Systematic Training for Effective Parenting Program (STEP) Social Studies test (Series II, form 4A) to compare their general social studies knowledge. No differences were found between the two groups on this measure, nor were there differences between the groups on their understanding and use of inquiry skills. The MACOS classes also tended to like social studies more and to rate social studies higher in comparison to other subjects than did the non-MACOS classes. These findings parallel those of Peckham and Ware (1973) and Herlihy (1974). It would appear that the content from anthropology not only can be learned by elementary school children, but that it can make social studies interesting.

One of the major findings from the Georgia Anthropology Curriculum Project was that there is not an inherent structure to the content of anthropology, but that decisions concerning the selection of content are more logical in nature. The findings of Hunt (1969) and Potterfield (1966) support this point of view. Rice (1968) indicates:

> Originally, it was thought that an analysis of the concepts of anthropology would reveal an hierarchic structure of complexity that would serve as the basis for a graded "sequential curriculum." It was found, however, that complexity is a function of the level of explanation, rather than of the concept *per se.* The sequencing now reflects merely the logic of the curriculum builders, and no claim is made that grade unit arrangement is inherent in the concepts of anthropology. For example, the Grade 7 unit "Life Cycle" might just as well serve as a point of entry to anthropology in Grade 1 instead of "The Concept of Culture," except that "culture" is a more significant organizing concept than is "life cycle." Learner maturity, however, would require modifications in the verbal input load at any grade level. (p. 254)

The role of anthropology in elementary school social studies has received little attention outside the two major curriculum projects—the Georgia Anthropology Curriculum Project, and Man: A Course of Study. The concepts of culture and cultural change often receive attention in curriculum guides and to some extent in commercial textbooks. Anthropology was the focus of the elementary section of the March, 1968 issue of *Social Education;* and the May, 1974 issue focused upon Man: A Course of Study. Although there is little empirical evidence to provide elementary school teachers with specific guidance in making content decisions to incorporate anthropology in their social studies, there appears to be sufficient information that the key ideas can be taught and learned if they are made meaningful to students.

INSTRUCTIONAL APPLICATIONS

Sociology and anthropology have an important place in elementary school social studies. Once the content decisions have been made, the teacher needs to select appropriate teaching strategies to provide for efficient learning of the main ideas from these two social science disciplines. Strategies that relate to concept formations and comprehension monitoring have been successfully employed by classroom teachers in other content areas. It is assumed that these strategies ought to be equally effective in promoting learning of the main ideas from anthropology and sociology. Children do not label the content that they are exposed to as belonging to a specific social science discipline. Rogers (1977) wrote:

> Children do not deal (voluntarily!) with "social studies" or "social science" questions. They view the world in a more wholistic way, and the questions they raise

(if they are genuinely children's questions) deal with concerns that are difficult to categorize exclusively as "geography," "sociology," "economics," etc. (p. 180)

It is important to note that cultivation of concepts in children requires that attention be given to their developmental abilities. Egan (1979) argued that the prominent thinking patterns of children should serve as a basis for curriculum selection and presentation. In teaching elementary school students, certain Piagetian learning characteristics may be readily discernible.

Elementary age children are generally engaged in concrete operational thought processes. They are developing their ability in the areas of logic, classification, conservation of quantities, and operational thought or the ability to organize and relate experience into an ordered pattern. They utilize both the enactive and iconic modes of learning (Bruner, 1966). Also, while they are eager for the new, they seldom relate it to the old without direction (Penrose, 1979). Learning at this age requires active participation of learners combined with some guidance to enable them to absorb the experience and to integrate it into their internal permanent store of understanding.

Taba (1965) was among the pioneers in social studies education to advocate the development of concept formation skills in children, while remaining within their developmental limitations. To successfully develop concepts, Taba wrote, children had to complete three processes. First, they had to differentiate the properties or characteristics of the objects or events under consideration. Second, children had to be able to abstract certain of these common characteristics into groups. Finally, children had to be able to categorize or provide labels that encompassed and organized the objects or events.

During the previous decade, researchers developed and tested strategies designed to foster conceptual development. Martorella's (1982) review of the research on concept formation models effectively summarized the principles required for effective instruction. These principles can be easily applied to the development of sociological concepts. Consider the following illustration using the sociological concept of family.

Martorella (1982) stated that the instructor should "begin with a clear and conventionally accepted definition of the concept" (p. 7). This definition should be developed with the students and be written using understandable vocabulary. Since family is a primary concept, a definition similar to the following may be suitable:

Family—A group of people, such as a mother, father, brother, sister, who usually live together.

This definition, based on the aforementioned research, is within the developmental level of understanding of primary students. It can be readily expanded to include lineage, grandparents and domestic function, while at the same time allowing for childless couples, single parents and split households.

Martorella suggested that once the definition has been established, the teacher should review and teach, if necessary, the critical attributes of the concept. Normally, these can be summarized as the most important words in the definition. For example, the child should have a thorough understanding of the terms "group," "mother," "father," "brother," "sister," and others in the family. Teaching critical attributes could involve a discussion of such individual terms and the role that each person plays in a family. It could also include the presentation of pictures or other visual stimuli.

The next step, according to Martorella, should be to list examples and non-examples of the concept. For the concept "family," students should be able to generate numerous examples from their personal history. This should provide an excellent opportunity for the instructor both to make the concept concrete and to expand the definition. Perhaps an interracial family or a communal family example can be presented to demonstrate the variety of patterns. In listing non-examples, the reader is cautioned that the non-example should be closely related to the concept being considered. (A "Big Mac," while being a non-example of everything but a hamburger sandwich, would not be considered an appropriate non-example of the concept "family!" Rather, the students should be deciding if groups such as their class, or neighbors are part of their family.) As with examples, the non-examples are judged according to the critical attributes of the definition.

Finally, Martorella (1982) wrote, "opportunities to experiment with identifying examples and non-examples should be incorporated, along with feedback on the correctness or incorrectness of the response" (p. 7). This testing to determine if the concept has been internalized can be accomplished using webbing, discussion, questions, drawings, pictures or any of a variety of methods.

The value of such an approach to concept instruction cannot be overstated. It has a wealth of empirical evidence to support its effectiveness, it is easily matched to the developmental capabilities of the students being instructed, and it can be used with any concept without the need for expensive or special materials.

Another valuable strategy designed to increase conceptual understanding is that of comprehension monitoring. Just as feedback was required with Martorella's (1982) model, ongoing feedback is required to monitor the child's understanding of material read or studied (Brown, 1980; Myers & Paris, 1978).

Comprehension monitoring is considered to be a conscious process designed to enhance comprehension. As such, it involves skills and strategies that can be taught to assist in the monitoring and remediation of material to be comprehended. Because social studies learning traditionally involves an inordinate amount of written material to be comprehended, the instructor should have knowledge of these monitoring skills and strategies. In addition, research has confirmed that children often do not monitor their listening or reading comprehension and therefore suffer an illusion of understanding (Markman, 1977; Brown, Bransford, Ferrara, & Campione, 1983; Wagoner, 1983).

Raphael (1982) wrote, "Once a passage is read, students assume that the information presented in the passage should be part of their knowledge base and therefore do not refer to the text when it would be appropriate to do so" (p. 18). The effective social studies teacher should realize this and use teaching strategies that compensate for students' false assumptions.

One such strategy that has been shown to facilitate understanding is the practice of supplementing textual presentations with teacher-generated questions (Pearson & Johnson, 1978). These questions normally require students to reread sections and to process the information at deeper levels, thus enhancing the possibility of relating the newly presented material to their prior knowledge.

The Follet Social Studies text series (Quigley et al., 1980) not only provides suggested teacher questions, but also specifically directs students to read the text questions, presented at the end of each unit, prior to reading the selection itself. Student-generated questions have also been shown to increase students' interaction with the text (Garner, Wagoner, & Smith, 1983).

Besides the use of questions to check comprehension, social studies teachers may employ other strategies that require further student interaction with the text. Suggested comprehension monitoring activities that have been demonstrated as being effective include the following:

1. Having students locate and orally read answers to classroom discussion questions.
2. Webbing information presented during the unit to other information presented in the unit or text.
3. Constructing a personal outline of the material read.
4. Answering who, what, where, when and why questions.
5. Asking for an individual or committee report that provides a summation of the material read.
6. Attempting to relate the data presented to the students' personal situation.
7. Further reporting that requires additional research.
8. Quizzes and tests.
9. Charting or graphing pertinent information.
10. Creating murals, dioramas, or montages that highlight concepts studied.

Space does not permit a discussion of each of these techniques. Webbing has been selected for presentation because it is a cognitive process that can be used by teachers to aid students in organizing and integrating text information. The web provides a visual representation of the materials being presented. Webs can provide students with an effective retrieval cue by having learners actively involved in encoding the content in a meaningful way (Clewell & Haidemus, 1983). The principles upon which webbing is based are similar to those of semantic mapping. This process requires semantic involvement with the text by the learner, is based upon the instructional effectiveness of diagrams, and is related to the effect of text structure on learning retention (Armbruster & Anderson, 1980).

A semantic web provides a visual image of the characteristics and relationships generating from a core. Dennyson (1979) provided a conceptual web that demonstrated the organization and integration of the roles and functions of families. This model is contained in Figure 1.

There are four parts in constructing a semantic web (Freedman & Reynolds, 1980). The first part is the core, which is the focus of the web and the question for inquiry. In the model presented, the question might be, "What are the roles and functions of families in the Amish culture?" The second part of the web are the strands that connect the core with its principal parts. These strands may provide the general answers to the questions. In the model presented, two strands are the Family As an Economic Unit, and Marriage and Courtship.

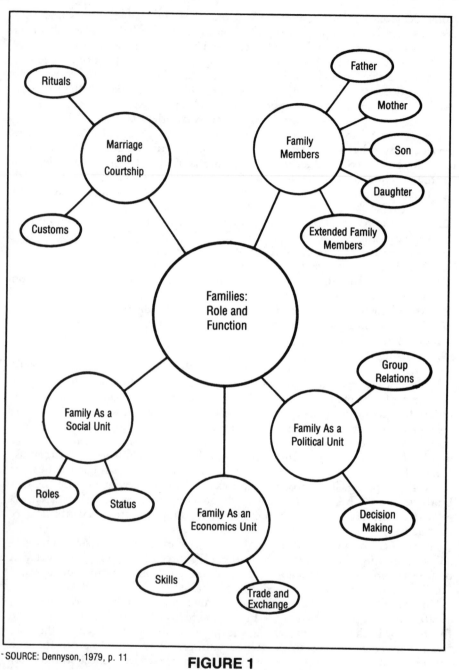

SOURCE: Dennyson, 1979, p. 11

FIGURE 1
Conceptual Web of the Family

The third part of the web are the strand supports. These help differentiate one strand from another. For example, Status and Roles are strand supports for the Family As a Social Unit. Strand ties are the fourth part of the web. These are the relationships that strands have with each other. For example, Daughter As a Family Member may at some time become involved in the rituals and customs of Marriage and Courtship.

The implications of comprehension monitoring for the social studies teacher are clear. It is evident from the research completed that merely reading the social studies text does not ensure automatic comprehension. Since facts, concepts and generalizations are usually presented in a spiral fashion, it becomes imperative that comprehension occur at the earliest levels. Often this requires that social studies teachers adopt reading strategies to enhance comprehension in the social studies area. Careful and continuous monitoring of the students' comprehension is needed if true conceptual understandings are to be developed. Students who fail to comprehend material must be provided with strategies to help them comprehend. Further information on strategies to improve the learners' comprehension of social studies materials can be found in McKenzie's chapter in this bulletin.

CONCLUSION

The purpose of this chapter was to provide classroom teachers with guidance in making content decisions concerning anthropology and sociology as these disciplines are related to elementary school social studies. In addition, some suggestions were made to increase teacher effectiveness in developing for students the key understandings from these disciplines. The following conclusions are based upon this review:

1. There is little empirical evidence to guide elementary classroom teachers in making content decisions about what should be taught, and when, in the areas of anthropology and sociology.
2. Some guidance in making these decisions can be found in the social studies curriculum development projects from the 1960s and early 1970s and in the literature on children's knowledge of social roles.
3. At the elementary school level, sociology and anthropology are most often taught with an interdisciplinary approach; ideas are not labeled as belonging exclusively to these two disciplines.
4. There is some evidence that teachers can provide instruction in these two areas without extensive training in the disciplines, and that children can learn the major understandings from these two disciplines.
5. Children's rankings of social studies with other areas tend to rise when the programs are systematically taught.
6. Strategies involving conceptual development and comprehension monitoring that have been successful in promoting student learning can probably be applied to learning the content from anthropology and sociology.

Analysis of the concepts of the Georgia Anthropology Curriculum Project indicated that the complexity of the content was more a function of the level of explanation than of the concepts involved. Decisions about the placement of content in the curriculum should be made more on the logic of the curriculum than on an inherent sequence of the discipline (Rice, 1968). This argument is probably true for those concepts from sociology as well. If this is assumed to be true, then future research efforts in elementary social studies involving anthropology and sociology should focus on teachers' behaviors that can facilitate students' learning of key understandings. Research also should be conducted on strategies that encourage the learning of key concepts from these two disciplines. Because much of the instruction in social studies involves text materials, research is also needed on ways to assist less able readers to monitor their comprehension of elementary social studies text-based materials.

Although anthropology and sociology appear to be neglected areas in elementary social studies instruction, they hold promise for making the curriculum exciting and motivating for students. When exposed to the content from these two disciplines, children appear to develop a more positive attitude towards social studies, and they rank it higher as a desirable school subject. Thus, by making appropriate content decisions for incorporating sociology and anthropology into elementary school social studies, and by employing effective teaching strategies, teachers can enhance students' attitudes toward school learning.

REFERENCES

Armbruster, B., & Anderson, H. (1980) *The effect of mapping on the free recall of expository text* (Tech. Rep. No. 160). Champaign, IL: Center for the Study of Reading. (ERIC Document Reproduction Service No. ED 182 735)

Brown, A. L. (1980). Metacognitive development and reading. In R. J. Spiro, B. C. Bruce, & W. F. Brewer (Eds.), *Theoretical issues in reading comprehension* (pp. 453–481). Hillsdale, NJ: Erlbaum.

Brown, A. L., Bransford, J. D., Ferrara, R. A., & Campione, J. C. (1983). Learning, remembering and understanding. In J. H. Flavell & E. M. Markman (Eds.), *Handbook of Child Psychology*, 4th ed. Vol. III (pp. 77–166). New York: Wiley.

Bruner, J. (1966). *Toward a theory of instruction.* Cambridge, MA: Harvard University Press.

Butzin, S. M. (1982). Learning experiences to promote sex equity. *Social Education, 46,* 48–53.

California State Department of Education (1975). *Social science education framework for California public schools, kindergarten and grades one through twelve.* Sacramento, CA: California State Department of Education. (ED 120 079)

Cataldo, C., & Geismar, L. (1983). Preschoolers' views of parenting and the family. *Journal of Research and Development in Education, 16,* 8–14.

Chase, W. L., & John, M. (1972). *A Guide for the elementary social studies teacher* (2nd ed.). Boston: Allyn and Bacon.

Clewell, S., & Haidemos, J. (1983). Organizational strategies to increase comprehension. *Reading World 22,* 314–21.

Cort, Jr. H., & Peskowitz, N. (1977). *Final report: A longitudinal study of Man: A Course of Study (Volume 1).* Washington, DC: Social Studies: Research Project, Antioch College.

Dynneson, T. (1977). *A conceptual/cross-cultural model for teaching anthropology in the elementary school.* University of Texas of the Permian Basin. (ED 137 171)

Egan, K. (1979). What children know best. *Social Education, 43,* 130–134.

Fairfax County Schools (1970). *Man in a changing world.* Fairfax, VA: Fairfax County Schools. (ED 048 045)

Freedman, G., & Reynolds, E. (1980). Enriching basic reader lessons with semantic webbing. *The Reading Teacher, 33,* 677–684.

Garner, R., Wagoner, S., & Smith, T. (1983). Externalizing question-answering strategies of good or poor comprehenders. *Reading Research Quarterly, 18,* 439–447.

Garvey, C. (1983). Some properties of social play. In William Damon (Ed.), *Social and personality development* (234–248). New York: W. W. Norton.

Hartup, W. W. (1983). Peer interaction and the behavioral development of the individual child. In William Damon (Ed.), *Social and personality development* (220–233). New York: W. W. Norton.

Herlihy, J. (1974). Prologue to change. *Social Education, 38,* 451–455.

Herman, W. (1983). What should be taught where? Scope and sequence in social studies education. *Social Education, 47,* 94–100.

Hunt, A. (1969). *Anthropology achievement of normal and disadvantaged kindergarten children.* Unpublished doctoral dissertation, Athens, GA: University of Georgia.

Jantz, R., Galper, A., Serock, K., & Seefeldt, C. (1976). *Children's attitudes toward the elderly: Final report.* Washington, DC: American Association of Retired Teachers, National Retired Teachers Association, Andrus Foundation. (Resources in Education, ED 142 860.)

Katz, P. (1983). Developmental foundations of gender and racial attitudes. In R. Leahy (Ed.), *The child's construction of social inequality* (41–78). New York: Academic Press.

Markman, E. M. (1977). Realizing that you don't understand: A preliminary investigation. *Child Development, 43,* 986–992.

Martorella, P. H. (1982). Cognition research: Some implications for the design of social studies instructional materials. *Theory and Research in Social Education, 10*(3), 1–16.

Moore, N. V. (1977). Cognitive levels, intactness of family and sex in relation to the child's development of the concept of family. *Dissertation Abstracts International, 37,* 4117B–4118B.

Myers, M., & Paris, S. G. (1978). Children's metacognitive knowledge about reading. *Journal of Educational Psychology, 70,* 680–690.

New York City Board of Education (1969). *Social studies, grade 3. Cultures around the world: Cultural and geographical relationships.* Brooklyn, NY: Bureau of Curriculum Development. (ED 064 181)

Pearson, P. D., & Johnson, D. D. (1978). *Teaching reading comprehension.* New York: Holt, Rinehart, and Winston

Peckham, P., & Ware, A. (1973). *An evaluation of Man: A Course of Study.* Bellevue, WA: Bellevue Public Schools. (ED 081 662)

Penrose, W. O. (1979). A primer on Piaget. Bloomington, IN: *Phi Delta Kappa.* Educational Foundation.

Potterfield, J. (1966). *An analysis of elementary school children's ability to learn anthropological content at grades four, five and six.* Unpublished doctoral dissertation, Athens, GA: University of Georgia.

Powell, J., & Thompson, D. (1981). The Australian child's concept of family. *Australian Journal of Early Childhood, 6,* 35–8.

Quigley, C. N., McKay, S. W., Santell, M. A., & Sears, T. G. (1980). *Follett social studies*. Chicago, IL: Follett Publishing Company.

Ragan, W., & McAulay, J. (1973). *Social studies for today's children* (2nd ed.). New York: Appleton-Century-Crofts.

Raphael, T. E. (1982). *Improving question-answering performance through instruction* (Tech. Rep. No. 32). Urbana, IL: University of Illinois, Center for the Study of Reading.

Rice, M. J. (1972). *Premises for structuring ethnic curricula*. Georgia Anthropology Curriculum Project. Athens, GA: University of Georgia. (ED 081 660)

Rogers, V. (1977). Reaction. In W. W. Joyce & F. L. Ryan (Eds.), *Social studies and the elementary teacher: Promises and practices* (179–181). Washington, DC: National Council for the Social Studies.

Rubin, Z. (1983). What is a friend? In William Damon (Ed.), *Social and personality development* (249–257). New York: W. W. Norton.

Schreiber, J. (1979). *Social studies, second grade book*. Glenview, IL: Scott, Foresman.

Scott, K. P. (1982). Sex fair education and the male experience. *Social Education, 46,* 53–57.

Semaj, L. (1980). The development of racial evaluation and preference: A cognitive approach. *The Journal of Black Psychology, 6,* 59–79.

Superka, D. P., & Hawke, S. (1982). *Social roles: A focus for social studies in the 1980's* (A Project SPAN Report). Boulder, CO: Social Science Education Consortium, Inc.

Taba, H. (1962). *Curriculum development: Theory and practice*. New York: Harcourt Brace Jovanovich.

Taba, H. (1965). The teaching of thinking. *Elementary English. 42,* 534–542.

Thornburg, K. R. (1983). Young childrens' understanding of familial concepts with implications for social studies units. *Social Education, 47,* 138–141.

Wagoner, S. A. (1983). Comprehension monitoring: What it is and what we know about it. *Reading Research Quarterly, 18,* 328–346.

Youniss, J. (1983). Understanding differences within friendships. In R. Leahy (Ed.), *The child's construction of social inequality* (161–177). New York: Academic Press.

CHAPTER 8

LEARNING AND INSTRUCTION

Gary R. McKenzie

S ocial studies grew out of history and geography three-quarters of a century ago. At the time, some people believed that young children's minds were inadequately developed to enable them to understand or reason with ideas, and that their minds would evolve if (and only if) the children engaged in activities like those that caused the minds of our primordial ancestors to evolve (Hall, 1904; Partridge, 1912). From the beginning, then, a number of social studies theorists de-emphasized the teaching of information and ideas, and stressed activities and experiences to enable minds to evolve naturally (Kilpatrick, 1921).

In the 1920s, taxpayers were willing to pay for schools where natural development would occur; but today, in a High Tech era when survival depends on technical knowledge, they demand more. Thus, in Texas, primary social studies was nearly dropped from the curriculum when critics reasoned that if children cannot learn significant ideas until 4th grade and learn best from direct experience in the real world, then primary social studies must be nonessential busywork (Senate Education Committee, 1981). Primary social studies was not dropped, however, because parents demanded that the information of history, geography, government and economics should be taught to all children.

Two relatively new lines of theory and research address these criticisms of social studies effectively, and help to identify traits of social studies that make it basic and more teachable than reading or writing. First, modern information processing and schema theories of learning and thought strongly suggest that children must learn stories, information and ideas of precisely the sort that is included in history and the social sciences before they can comprehend the sketchy statements they hear or read every day, and before they can solve problems by logical reasoning. Instructional design research has done a great deal to define variables that teachers can manipulate to elicit this learning. Second, an impressive array of studies has been completed in the last decade about what effective teachers do in classrooms to elicit unusually high levels of pupil achievement in learning of the sort that parents demand and teachers emphasize. The combination of studies on instructional design and teacher effectiveness has dominated the last decade of educational research.

Readers should note that this chapter omits discussion of descriptive research based on the assumptions of developmentalists like G. S. Hall or Jean Piaget. As Di Vesta points out in his authoritative summary (1982), children's abilities

to learn from instruction have been underestimated. Stage theories are undergoing revision, and principles and implications are presently unclear. Readers interested in traditional developmentalist implications for social studies should read McCartin's (1970) comments, but also should check recent trends summarized in Di Vesta's 1982 review.

Perceptions of societal demands and needs, of practical needs of elementary teachers, and of the theories of learning lead one to stress the teaching of information by powerful, direct methods. This is not to suggest that information is all that should be taught, or that all lessons should be taught by direct methods. There are other important goals of elementary social studies, including attitude formation, social skills, and creative thinking; and they may well require different methods. These other social goals are treated in other chapters of this volume, however. Teachers need different methods to do different jobs.

LEARNING AND CURRICULUM

Learning theories now hold that when new data are presented, learners focus attention on a few details according to the goals established for the learning task at hand. At first, these details register in short-term or working memory as meaningless stimuli; they become meaningful when the learner searches through long-term memory and finds related information that adds associated meanings. When the new data are related to a known system of ideas, they are encoded, comprehended and added to the memory file. For example, if one says, "Separatists faced many difficulties," the statement may not prompt much meaning; but if one uses a more familiar name, "Pilgrims," a dozen or so images, stories and ideas may be immediately recalled into working memory, and the reader comprehends more than was actually said (Ausubel, 1962; Gagné, 1977). Schema theorists, who are particularly interested in reading comprehension, agree that background knowledge is learned and later used in understanding new text. Furthermore, their work indicates that if relevant background information is not available, people will have trouble comprehending text, regardless of age (Anderson et al., 1977; Bransford, 1979; Hansen & Pearson, 1983; Pearson, Hansen, & Gordon, 1979; Silver, 1981; Schallert, 1982).

Problem solving is thought to occur in much the same way: by selecting cues in the problem statement and using them to search memory files for previously learned principles or factual analogues that imply or compose a solution. For example, if one asks, "How can you determine the volume of an irregularly shaped object like a statue?", the term "volume" probably produces a search for principles from geometry—which are rejected because the shape is irregular. If, however, one happens to know that volume is related to displacement, one can shift to an alternate memory file and deduce a solution. Similarly, if one happens to know the legendary story of Archimedes in the bathtub, the story will serve as a specific analogue for solving the problem. Expert and novice problems solvers appear to differ primarily in that novices must laboriously work through problems by trial and error, but experts use domain-specific knowledge to recognize familiar aspects of the problem and then recall principles or analogues to known solutions. By doing so, experts can move to a hypothesis (Akin, 1980; Chi, Glasser, & Rees, 1982; Feltovitch, 1981; Gagné, 1985). Differences in adult and young children's problem solving ability are said by these theorists to exist mainly in the amount and clarity of knowledge and the processing tricks that have been learned (Brown & De Loache, 1978; Gagné, 1980).

There is general agreement among learning theorists that different kinds of useful learning exist. Simple S-R associations (e.g., memorizing term-referent pairs) probably help people translate from one symbol system (like a place name or map symbol) to an image or referent in memory (McKenzie, 1980). Verbal information or chains (such as stories) are easy for children to remember and seem to link events together into structures that can be used as analogies (Schallert, 1982). Concepts (abstract definitions of categories, ideas for terms) enable classification and thus facilitate comparison (McKenzie, 1972). Principles (general patterns or cause-effect relations) probably serve as the major premise in deductions and inferences (Gagné, 1985). And cognitive strategies (generalizable routines for tackling different types of problems or processes) are probably used by learners as routines to guide themselves through complex learning or problem-solving tasks (Gagné, 1977; 1980).

Gagné (1977) suggests that these different kinds of learning form a hierarchy in which the easily learned lower level bits of knowledge are prerequisites to, and rearranged in, understanding of more complex ideas or solving problems. A number of studies analyze complex concepts into simpler component ideas and either pretest or teach the component ideas. These studies generally demonstrate that subjects who know the component ideas are much more likely to learn or apply the complex ability (Cancelli, Bergman, & Taber, 1980; Caruso & Resnick, 1972; Mayer, 1975; Resnick & Ford, 1981; White, 1973). Most of this work used older subjects, but Crabtree (1974) demonstrated the same effect in 2nd grade social studies, and it is believed that the phenomenon applies to young children.

Several practical implications for social studies curriculum can be derived from these modern cognitive theories. First, children need knowledge of ideas and information before they can make sense of complex experiences or solve problems rationally, and children who know more information will learn new ideas and solve problems more efficiently and effectively than less-informed children. The corollaries to this point are interesting.

A major goal and justification of elementary social studies in this era of "basics" is that social studies provides the information and ideas about people, places and events that children must know if they are to comprehend meanings of sketchy news reports or brief paragraphs, such as those that occur on reading comprehension tests. It is possible to argue from this theory and research that comprehension of paragraphs about unfamiliar people or places will increase more as a result of carefully explaining information than from extra word-attack or question-answering drills in reading. Thus, social studies is not merely "basic," it is prerequisite to "basic skills."

The same principle should apply in planning for and teaching social studies lessons. Before elementary children are engaged in grappling with and attempting to resolve problems involving the complexity of conflict, racism, economic injustice and environmental imbalance (Manson, Marker, Ochoa, & Tucker, 1970), the teacher must identify and teach the information the children need as background evidence, models, or premises.

Mental schema, or files of background knowledge, can be developed in two ways that have implications for curriculum design. First, they can be developed and elaborated by reminding children briefly of events and phenomena they already know and then showing or telling new examples or details or applying information. The other basic approach is to task analyze the new information into component facts and ideas, and then to teach the simpler images, facts and ideas in a way that relates them to a story or principle that pupils can recall and use. Thus, new ideas must be carefully added or built onto known or simple ideas.

Another principle is that children must learn strategies for analyzing stimuli, searching for relevant knowledge, and applying that knowledge systematically. These strategies probably develop at two different levels. At the simplest level, pupils must learn when and how to apply each idea in new cases. As will be noted below, the odds that children will be able to apply an idea are increased if the idea is stated in special forms, and also if children practice applying it to new cases. At a higher level, there have been some cases in which children have been taught systematic and transferable strategies that they can use to learn new ideas or solve new problems.

INSTRUCTION

An important series of 14 fairly large-scale, atheoretical "teacher effectiveness" studies have identified what amounts to a national sample of teachers of students who produce unusually high or low scores on standardized mathematics and reading achievement tests. Researchers observed the classrooms to define patterns in the methods of the two groups. When all types of students are combined into a heterogeneous sample, these studies consistently show that child-centered, process-oriented classes with high pupil choice of activity and an indirect teacher correlate with reduced pupil achievement on these tests. On the other hand, effective teachers are highly content-oriented, impose high structure on the class, explain new material to groups of pupils, have pupils practice on common assignments, ask frequent recall and comprehension questions, and monitor and correct pupil errors carefully during lessons (Rosenshine, 1977). A second generation of these studies shows that average teachers can be taught the methods extracted from the first studies to produce gains in pupil achievement (see Barnes, 1981; Brophy & Good, in press; Medley, 1982).

The uses and limitations of these studies should be carefully understood. One limitation is that the standardized tests used in reading and mathematics measure up to the level at which pupils apply skills and principles to solve problems similar to those that have been taught and practiced. They do not test creativity or the ability to solve novel problems. Thus, the teacher effectiveness studies do not show that direct methods are the best way to teach higher order thinking skills.

It is also true that effects of direct instruction are greater with lower SES pupils, and that correlations become insignificant with middle-class pupils (Medley, 1982). That is, there is no clear pattern in what methods work best for middle-class pupils. These studies should be attended to as models when teachers wish to teach facts, concepts, principles and routine skills up to the application level in elementary social studies, and when they are teaching a low ability or heterogeneous class. On the other hand, other methods may be necessary when teachers attempt to teach attitudes or novel problem-solving skills.

In an unusual coincidence, findings from the atheoretical classroom-based teacher effectiveness studies and the theory-based instructional design work seem to be converging on a common model of instruction. Indeed, at a general level, the steps in Gagné's (1977) model of instruction are the same as those of synthesized models of instruction from the teacher effectiveness studies (Barnes, 1981; Brophy & Good, in press). The lack of theoretical rationale in the teacher effectiveness studies is compensated for by the theory of the design studies, and the lack of classroom testing of design studies is ameliorated conversely.

Correlations between teacher behavior and pupil achievement are even higher when instructional design principles are added to the general teacher effectiveness findings in teaching 6th grade social studies facts, and application of concepts and principles (Bass, 1980). The emerging model is quite teacher-centered. It suggests ways that teachers can focus pupil attention, control clarity, elaborate information, and guide practice. This kind of model will prove more practical to classroom teachers than models that focus on factors within children that teachers cannot influence.

Introduce Lessons with Clear Goals

Modern conceptions of academic motivation de-emphasize the notion of fitting curriculum to instinctive interests or the use of extrinsic reinforcement. Achievement motivation and attribution theories take the position that all children are naturally motivated to succeed, or at least to avoid failure, and propose that whether or not a child will try in a given task depends upon (1) the child's history of success in similar tasks, and (2) the child's awareness of specific things that he or she can do during study to increase success (Atkinson & Raynor, 1974; Butkowsky & Willows, 1980; Thomas, 1979). In classrooms, for example, children will cooperate if tasks are clear or there is low risk of failure; but when instructions become ambiguous and pupils perceive a high risk of failure, anxiety increases and children may actually misbehave to force the teacher to abort the lesson and shift to an easier or clearer task (Doyle, 1983). Indeed, we know that background knowledge to assist understanding (Butkowsky & Willows, 1980; Carno & Mandinach, 1983; Chou, Hare, & Devine, 1983) or accessibility of necessary information in the lesson (Rothkopf & Koether, 1978) relates directly to student effort. Thus, poorly designed lessons of any sort can reduce motivation, and the danger increases as information and structure are reduced (McKenzie, 1979).

This conception of "motivation" is actually rather practical. It does not rely on natural interests, which often do not correspond to assigned curriculum; and it suggests that by making lessons clearer and by prompting correct study behavior, a teacher can increase pupil success on Monday so that pupils will be easier to engage in new lessons on Tuesday. Thus, the problem of motivation is not so much to make the lesson sound like fun as it is to make the lesson goal and study methods clear.

Effective teachers introduce lessons quickly and efficiently by informing pupils of a clear goal and rationale or by stating the objective to pupils (Brophy, Rhorkemper, Rashid, & Goldberger, 1983). Instructional design studies suggest that displaying a list of questions to be answered, or previewing a quiz, is effective and powerful in focusing pupil attention and eliciting learning of specific data—at least when pupils cannot answer the questions at the outset, and the necessary information is clearly available. However, prequestions focus attention on the extent that students will actually ignore information incidental to the questions (Faw & Waller, 1976; Hartley & Davies, 1976; Rothkopf & Bisbicos, 1967). Prequestions are the best way to introduce a lesson in which the teacher has determined that a specific set of question-answer pairs are to be learned, such as when children are to memorize the locations of major rivers or regions or landmarks or where children are to learn to match names or events with specific achievements.

Informing pupils of a behavioral objective is also quite effective in eliciting and focusing attention and increasing objective-relevant learning (Duchastel & Merrill, 1973; Hartley & Davies, 1976; Wong, Wong, & Le Mare, 1982). Because objectives are somewhat less precise than specific questions, they tend to direct attention to a broader range of material that might be relevant (Frederickson, 1975). Khoynejad (1980) found that using a combination of objectives and illustrative prequestions with high school students produced high question-relevant achievement and also high achievement on learning incidental information. Telling pupils the objectives and sample prequestions makes reading or explanation lessons clearer to children down to 1st grade, probably because younger children need more cues for deciding what and how to study.

Descriptive titles and advance organizers that either relate new material to previously learned knowledge or show relations between ideas to be introduced are also effective (Faw & Waller, 1976; Mayer, 1979; Royer & Cable, 1975; Stone, 1983). Giving an outline of points to be made in the lesson also helps (Hansen & Pearson, 1983).

When a teacher wishes to introduce the often superficial, disjointed, rambling chronicles of invasions or settlements, or descriptions of cities or families as they appear in elementary texts or films, he or she should recognize that there may be too much poorly organized information for pupils to understand what is worth learning. To focus attention and simplify the task, the teacher should study the content, isolate a set of a dozen or fewer fact questions and/or a general pattern or organizing principle in the material, and build objective and illustrative prequestions around this content. Then the teacher should plan to spend five minutes or so describing the goals to pupils, and providing hints about how to study. The clearer the introduction is about goals and procedures, the easier the lesson will appear to pupils, and the more likely they will be to try to learn and to feel successful.

Make Ideas Clear and Useful

There is no longer any serious question about whether young children can learn ideas from verbal instruction. They can and they do (Ausubel, Novak, & Hanesian, 1978; Barnes, 1981; Brophy & Good, in press; Di Vesta, 1982; Rosenshine, 1977). Often, however, statements that appear in elementary social studies texts or curriculum guides have been broadened and diluted until they are difficult to understand or impossible to apply. For example, a statement such as "Families are alike in many ways" is very vague. The problem is to narrow down such ideas into more definite statements that are easy to use as premises in logical reasoning.

There is also considerable information on how to state ideas with maximum clarity. The rule is that precision and specificity improve clarity and understanding. First, teacher use of indefinite or ambiguous terms ("somewhere," "several," "often," "a few," "maybe"), bluffing ("etc., etc.") and mazes (jumbles of words that do not make sense) inhibit pupil achievement (Dunkin, 1978; Dunkin & Doneau, 1980; Smith & Land, 1981).

Facts will be easier to remember if the same cue term is used in questioning as in instruction (Glenberg, 1976; Tulving & Watkins, 1975). This implies that it is worthwhile to use some care in selecting the most frequently used name or cue when teaching facts, and sticking to it during the lesson and questioning. If, for example, pupils must memorize map symbols (e.g., for elevation), a universal code (like the international colors for elevations) will be more valuable to them than homemade or nonstandard codes.

Defining concepts in the syntactic style of dictionaries is less clear and transferable than stating definitions in the operational form of vertical list, such as the following:

Term: Democracy

Domain	a form of government in which
Critical Attribute	(1) all citizens may vote on policy;
Critical Attribute	(2) there is free speech and debate;
Critical Attribute	(3) the majority rules.

Apparently, the list form is easier to recall and use when a definition is needed to classify new cases (Markle, 1975; Tennyson & Parks, 1980).

Principles or generalizations that do not stipulate exactly when the rule applies or exactly what is implied by the rule are difficult or impossible to use as major premises in deductive applications. Ellen Gagné (1985) indicates that principles or generalizations should be stated in definite "if-then" form so that students can examine the facts of a problem case and determine whether the necessary and sufficient conditions are present to warrant prediction from the rule. That is, a generalization such as "Deserts occur where prevailing winds bring little rain" is not as useful as a more precise proposition such as "If prevailing winds blow from an ocean across high mountains, then the downwind side of the mountains will be a desert."

Routine skills are easier to teach, learn and use if a defininte step-by-step procedure can be outlined "by the numbers" or as an algorithm from a definite and predictable starting point (Gagné, 1985; Landa, 1974). For example, "If you wish to orient a city map with no compass:

1. Go to an intersection with marked street names.
2. Use the map index to locate both streets on your map.
3. Find the intersection of the two street lines on the map.
4. Rotate the map until the two street lines on the map are parallel to the real streets."

A general recommendation that can be drawn from these findings is that teachers should carefully avoid planning to "cover a topic" merely in the hopes that someone will learn something. Rather, the teacher might write a list of question-answer pairs in planning fact lessons, a concept's definition in list form, or a statement of principle in "if-then" form. These statements of ideas could than be checked for unfamiliar or ambiguous terms to reduce confusion when they are presented to children. They could also be used to select appropriate examples and application questions later in the lesson.

Ensure Elaboration

Even when the information is stated in clear form, it is necessary to help pupils relate the new information either to something already understood or remembered and to show just how broadly the idea can be applied. Effective teachers are known to give examples or to model steps of a skill or process (Barnes, 1981; Brophy & Good, in press). Instructional design research suggests a variety of specific possibilities to mold information into ideas.

When texts or lessons introduce a period, place or culture that is unfamiliar to pupils and "cover" the topic in only one or two paragraphs, it may be that too little information is given to enable even good readers to form a meaningful image or idea. Teachers can help by telling how the to-be-read passage relates to a previously learned theme (Newman & Mayer, 1983; Schallert, 1982). Also, because the structures of stories are easy to remember (Mandler & Johnson, 1977; Schallert, 1982), a vague or abstract principle can be clarified by a dramatic illustrative story or mural-like picture that links discrete features into an integrated sequence or scene. For example, texts generally treat hardships of pioneers in a brief, generalized form that has little meaning or human interest to pupils. In such cases, the teacher should take time to tell a specific story or read illustrative excerpts from a narrative, like Virginia (Patty) Read's account of the Donner Party tragedy.

A second approach to elaboration, use of mnemonics, is particularly useful when a large number of specific name-place or name-event pairs are to be memorized. "Intrinsic" mnemonics are custom-made to begin with a term or name that will appear frequently in text or news and to link some distinctive feature of that cue term to a distinctive feature of the correct response. For example, if "Pizarro" is often mentioned in history, and the association desired is "conquered Peru" or "1532," a sentence linking the P's with an alliteration will be helpful: "Pizarro pillaged Peru in 1532." Mnemonic devices serve as artificial prompts for locating information in long-term memory, and greatly aid acquisition and long-term recall (Bellezza, 1981; Prestley, Levin, & Delaney, 1982).

A recent study required 5th graders to learn to match names to landmarks (such as bays and mountain ranges) of the Pacific states. Use of mnemonics that matched a feature of the name to a shape printed on an outline map (e.g., "Puget Sound—sound reminds you of ear—is the ear-shaped bay") increased retention by more than 100 percent; and use of both mnemonics and test-like practice increased retention by 200 percent (McKenzie & Sawyer, 1985). Although most young children do not invent effective original mnemonics, older children can do so with training; and all age groups benefit from having them supplied by the teacher (Prestley & Dennis-Rounds, 1980; Prestley, Levin, & Delaney, 1982; Rohwer & Cable, 1983).

Levin, Schriberg, and Berry (1983) used mnemonics linking names of 10 cities to some feature of specially constructed pictures representing attributes of the cities. They found that the mnemonics enabled recall of the correct scene for each city. In addition, the mental image of the integrated scene enabled recall of multiple attributes of each city, thus teaching literally dozens of facts very quickly. Gary McKenzie used this "mural method" in a 40-minute lecture (to 84 5th graders) on traits of each of six culture groups of Indians in September. In April, pupils recalled an average of 36 traits. Most reported that, after six months, they still could visualize each of the six village scenes.

When a concept, generalization or skill is stated in verbal form, pupils may not know the meanings of the words used, or may have difficulty remembering how the parts fit together. Thus, after the main idea (or step) is stated, it is very useful to provide a classic (or the best) example, either as a picture, an exploded diagram, a case study story or a demonstration; and then point out exactly how the terms in the rule correspond to specific concrete features of the example (Reder, 1980; Schallert, 1982; Tennyson, Chao, & Youngers, 1981; Tennyson & Park, 1980; Tennyson, Youngers, & Suebsonthi, 1983). This "best example" step apparently accomplishes several things: the example is concrete, (or memorable in the case of a story) and may be directly recalled and used later as a prototype in analyzing new situations. The verbal linking of terms to features of the case (Kunen & Duncan, 1983) cues attention to conceptual details or causal links that may otherwise be overlooked by unsystematic pupils (Hansen & Pearson, 1983; Newman & Mayer, 1983). The explicit matching helps to define words in terms of features of the example, or to prompt recall of prior learning.

If children are to be able to use a concept or generalization in new situations, the definition and best example must be extended or elaborated with a variety of examples that are selected and presented to demonstrate how broadly the idea applies. This is essential if children are to use ideas to solve new problems. It is not necessary to show every example. So, in analyzing democracy, the teacher can focus on illustrative forms: the government of the ancient Germans, as described by Tacitus, as a simple and informal democracy; the Athenian city-state as a direct democracy for citizens; and the United States as a democracy of representative government and separation of powers.

Similarly, children will consistently overgeneralize abstract ideas unless the teacher selects and explains a set of similar non-examples—cases that have many but not all of the essential characteristics of the concept or generalization (Tennyson & Park, 1980). Again, texts are extremely inadequate in the array of examples presented, and almost never provide an explicit non-example. Thus, the classroom teacher or local authors of curriculum guides must identify and supply these elaborations as supplements to texts or to games and activities that focus on only one specific example.

Guide Processing with Questions

Learning requires pupils to attend to and process new information in some appropriate way, and questioning gives teachers indirect means to elicit and direct how pupils think and practice. Some assumptions about questioning have changed.

Although teachers frequently insert questions into reading and discussion in an attempt to elicit or hold attention, there is some evidence that oral questions addressed to individuals or volunteers in large groups produce more off-task behavior than teacher explanations (Kounin & Doyle, 1975). Children learn to play the odds of being called on, and may tune out. Even when pupils appear to be attentive, they may be thinking about something unproductive, such as "I want to talk," rather than rehearsing answers to questions (McKenzie & Schadler, 1980.) However, test-like events (questions inserted into instruction that all learners must answer without looking back) maintain attention, raise achievement on question-relevant material, and may also develop habits of careful or selective study (Frase, 1968; McKenzie & Herrington, 1981; Roth-kopf, 1970; Rothkopf & Bisbicos, 1967).

One very effective classroom device is for the teacher to plan a way that all pupils can signal an answer by a nonverbal gesture in unison (e.g., ditto a list of answers, a blank map or an unlabeled timeline that pupils can point to and "show" answers to oral questions; or phrase questions in the form, "Raise your hand if this is an example of (the concept name). (pause) Why do you think so (pause) . . . Geraldine?" (McKenzie & Henry, 1979; McKenzie & Schadler, 1980).

Research on type of questions continues to be contradictory, which may indicate that different kinds of questions do different jobs that may be necessary in different situations. However, some interesting patterns seem to be emerging. It is clear that respect for recall and comprehension questions has dramatically increased among researchers in the last decade. Effective teachers emphasize recall and comprehension questions, especially with low SES pupils. Their questions are clear to pupils, the teachers insist on an answer, and pupils give correct responses most of the time: 75 percent on initial practice questions, 90 percent on seatwork or homework (Brophy & Good, in press). Most of the studies indicate that higher order questions are not more effective than lower order questions in developing recall, comprehension or application of a principle to a new case (Andre, 1979, 1980; Barnes, 1982; Brophy & Good, in press; Gall et al., 1975; Winne, 1979). Presumably this finding is consistent with the current belief that students must be guided to acquire accurate statements of basic information before they can be expected to apply it logically in thinking or problem solving (Frase, 1968; Rothkopf, 1970). It also fits with the belief that recall of a factual example may be quite as useful in problem solving as the exercise that may occur from "thinking" questions, at least up to the application level (Tennyson et al., 1983; Barnes, 1982).

On the other hand, some studies of concentrated use of application questions have produced somewhat encouraging results. Pupils learn to apply ideas to new situations better if a rule statement is followed by several application questions about new situations (Andre, 1979; McKenzie & Henry, 1979; Watts & Anderson, 1971). When a concept or principle is taught and the teacher wishes pupils to be able to transfer the idea to new cases, it appears to be helpful if the teacher phrases some application questions which (a) describe facts of the new case that indicate the presence or absence of each critical condition of the rule, and then (b) ask pupils if the rule applies and why or why not. For example, after explaining the principle that deserts develop on the lee side of high mountains, a teacher can say, "Prevailing winds blow from the Pacific across the Sierra Nevada Mountains to Nevada. Raise your hand if you can predict a desert in Nevada. . . . Why do you think so, Sam?" Teachers use application questions in teaching vowel or punctuation rules in language; the same kind of practice should help transfer in social studies.

Application of new concepts or rules to new cases is important to thinking in classical logic and modern psychology because it shows pupils when and how to use rules as major premises in deduction. Apparently even toddlers can apply rules with practice (Moskovitz, 1978). Kindergarten pupils have been taught to predict wind direction, customs of Indian tribes, or changes in cowboy's work by stating verbal rules and asking a series of application (prediction) questions.

One study (McKenzie & Herrington, 1981) detected signs of forward transfer of a basic thinking strategy after pupils were taught generalizations and asked application questions in the same way over a series of lessons. In each training lesson, the teacher began with a consistent cue ("Today I'm going to teach you a new generalization"), and stated a rule in the general form ("If A, and B, and C, then X."). Two examples and two non-examples were explained. Then pupils were given short descriptions of cases that had not been discussed that mentioned all or omitted one of the conditions A, B, C and the outcome. Pupils were asked after each case, "Raise your hand if you can predict X in this case. Why or Why not?" Treatment lessons on Monday, Tuesday and Wednesday dealt with geography, geology and meteorology generalizations. Pupils were tested on their ability to understand and apply an unrelated economics principle that was simply stated to experimental and control pupils on Thursday. Experimental pupils were better able to apply the new idea to new economics problems than were control pupils. All steps in the procedure were necessary. The cue warns pupils to expect application questions before the rule is stated; the rule statement provides the major premise necessary for the deductions; and the practice in applying different generalization statements teaches pupils that the same process will work in all tasks of this type.

More complex problem solving is also important, but apparently there is no evidence that asking children to grapple with hard problems or to exercise any specific faculty or region of the brain has any positive, transferable effect on rational thinking or effective problem solving. Children can and do learn to think in the highest sense of the word, but they seem to do so as a consequence of acquiring information and ideas, and of learning more or less systematic strategies for dealing with particular types of problems. Gagné's (1977) minimum conditions in teaching problem solving seem representative: the learner must first know and be able to use relevant ideas and information; then verbal instructions that state the goal and general form of a solution should be given. Modeling the process to be used in a step by step way is helpful. Then considerable practice at solving similar types of problems (not an occasional higher order question in isolation) is required.

Different approaches to teaching for thinking have been suggested, but research lags behind speculation. There are five studies that describe replicable treatments that demonstrate that elementary pupils apparently learned how to transfer to solve problems with new content in later lessons. Anderson (1965) taught 1st graders a systematic procedure for solving word problems in mathematics. Rohwer and Litrownik (1983) successfully taught upper elementary pupils a system for inventing mnemonics to aid in paired-associate learning (but failed to do so with primary grade pupils). Hudspeth (1983) taught 5th graders a system for analyzing and rewriting dictionary definitions into operational (list) form to produce more symmetric classifications and a better comprehension of new terms on a later test. McKenzie and Herrington (1981) trained 5th graders to use a strategy for learning and applying principles that enhanced later learning and application of a new principle. Finally, Olton and

Crutchfield (1969) trained 5th graders in a more complex routine for analyzing cues, forming hypotheses, and verifying hypotheses, and it produced transfer to enhance solution of new problems. Gagné's theory (1977) and these studies have common elements: a narrow (but generic) type of problem task is defined, the researchers generated a specific model of definite steps that fit the particular type of problem, the steps were explained and modeled, and repeated practice with corrective feedback was provided.

CONCLUSION

Elementary social studies is an essential subject, especially for young children with a limited knowledge of the stories, the concepts and the principles that people must have to comprehend what they see, hear or read, or to reason logically in problem solving. Modern information processing or schema theories of learning and thought suggest that the kinds of information that can be taught in elementary social studies are essential and prerequisite even for the "basic skill" of reading comprehension, and that learning these kinds of information may be a fundamental cause of mental development.

Classroom teachers have traditionally tried to teach facts, concepts, and principles; but social studies theorists from Kilpatrick to the present have emphasized various kinds of process goals and indirect methods of teaching that may not be very effective in helping pupils to learn and apply new ideas. Both groups were right and wrong in light of modern research. Teachers were right to try to teach information and ideas, but wrong in failing to be precise enough and in not requiring pupils to apply the ideas in new settings. Theorists were right to stress thinking and problem solving, but wrong to de-emphasize the direct teaching of information that pupils must learn before they can solve problems.

Research also suggests that once an idea is acquired, it should be elaborated; and pupils should be asked to apply it. Some studies demonstrate ways to teach even 1st graders logical, orderly "strategies" of thinking. This is only a modest extension into the domain of higher order objectives that are important in the eventual development of good citizens.

In brief, then, the research identified in this chapter has the potentiality to be of practical value to classroom teachers, provide an outside perspective on trends in learning and instruction that can stimulate thought about social studies traditions, and help to develop the unique information and ideas that give social studies a claim to an essential niche in the elementary curriculum.

REFERENCES

Akin, O. (1980). *Models of architectural knowledge.* London: Pion.

Anderson, R. (1965). Can first graders learn an advanced problem solving skill? *Journal of Educational Psychology, 56,* 283–294.

Anderson, R., Reynolds, R., Schallert, D., & Goetz, E. (1977). Frameworks for comprehending discourse. *American Educational Research Journal, 14,* 367–381.

Andre, T. (1979). Does answering higher level questions while reading facilitate productive thinking? *Review of Educational Research, 49,* 280–318.

Andre, T. (1980). Adjunct application questions facilitate later application, or do they? *Journal of Educational Psychology, 72,* 533–543.

Atkinson, J., and Raynor, J. (1974). *Personality, motivation and achievement.* New York: John Wiley & Sons.

Ausubel, D. (1962). A subsumption theory of verbal learning and retention. *Journal of General Psychology, 66,* 213–224.

Ausubel, D., Novak, J., & Hanesian, H. (1978). *Educational psychology: A cognitive view* (2nd ed.). New York: Holt, Rinehart & Winston.

Barnes, S. (1981, September). *Synthesis of selected research on teaching findings* (Report 9009). Austin, TX.: Research and Development Center for Teacher Education.

Bass, J. (1980). *Effects of an inservice program on teacher planning, and pupil achievement with middle school social studies teachers.* Unpublished doctoral dissertation, University of Texas at Austin.

Bellezza, F. (1981). Mnemonic devices: Classification, characteristics, and criteria. *Review of Educational Research, 51,* 247–275.

Bransford, J. (1979). *Human cognition: Learning, understanding, and remembering.* Belmont, CA.: Wadsworth.

Bransford, J., & Johnson, M. (1972). Contextual prerequisites for understanding: Some investigations of comprehension and recall. *Journal of Verbal Learning and Verbal Behavior, 11,* 717–726.

Brophy, J., & Good, T. (in press). Teacher behavior and student achievement. In M. Wittrock (Ed.), *Handbook of research on teaching* (3rd ed.). Rand McNally.

Brophy, J., Rhorkemper, M., Rashid, H., & Goldberger, M. (1983). Relationships between teachers' presentation of classroom tasks and student engagement in those tasks. *Journal of Educational Psychology, 75,* 544–552.

Brown, A., & De Loache, J. (1978). Skills, plans and self regulation. In R. Siegler (Ed.), *Children's thinking: What develops?* (pp. 3–37). Hillsdale, N.J., Earlbaum and Associates.

Butkowsky, I., & Willows, D. (1980). Cognitive motivational characteristics of children varying in reading ability: Evidence for learned helplessness in poor readers. *Journal of Educational Psychology, 72,* 408–422.

Cancelli, A., Bergman, J., & Taber, D. (1980). Relationships between complexity and hierarchical sequencing. *Journal of Educational Psychology, 72,* 331–337.

Carno, L., & Mandinach, E. (1983). Using existing classroom data to explore relationships in a theoretical model of classroom motivation. *Journal of Educational Research, 77,* 33–42.

Caruso, J., & Resnick, L. (1972). Task structure and transfer in children's learning of double classification skills. *Child Development, 43,* 1297–1308.

Case, R. (1975). A developmentally based theory and technology of instruction. *Review of Educational Research, 45,* 59–87.

Chi, M. (1978). Knowledge structures and memory development. In R. Siegler (Ed.), *Children's thinking: What develops?* (pp. 73–97). Hillsdale, N.J.: Earlbaum and Associates.

Chi, M., Glasser, R., & Rees, E. (1982). Expertise in problem solving. In R. Sternberg (Ed.), *Advances in the psychology of human intelligence* (Vol. 1) (pp. 7–75). Hillsdale, N.J.: Earlbaum & Associates.

Chou, V., Hare, & Devine, D. (1983). Topical knowledge and topical interest predictors of listening comprehension. *Journal of Educational Research, 76,* 157–160.

Crabtree, C. (1974). Some factors of sequence and transfer in learning the skills of geographic analysis. Part I of *Children's thinking in the social studies.* Unpublished manuscript, Graduate School of Education, University of California at Los Angeles.

Di Vesta, F. (1982). Cognitive development. In H. Mitzel (Ed.), *Encyclopedia of educational research* (2nd Ed.) (pp. 285–296). New York: Macmillan.

Doyle, W. (1983). Academic work. *Review of Educational Research. 53,* 159–200.

Duchastel, P., & Merrill, P. (1973). The effects of behavioral objectives on learning: A review of empirical studies. *Review of Educational Research, 43,* 53–70.

Dunkin, M. (1978). Student characteristics, classroom processes and student achievement. *Journal of Educational Psychology, 70,* 998–1009.

Dunkin, M., & Doneau, S. (1980). A replication study of unique and joint contributions to variance in student achievement. *Journal of Educational Psychology, 72,* 398–403.

Faw, H., & Waller, T. (1976). Mathemagenic behaviours and efficiency in learning from prose materials: Review, critique and recommendations. *Review of Educational Research, 46,* 691–720.

Feltovitch, P. (1981). *Knowledge based components of expertise in medical diagnosis* (Tech. Rep. PDS-2). University of Pittsburgh, Learning Research and Development Center.

Frase, L. (1968). Questions as aids to reading: Some research and a theory. *American Educational Research Journal, 5,* 319–322.

Frederickson, C. (1975). Effects of context induced processing operations on semantic information acquired from discourse. *Cognitive Psychology, 7,* 139–166.

Gagné, E. (1985). *The cognitive psychology of social learning.* Boston: Little Brown.

Gagné, R. (1977). *The conditions of learning* (3rd ed.). New York: Holt, Rinehart, & Winston.

Gagné, R. (1980). Learnable aspects of problem solving. *Professional Psychologist, 15,* 84–92.

Gall, M., Ward, B., Berliner, D., Cahen, L., Crown, K., Elashahoff, J., Stanton, G., & Winne, P. (1975, August). *The effects of teacher use of questioning techniques on student attitude and achievement.* San Francisco: Far West Laboratory for Educational Research and Development.

Glenberg, A. (1976). Monotonic and nonmonotonic lag effects in paired associate and recognition memory paradigms. *Journal of Verbal Learning and Verbal Behavior, 15,* 1–16.

Hall, G. S. (1904–1905). *Adolescence: Its psychology and its relations to physiology, anthropology, sociology, sex, crime and religion and education* (Vols. 1–2). New York: Appleton.

Hansen, J., & Pearson, P. (1983). An instructional study: Improving the inferential comprehension of good and poor fourth grade readers. *Journal of Educational Psychology, 75,* 821–829.

Hartley, J., & Davies, I. (1976). Preinstructional strategies: The role of pretests, behavioral objectives, overviews and advance organizers. *Review of Educational Research, 46,* 239–265.

Hudspeth, B. (1983, April). *Training elementary school pupils to process dictionary definitions.* Paper presented at the annual meeting of the American Educational Research Association, Montreal.

Khoynejad, G. (1980). *The effects of behavioral objectives, prequestions and a combination of both on intentional and incidental learning from written text by secondary students.* Unpublished doctoral dissertation, University of Texas at Austin.

Kilpatrick, W. (1921). *The project method, the use of the purposeful act in the educative process.* New York: Teachers College Press.

Kounin, J., & Doyle, P. (1975). Degree of continuity in a lesson's signal system and task involvement of children. *Journal of Educational Psychology, 67,* 159–164.

Kunen, S., & Duncan, E. (1983). Do verbal descriptions facilitate visual inferences? *Journal of Educational Research, 76,* 370–373.

Landa, L. (1974). *Algorithmization in learning and instruction* (V. Bennett, Trans.). Englewood Cliffs, NJ: Educational Technology Publications.

Levin, J., Schriberg, L., & Berry, J. (1983). A concrete strategy for remembering abstract prose. *American Educational Research Journal, 20,* 277–290.

Mandler, J., & Johnson, N. (1977). Remembrances of things parsed: Story structure and recall. *Cognitive Psychology, 9,* 111–151.

Manson, G., Marker, G., Ochoa, A., & Tucker, J. (1970) Social studies curriculum guidelines. *Social Education, 35,* 853–869.

Markle, S. (1975). They teach concepts, don't they? *The Educational Researcher, 4,* 3–9.

Mayer, R. (1975). Information processing variables in learning to solve problems. *Review of Educational Research, 45,* 525–541.

Mayer, R. (1979). Twenty years of research on advance organizers: Assimilation theory still the best predictor. *Instructional Science, 8,* 133–167.

McCartin, R. (1970). The cognitive and affective learning of children. In P. Bacon (Ed.). *Focus on geography: Key concepts and teaching strategies* (pp. 229–262). Washington, D.C.: National Council for the Social Studies.

McKenzie, G. (1972). *Some developmental trends in inferential thinking among elementary school children.* Paper presented at the annual meeting of the American Educational Research Association, Chicago.

McKenzie, G. (1979). The fallacy of excluded instruction: A common but correctable error in the logic of process oriented social studies lessons. *Theory and Research in Social Education, 7,* 35–48.

McKenzie, G. (1980). The importance of teaching facts in elementary social studies. *Social Education, 44,* 494–498.

McKenzie, G., & Henry, M. (1979). Effects of test like events on task behavior, test anxiety, and achievement in a classroom rule learning task. *Journal of Educational Psychology, 71,* 370–375.

McKenzie, G., & Herrington, L. (1981, April). *Effects of adjunct application questions on forward transfer of a cognitive strategy.* Paper presented at the annual meeting of the American Educational Research Association, Los Angeles.

McKenzie, G., & Sawyer, J. (1985, April). *Teaching geography facts: questions and mnemonics.* Paper presented at the annual meeting of the American Educational Research Association, Chicago.

McKenzie, G., & Schadler, A. (1980, April). *Effects of three practice modes on attention, attitudes and achievement on a second grade association learning task.* Paper presented at the annual meeting of the American Educational Research Association, Boston.

Medley, D. (1982). Teacher effectiveness. In H. Mitzel (Ed.), *Encyclopedia of educational research* (pp. 1894–1903). New York: Free Press.

Melton, A. (1970). The situation with respect to the spacing and repetition and memory. *Journal of Verbal Learning and Verbal Behavior, 9,* 596–606.

Moskovitz, B. (1978). Acquisition of language. *Scientific American, 18,* 92–4, 198.

Newman, N., & Mayer, R. (1983). Signaling techniques that increase understandability of expository prose. *Journal of Educational Psychology, 75,* 402–412.

Olton, R., & Crutchfield, R. (1969). Developing the skills of productive thinking. In P. Mussen, J. Langer, and M. Covington (Eds.), *Trends and issues in developmental psychology* (pp. 68–87). New York: Holt Rinehart & Winston.

Partridge, G. (1912). *Genetic philosophy of education: An epitome of the writings of president G. S. Hall.* New York: Sturgis and Walton.

Pearson, P., Hansen, J., & Gordon, M. (1979). The effects of background knowledge on young children's comprehension of explicit and implicit information. *Journal of Reading Behavior, 11,* 200–209.

Prestley, M., & Dennis-Rounds, J. (1980). Transfer of the keyword strategy at two age levels. *Journal of Educational Psychology, 72,* 578–582.

Prestley, M., Levin, J., & Delaney, H. (1982). The mnemonic keyword method. *Review of Educational Research, 52,* 61–91.

Reder, L. (1980). The role of elaboration in the comprehension of prose. *Review of Educational Research, 50,* 5–52.

Resnick, L., & Ford, W. (1981). *The psychology of mathematics for instruction.* Hillsdale, N.J.: Earlbaum Associates.

Resnick, L., Siegel, A., & Kersh, E. (1971). Transfer and sequence in double classification skills. *Journal of Experimental Child Psychology, 11,* 139–149.

Rohwer, W. Jr., & Litrownik, J. (1983). Age and individual differences in the learning of a memorization procedure. *Journal of Educational Psychology, 75,* 799–810.

Rose, S., & Blank, M. (1974). The potency of content: An illustration through conservation. *Child Development, 45,* 499–502.

Rosenshine, B. (1977). *Academic engaged time, content covered and direct instruction.* Paper presented at the annual meeting of the American Educational Research Association, New York.

Rothkopf, E. (1970). The concept of mathemagenic activities. *Review of Educational Research, 40,* 325–336.

Rothkopf, E., & Bisbicos, E. (1967). Selective facilitative effects of interspersed questions on learning from written material. *Journal of Educational Psychology, 58,* 56–61.

Rothkopf, E., & Koether, M. (1978). Instructional effects of discrepancies in content and organization between study goals and information sources. *Journal of Educational Psychology, 70,* 67–71.

Royer, J., & Cable, G. (1975). Facilitated learning in connected discourse. *Journal of Educational Psychology, 67,* 116–123.

Russell, J. (1983). Nonverbal and verbal performance on a number conservation problem and a proposal about the determinants of nonconservation. *Educational Psychologist, 3,* 107–113.

Schallert, D. (1982). The significance of knowledge: A synthesis of research related to schema theory. In W. Otto (Ed.), *Reading expository material* (pp. 13–34). New York: Academic Press.

Senate Education Committee. (1981, March). Hearings on H.B. 246. State of Texas.

Shank, R., & Ableson, R. (1976). *Scripts, plans, goals, and understanding: An inquiry into human knowledge structures.* Hillsdale, N.J.: Earlbaum Associates.

Silver, E. (1981). Recall of mathematical problem information: Solving related problems. *Journal of Research in Mathematics Education, 12,* 54–64.

Smith, L., & Land, M. (1981). Low inference verbal behaviors related to teacher clarity. *Journal of Classroom Interaction, 17,* 37–42.

Stone, C. (1983). A meta-analysis of advance organizer studies. *Journal of Experimental Education, 51,* 194–200.

Tennyson, R., Chao, W., & Youngers, J. (1981). Concept learning effectiveness using prototype and skill development presentation forms. *Journal of Educational Psychology, 73,* 326–334.

Tennyson, R., & Park, O. (1980). The teaching of concepts: A review of instructional design research literature. *Review of Educational Research, 50,* 55–70.

Tennyson, R., Youngers, J., & Suebsonthi, P. (1983). Concept learning by children using instructional presentation forms for prototype formation and classification skill development. *Journal of Educational Psychology, 75,* 280–291.

Thomas, A. (1979). Learned helplessness and expectancy factors: The implications for research on learning disabilities. *Review of Educational Research, 49,* 208–221.

Tulving, E., & Watkins, M. (1975). Structure of memory traces. *Psychological Review, 84,* 261–275.

Watts, G., & Anderson, R. (1971). Effects of three types of inserted questions on learning from prose. *Journal of Educational Psychology, 62,* 387–394.

White, R. (1973). Research into learning hierarchies. *Review of Educational Research, 43,* 361–375.

Winne, P. (1979). Experiments relating teacher use of higher cognitive questions to student achievement. *Review of Educational Research, 49,* 13–49.

Wittrock, M. (1967). Replacement and nonreplacement strategies in children's problem solving. *Journal of Educational Psychology, 58,* 69–74.

Wong, R., Wong, R., & Le Mare, L. (1982). The effects of knowledge of criterion task on comprehension and recall in normally achieving children. *Journal of Educational Research, 76,* 119–126.

CHAPTER 9

ELEMENTARY TEACHER EDUCATION AND CERTIFICATION

Thomas Weible and Wayne Dumas

The processes and criteria by which elementary teachers are selected, prepared and certified is under attack today in ways that are perhaps without precedent. The recent report of the President's Commission on Excellence in Education laments the observation that students majoring in education are among the least able high school graduates and are prepared for their profession in programs heavily weighted toward educational methods at the expense of courses in subjects to be taught (Commission on Excellence in Education, 1983). The criticisms have been extended, and perhaps exaggerated, to the more general charge that "some states have more requirements for getting a driver's license than for teaching" (Williams et al., 1981).

A second and distinct observation is that the last decade has seen a steady diminution of the time and emphasis given to social studies and civic education in the curricula of elementary schools nationwide. This decline has resulted generally from expansion of instruction in "basic skills," a category which in many states or schools does not include the social studies. Most social studies educators, as might be expected, feel that social studies contributions to civic and social competence qualify it, along with mathematics and reading, as basic. Since elementary teachers are most likely to teach what they know well and what they have been taught to believe is important, a major factor in bringing about a social studies renaissance in elementary curricula is to strengthen its degree of emphasis within teacher preparation programs.

The purpose of this chapter is to assess the social studies aspects of elementary teacher education and certification nationally. This will be accomplished by:
1. Reviewing five relevant sets of standards, developed by national professional organizations or learned societies, for the preparation of teachers.
2. Examining existing programmatic standards for teacher certification established by state education agencies. In some cases, this includes processes for the approval of college and university programs for the preparation and certification of teachers.
3. Highlighting selected university programs that place a unique emphasis on social studies in the teacher education curriculum.

NATIONAL STANDARDS

Several key professional organizations have adopted standards which constitute points of reference for state education agencies and, ultimately, for

colleges and universities in the development of programs for the preparation of elementary teachers. The document which most influences state education agency decisions is the *Standards for State Approval of Teacher Education* of the National Association of State Directors of Teacher Education and Certification (NASDTEC, 1981). NASDTEC makes no distinction between the "general education" components of elementary and secondary teacher education programs. It recommends that all state education agencies require that "general education" studies include "the historical and cultural values, customs, and social institutions, of both western and nonwestern cultures and both minority and majority cultures in our own society, integrating this study whenever possible." Furthermore, NASDTEC asks that teacher certification programs require the study and application of modes of inquiry and characteristics of the social science disciplines. In the area of "professional education," NASDTEC clearly insists upon special methods instruction in the teaching of social studies by requiring "study in the use of methods and materials to promote effective student skills in the subject areas normally found in the elementary school curriculum." This phrasing does not, of course, necessarily imply the need for a distinct methods course in social studies education.

Four significant sets of national guidelines apply more directly to teacher education institutions than to state education agencies, although they probably exercise some influence with both. Perhaps the most current statement is that of the American Association of Colleges of Teacher Education (AACTE) titled *Educating a Profession: Profile of a Beginning Teacher* (AACTE, 1983). Like the guidelines of NASDTEC, the AACTE guidelines do not distinguish separate "general education" requirements for elementary and secondary teachers.

According to AACTE all teachers should:

Understand the importance of groups and institutions—"their origins and development, organization, functions, strengths and weaknesses, historical impact and relationship to cultural characteristics."

Understand the relationship between society and work—"the study of . . . historical, philosophical, religious and social attitudes toward work, and the relationships of individuals and groups to production."

Understand the relationship between time and civilization—"the interrelationships of the past, present, and future events; convergence of social, cultural, religious, political, economic, and intellectual forces; the contributions and decline of major civilizations; and the emergence of global interdependence; and understanding of the laws, customs, traditions, and values in relation to a variety of cultures, including pluralistic culture of the United States; the derivation of social ethics and morality; and the derivation of individual values and beliefs."

AACTE's guidelines for "professional studies" contain suggestions relating to generic methods, but these acknowledge only that generic knowledge of teaching "provides the basis for more specialized pedagogical knowledge and skills, some of which relate specifically to the subject or content to be learned," Whether or not this statement may be interpreted as actually requiring specific instruction in social studies methods is not clear.

Certainly, the most influential document for Colleges of Education is the National Council for the Accreditation of Teacher Education's *Standards for Accreditation of Teacher Education* (NCATE, 1981). NCATE requires that at least one-third of each prospective teacher's program be designated for "general studies" consisting of "symbolics of information, natural and behavioral sciences, and humanities." In what ways and to what extent this may be interpreted as requiring history and/or social studies is obviously open to conjecture. However, NCATE emphasizes nothing more heavily than the need for multicultural studies, insisting on this inclusion within both the "general" and "professional" components. Such multicultural studies, says NCATE, should (1) promote analytical and evaluative abilities to confront issues such as participatory democracy, racism and sexism, and parity of power; (2) develop skills for values clarification, including the study of manifest and latent transmission of values; and (3) examine the dynamics of diverse cultures and the implications for developing teaching strategies. Beyond these specifications, NCATE refers institutions to the guidelines developed by national learned societies and professional associations affiliated with NCATE.

The qualification that NCATE's concerns be restricted to guidelines of national organizations affiliated with NCATE is particularly significant for social studies, because the National Council for the Social Studies (NCSS) is no longer affiliated with NCATE. The importance, therefore, of NCSS standards to the accreditation process is placed somewhat in limbo. Nevertheless, NCSS released new guidelines in 1984, replacing its 1970 standards.

The newly released NCSS standards (NCSS, 1984) provide some guidance, however, with regard to the social studies aspects of certification for a teacher in a self-contained classroom at the elementary level, although considerably less than for secondary social studies teachers. NCSS proposes that at least 72 semester hours (60 percent of a 120-hour degree program) of such programs be devoted to "general education" with roughly an "equal distribution" among the major disciplines, except that one area of study should be selected for "significant in-depth and analytical study." Elementary teachers are expected by NCSS to complete 15 percent (18 semester hours) of their program in history and the social sciences, not necessarily exclusive of the "general education" requirement. NCSS explicitly recommends that all elementary teachers have "a course of at least 3 semester hours in the teaching of social studies at the level for which certification is sought." Finally, the NCSS standards indicate that among the necessary dimensions of preservice programs is the provision for an understanding of the meaning of culture "both in the global context as well as cultures that constitute the American heritage."

It must be noted that the NCSS Early Childhood Advisory committee has submitted a resolution to the NCSS Board of Directors to include in the new standards that teachers in Early Childhood and Elementary Education have a minimum of three semester credit hours (or equivalent) in the teaching of social studies. The Board has approved this resolution.

Finally, the Association for Childhood Education International has produced a set of guidelines (ACEI, 1983) for the preparation of early childhood teachers which requires a "general education" component including a "knowledge and understanding of differences and similarities among societies and culture, both at home and abroad, and an awareness of the social and political forces affecting education." ACEI also asks that all teachers be prepared to "implement a developmentally appropriate program of learning for children that includes social studies."

Cutting through the differences and subleties in the phrasing of these statements, what can be said with confidence about the general expectations of these organizations regarding social studies aspects of elementary teacher certification? First, there can be no question that "general education" components for elementary teacher candidates must include some instruction in history and/or the social sciences. Second, though the emphasis placed varies, there is a consistent expectation that students receive a solid grounding in the characteristics and values of minority cultures and a preparation for dealing with cultural diversity in classrooms. Third, it seems to be generally expected that studies in history and social science include both national and global aspects. Finally, there appears to be a general intent that elementary teacher candidates receive specialized instruction in the teaching of social studies in the "professional education" curriculum, although the extent or context of the instruction is consistently unspecified.

STATE CERTIFICATION STANDARDS

An intermediate agency contributing to the form and substance of teacher education programs is the education department of each of the 50 states. Each agency prescribes either a list of minimum standards, a process for the approval of institutional teacher education programs, or, in some cases, a combination of both. In establishing standards and/or processes, the state agencies generally pay considerable attention to several of the national guideline statements mentioned in the previous section. The NASDTEC standards, as mentioned earlier, are by a considerable margin the most influential at the state agency level.

A 1983 survey of state standards for certification of elementary teachers (Dumas & Weible, 1983) revealed various definitions of comprehensive elementary certificates including K–6, 1–6, 1–8, and K–8. Two states, North Carolina and Virginia, grant only early childhood and middle school certificates; and several other southeastern states seem to be moving toward elimination of the comprehensive certificate. Of the remaining states, two depend entirely upon a program approval process. This results in only 46 states specifying program minimums for comprehensive elementary certification, necessary characteristics of teacher education programs at colleges and universities, or necessary minimum competencies of graduates of their programs.

The study revealed that, of the 46 states with programmatic guidelines or principles, only 34 established minimum standards for the "general education" component. The remainder either left "general education" questions to the program approval process or, in several cases, to the discretion of colleges and universities. History/social science was the only category of disciplines requiring instruction in all 34 states specifying minimums. Comparatively, science instruction was required in 30 states, English/composition in 28, mathematics in 27, fine arts/humanities in 25, oral communication in 17, and physical education/health in only 16 states.

Of the 34 states requiring instruction in history/social science, only 20 specify a minimum number of semester credit hours. The range among the 20 states was 2–18 hours. By way of comparison with other disciplines, 16 states report minimum semester hour requirements in English/composition ranging from 2 to 15 hours; 14 states require a range of 3 to 15 semester hours in sciences; 14 states require between 3 and 8 hours of instruction in mathematics; 12 states require between 3 and 18 hours of fine arts/humanities; 9 states require 2 to 8 hours of study in health/physical education, and 8 states require a 2- to-3 hour course in oral communication. Although the above statistics are accurate for requirements designated as "general education," the effect is substantially different for both mathematics and fine arts. In the case of mathematics, 7 states require 3 to 6 hours of *specially adapted* courses for elementary teachers, while 6 states require specially adapted courses in both art and music. From state certification documents, it is difficult to determine whether these requirements are in addition to "general education" requirements or whether specially adapted courses may be used to meet the "general education" standards.

It would appear that state agencies place a high priority on the history/social science aspect of teacher certification in "general education." However, on careful inspection, this priority appears substantially different in purpose and content from the expectations of national professional guidelines. In a majority of states that specify coursework, it is also indicated that the coursework include U.S. history and/or U.S. government and, in several instances, study of state and/or federal constitutions. References to multicultural studies within the general education component are few, vague, and essentially noncommittal; there are no requirements of international or global studies. The priority status of social studies is clearly based largely on the states' interest in promoting a special citizenship consciousness in its teachers. The conventional view continues to assume that citizenship preparation is solely dependent upon national studies; and it denies the possibility, or probability, that growing world interdependence begs that civic education balance knowledge and values of the national with those of the global.

With regard to the "professional education" component, 46 states make substantive requirements. Dumas and Weible (1983) found that of these, 17 states specify that prospective elementary teachers have instruction in methods or materials for teaching social studies and only 8 states mandate instruction in how to teach multicultural students. Yet instruction in both of the above areas is generally demanded in some form by the standards of most professional organizations. In order to put this information into perspective, the following requirements by the states are offered for contrast: educational psychology (38 states), social foundations of education (23 states), teaching of reading (41 states), teaching of mathematics (20 states), teaching of science (18 states), teaching of health/physical education (21 states), teaching of English (20 states), and children's literature (20 states). It seems possible that the lack of value placed on social studies within the "professional" component may more realistically indicate the relative status of social studies in state education agencies than its apparent priority under the "general education" component.

The relatively light mandating of multicultural studies by state education agencies is almost certainly a result of two factors. The NASDTEC guidelines, quoted earlier, incorporates multicultural requirements within the history/ social science context, and it does so in terms that might well be interpreted as being met by conventional courses in U.S. or world history or cultural geography—unlike the NCATE mandate, which is distinct and beyond misinterpretation. Second, the NASDTEC upgrading of the multicultural requirement occurred only in 1981, a year before the survey.

SOCIAL STUDIES DIMENSIONS OF PROFESSIONAL EDUCATION PROGRAMS

An additional dimension of this report is a brief description of selected professional education programs that have adopted innovative approaches to preparing teachers to teach social studies in early childhood and elementary education. The aim will be to highlight some interesting features of the "professional education" components as they relate to social studies, multicultural education, and global education. As previously mentioned, the NASDTEC, AACTE, NCSS, and NCATE guidelines stress the importance of providing multicultural and global experiences in training teachers. Both NASDTEC and AACTE clearly state the need for coursework or competences in the "general education" component, while NCATE is specific in requiring multicultural studies in "general" and "professional" education.

Ohio State University

This field-based professional education program on the Mansfield Campus features social studies experience for preservice teachers in early childhood, elementary, and middle school education. The experience is designed to give students an opportunity to implement strategies and techniques acquired in social studies, reading, and language arts methods classes. Upon completing methods coursework in these areas, and prior to student teaching, all students enter a field component called the Integrated Block. This component provides an opportunity to teach social studies units specially designed to enhance concept development through reading and language activities. A wide variety of reading resources are coordinated with unit topics, and language activities stress writing, oral communications, and listening.

The Integrated Block typically consists of three weeks of university classroom instruction directed by professors in the areas of social studies, reading, and language arts. This is followed by a seven-week field component arranged to provide blocks of teaching time followed by a one-hour planning/evaluation session. The field experience is supervised at all times by university personnel. Selected school sites represent diversity in culture and socioeconomic status. Multicultural and global education is included through the use of resource persons, children's literature, and activities which are designed to decrease ethnocentricism.

University of Missouri–Columbia

A newly implemented program in early childhood education features a field-based, interdisciplinary approach to social studies methods instruction. All early childhood majors take a course developed by a team of professors who specialize in social studies, art, and music. Social studies units, compatible with the curriculum of selected schools, are developed by university students early in the semester. Throughout the developmental stages of the unit, stress is placed on integrating language, art, and music experiences to teach social studies concepts. Activities are designed to promote interest and active learning, and to foster an appreciation of the fine arts. Art and music activities are also used as means to promote education that is multicultural and global. Units are taught in grades K–3 by teams of undergraduate students under the supervision of university professors. Teaching periods are followed by class discussions focusing on evaluating the successes and failures of various teaching strategies.

To broaden multicultural understandings for both early childhood and elementary majors, the children's literature course requires students to create a unit on a culture of personal interest. Students must establish a rationale as to why they selected this culture and read ten books dealing with the culture. Two book selections from the following areas must be included: historical fiction, folklore, information books, and literature describing the fine arts and clothing of the culture. Students write a review for each book and a summary explaining how this reading experience changed their understandings and perceptions of the culture.

New Mexico State Univesity

Elementary education majors are required to take a block of courses including social studies, language arts, reading, and computer literacy. Students typically enroll in the block during their junior year. The College of Education has made a commitment to integrate multicultural education, special education, rural education and computer applications throughout this block. Plans are also being made to integrate or correlate children's literature and creative writing with the social studies.

Considerable emphasis is placed on integrating instruction. Typically this involves six or seven students working in groups planning a unit that integrates significant aspects of history and the social sciences as well as concepts from the fine arts and humanities. Students then select lessons from the units and present these to their peers. A VCR is used to record peer teaching lessons, and a file of these is kept in the Learning Resource Center for viewing. Analysis of the recorded lessons takes place immediately after teaching. Preservice teachers in the block are then assigned to pilot schools to teach their lessons to small groups of students.

SUMMARY

The first two parts of this chapter were devoted to: (1) identifying various national standards established by key professional associations for the preparation and certification of teachers, and (2) reporting minimum state certification standards for elementary teachers in the areas of general and professional education. Particular emphasis was given to the social studies aspects of such requirements. Discussion centered on the relationships between state minimums and national guideline statements of NASDTEC, NCATE, AACTE, ACEI, and NCSS.

While all states specify minimums in "general education" and require coursework or competencies in history and social science, it is obvious that there are discrepancies between state requirements and expectations of the professional associations previously discussed. For the most part, state requirements are much less rigorous than those established by professional associations. A glaring example is the fact that while each national statement stresses global and multicultural coursework or competencies in general education, only eight states mandate multicultural studies, and no states require studies in global education.

Greater discrepancies appear to exist in relation to "professional education" expectations. Guideline statements for all of the associations indicate that preservice teachers in early childhood and elementary education should receive some specialized instruction in the teaching of social studies. However, only 17 states require instruction in methods and materials for teaching social studies. The NCATE guidelines clearly state that multicultural studies should be included within both "general" and "professional education" components. Only eight states currently mandate such instruction in the "professional education" component.

Many colleges and universities have developed program requirements for early childhood and elementary teacher candidates that surpass minimum certification standards and, thus, are likely to be more compatible with national guideline statements. The third part of this chapter, therefore, identified selected professional education programs and provided a brief description of how each addressed the areas of social studies methods, multicultural education, and global education. These innovative programs emphasized an interdisciplinary approach to social studies methods, all using locally developed units as a basis for instruction. The inclusion of field-based social studies experiences was another common factor. Multicultural and global topics were often integrated with unit topics, and multicultural education was woven into each of the social studies methods courses.

Finally, this chapter makes clear that there is a pressing need for further research into what constitutes effective preparation for teachers of early childhood and elementary social studies. Two concluding recommendations seem fully justified:

1. The National Council for the Social Studies should promote research efforts that will provide information concerning the relationship between teacher preparation components and teacher effectiveness in early childhood and elementary social studies.

2. The National Council for the Social Studies should take a leadership role in establishing and disseminating to decision makers specific guidelines for the social studies aspects of preparation of early childhood and elementary social studies teachers.

REFERENCES

A nation at risk: The imperative for educational reform. (1983). Washington, D.C.: National Commission on Excellence in Education.

Dumas, W., & Weible, T. (1984). Standards for elementary teacher certification: A fifty-state study. *The Elementary School Journal, 85,* 177—183.

Educating a profession: Profile of a beginning teacher. (1983). Washington, D.C.: American Association of Colleges for Teacher Education.

Preparation of early childhood teachers. (1983). Washington, D.C.: Association for Childhood Education International.

Standards for accreditation of teacher education. (1981). Washington, D.C.: National Council for Accreditation of Teacher Educators.

Standards for state approval of teacher education. (1981). Salt Lake City: National Association of State Directors of Teacher Education and Certification.

Standards for the preparation of social studies teachers. (1984). *Social Education, 48,* 357–361.

Williams, D. A., et al. (1981, April 27). Teachers are in trouble. *Newsweek,* 78–84.

CHAPTER 10

PARENT INVOLVEMENT IN SOCIAL STUDIES PROGRAMS

Cynthia Szymanski Sunal

During the past 25 years, parents have become the schools' highly active, and often vocal, partners in education (Anselmo, 1977). Research during this period has indicated that high levels of parent involvement produced positive results in students' achievement and attitudes (Gilliam, Schooley, & Novak, 1977). However, research has also shown that schools have only just begun their journey down the road to equal parent-teacher participation in education.

The impetus for increased parental involvement has come from two sources: parents and preschool program research. Since the 1960s, many parents have felt that their children's education should not be solely the preserve of professional educators. Parents have pushed for, and obtained, a greater role in the workings of schools. They have gained the right to visit classrooms, to serve on textbook selection committees, and to read their children's records. As a result, education has become a much more public enterprise.

Research on the effects of preschool programs which involved parents in a variety of ways has indicated highly positive results for children. Support for the involvement of parents at the elementary school level has resulted from research indicating the potential long-lasting impact of home and family on the development of cognitive functioning and academic performance (Keeves, 1975; Schaefer, 1971; Walberg & Marjoribanks, 1976). Educators have supported the parents' push for a more active role in education, in part because of the positive results indicated in preschool program research, and elementary school parent-involvement programs have been developed which adapt successful preschool forms of parent involvement to the elementary schools.

Social studies education offers many occasions for parent involvement, opportunities which can provide for those high levels of involvement which yield positive results.

Research on parent involvement, which has implications for social studies education, can be organized into three major categories:

1. Studies of parent/family/home environmental factors that significantly influence children's achievement and adjustment in school.
2. Surveys documenting parental interest in schools.
3. Studies and projects designed to improve home-school relations.

Research on parent involvement tends to be generic. When a specific area of elementary school endeavor is studied, it is usually reading. Social studies education has been rarely studied in regard to the effects of parent involvement. Much of the literature, however, can be applied to the teaching of social studies, and it can be used to enhance the quality of social studies programs.

HOME ENVIRONMENT FACTORS

"Schools do not change the child's level of functioning, they merely educate him at the level of functioning established and maintained by the family and community" (Schaefer, 1971, p.18). A child's family, home environment, and community are more important to academic achievement in all areas than are teacher-related or school-related variables (Dobson & Dobson, 1975; Mize, 1977; Nedler & McAffee, 1979; Schaefer, 1971; Walberg & Marjoribanks, 1976). Family effects on achievement also have been noted outside the United States. Schaefer (1971) reported a study of 5,000 children in the United Kingdom that "found that [family] interest and involvement with children's education were far more important than the quality of schools, even after statistically controlling for family socioeconomic status" (p. 19). Mize (1977) summarized independent research studies by Bissent and Webb; and Dave, Marjoribanks, and Wolf. These researchers found that 50 percent to 85 percent of the variance in achievement test scores, IQ, and verbal ability could be attributed to parent, home, and family variables. Since the impact of home environment factors is powerful, schools need to be aware of families' attitudes and abilities. One means of developing this awareness is through parent-school contacts which can foster mutual understanding (Sunal, 1983).

Keeves (1975) investigated the ways in which the educational environments of the home, the peer group, and the classroom accounted for changes in performance in mathematics and science over a one-year-period. In a discussion of findings, Keeves noted that some variables of home environment cannot be changed; for example, income level, family size, and parent education level. Keeves also reported that factors such as home-school relationships, use of books and library facilities, and an environment conducive to the completion of homework influenced achievement in content areas. He found that parental attitudes and ambitions for the student contributed to achievement in both mathematics and science. Keeves inferred that parental attitudes and interest in school can be increased. As a result, these attitudes may affect positively the student's level of achievement. This hypothesis can be extrapolated to include the social studies.

Mize (1977) supported Keeves' conclusions indicating that students whose parents had positive attitudes about school had higher academic achievement, social adjustment, and emotional stability. He concluded that if parents become involved in school activities, not only would their own attitudes improve, but their children's attitudes and achievements would likewise improve. Brookover (1979) also demonstrated the effects of change in parent attitudes. In his study, parents were helped to increase the academic expectations they held for their children. With this change in parental attitude, students' self-perceptions improved, as did their school grades.

Research on home environment factors strongly suggests that these factors have major impact on students' ability to achieve in school. The strength of home environment factors must be considered in relation to social studies. Would high levels of parental involvement in social studies education affect positively the attitudes of parents toward the social studies? Research has demonstrated, in general, that increased parental valuing of education results in high student performance and interest levels. Would the same result occur in social studies education? These are questions that warrant investigation.

PARENTAL INTEREST IN SCHOOLS

Parents believe education is important and want to stay informed of their children's progress (Etheridge, Collins, & Coats, 1979; Hubbell, 1979; Valentin & Alston, 1978). Parents also want to be more involved in the schools.

Eighty-four percent of the parents participating in the 1980 Gallup poll of the public's attitudes toward schools favored involving parents in a home-school educational program. The model used in the poll was the Fail-Safe program in Houston, Texas. This program encouraged parents to meet with their children's teachers at the beginning of each semester. At this meeting the child's achievement was reviewed and plans for a cooperative home-school program, tailored to the child's needs and abilities, were developed. The program involved parents in reinforcing the school's efforts through remediation activities and through extension of school activities. Forty-five percent of the parents sampled in the Gallup poll approved of parent training "to help parents become more fully involved in their children's education" (p. 41). Apparently, teachers are also interested in parent involvement in education. According to a 1981 NEA poll, over 90 percent of the teachers who responded thought more home-school interaction was desirable.

Conversely, while many parents want improved school-home communication and contact, most are quite uninformed about their schools. Hubbell (1979) found that two out of every three adults surveyed had no contact with public schools. His respondents, however, wanted to stay informed of student test results, curriculum, and teaching methods. This frustrated desire for communication, Hubbell reported, has eroded public confidence in the school, especially among adults without children.

The 1984 Gallup poll found that 43 percent of adults with children in school had little or no involvement with the schools during the 1983–84 school year. Among adults without children in school, 56 percent had little involvement with schools. School involvement was broadly defined; among the specific activities were: receiving a school newsletter, attending a school athletic or cultural event, writing a letter to the school board, and meeting with a teacher about one's child. Perhaps as a result of the low level of involvement many adults had with schools, the Gallup poll also found that only 22 percent of adult respondents thought they knew "quite a lot" about the local schools, and 42 percent thought they knew "some." Adults are interested in the schools, but most have little communication with schools and are unable to satisfy their interest.

Ingram (1978) investigated the means of communication most preferred by parents. He reported that parents preferred to be informed about school activities through: (1) the school newspaper, (2) parent-teacher conferences, (3) PTA, (4) their children, and (5) phone call or note from the teacher.

The 1984 Gallup poll found that parents with children in school got most of their information about the schools from their own children. Adults who did not have children in school indicated that their best source of information about schools was the local newspaper. It appears that most adults are not being informed about their school via their preferred means.

Although parents prefer acquiring information about what is happening in schools from a traditional source, they have proven to be amenable to new methods if they are given a little time to adjust (Sunal, Strong, Wilmoth, & Fassig, 1983). Neighborhood meetings, radio announcements, letters from their children about specific social studies activities, round-robin letters to which students and parents each contribute a sentence about their efforts, all are less traditional information-sharing methods that parents have enjoyed. The implication is that parents may prefer traditional means primarily because they have not been exposed to other methods. In brief, communication between home and school, and between the larger adult community and the schools, is a prerequisite for parent involvement in the schools, but it is a prerequisite that has yet to be fulfilled.

HOME-SCHOOL RELATIONS

Home-school relations begin with the schools' attempts to respond to the interest that parents have in teaching, instruction, and their children's progress. Methods of informing adults about each of these areas are a part of home-school relations. However, home-school relations extend beyond information-giving activities to include programs that range along a continuum of parent involvement. This continuum moves from programs that view the school as the primary focus of education to those that view the home as the primary focus. Programs along this continuum can be organized into the following categories:

- Training parents to be tutors of their children
- Increasing home-school communication which encourages more parent contacts with schools
- Making efforts to strengthen the home environment through parenting training
- Involving parents in decision-making or policy-making roles within the schools
- Using parents as school volunteers.

While the continuum along which home-school relations efforts occur is broad, typically there are at least two distinctive stages of parent participation (Moles, 1982). Each stage implies an equality between parents and school personnel. In the first stage, teachers inform parents of their children's school performance and ways they can assist. Teachers, in turn, learn of student capabilities and interests from parents. Teachers also learn about parents' abilities to help their children. Notes, conferences, home visits and joint participation in workshops and classes are among the forms parent-teacher contact may take.

In the second stage, home-learning activities occur with children acquiring information and skills useful for the classroom. At least four educational processes are utilized to help children become home learners: home instruction, enrichment activities, contracts to supervise homework or provide incentives for good work, and modeling of educational pursuits by family members (Moles, 1982).

Home-school relations incorporate a wide variety of activities by parents which develop gradually as they involve parents increasingly in their children's education. The use of parents as tutors is one of the strongest ways to involve parents.

Parents As Tutors

Tutoring takes many forms in home-school programs. Becker and Epstein (1982) identified 14 techniques for involving parents in teaching activities at home, and they examined the use of them in a statewide survey of 3,700 elementary teachers. The techniques clustered into four tutoring approaches:

- Activities emphasizing reading; for example, asking parents to listen to their children read,

- Activities emphasizing discussion; for example, asking parents to watch a television program with their children and to discuss it afterwards,
- Informal learning activities; for example, sending home ideas for a game or activity related to schoolwork, and
- Formal contracts in which the parent agreed to supervise and assist children with homework.

Involvement of the parent in activities emphasizing reading was the most popular technique. Between 1st and 5th grade it declined, as did the use of informal learning activities. Strategies which were utilized equally often with both older and younger students were: the use of contracts, television-stimulated family discussions, filling out of parent evaluation forms, and assignments to ask parents questions.

Parents of low-performing children can be trained as tutors. As a result, their children may outperform children tutored by untrained parents (Hofmeister, 1975; McKinney, 1975). After reviewing the research, Rich, VanDien, and Mattox (1979) advocated the parent-as-teacher approach. They stated that parents maintained involvement when they saw that what they were doing made a difference. They also noted that utilizing volunteer resources, rather than additional school personnel, was cost effective. In addition, McKinney (1975) noted that involvement in a training program affected significantly and positively parental attitudes toward the school.

The effect of training parents as tutors may be partially attributable to increased parent contacts with schools. Schiff (1963) trained parents, through parent-teacher conferences, to offer lessons at home. Students of these parents were compared with students whose parents had little contact with their children's teachers; the latter group of parents received standard report cards as their major source of contact with their children's teachers. Students in the experimental group had better school attendance records, better study habits, fewer school behavior problems, and greater gains in reading. Parents in the experimental group showed an increase in positive attitudes and interest in the schools. Thus, the research indicated that parent tutoring can assist children's progress in school.

Parents-Teacher Communication

Stronger communication between school personnel and parents has been shown to:

1. Increase school attendance (Duncan, 1969; Parker & McCoy, 1977; Sheats & Dunkleberger, 1979; Shelton & Dobson, 1973).
2. Improve school performance (Bittle, 1975; Duncan, 1969; Shelton & Dobson, 1973).
3. Increase parent-initiated contact with the schools (Bittle, 1975; Duncan, 1969; Mager, 1980; Parker & McCoy, 1977).

Mager (1960) identified characteristics that distinguish teachers with a high frequency of teacher-initiated parent contacts from those with a low frequency of teacher-initiated parent contacts. The high-frequency contact teachers reported a larger variety of reasons for parent contact, saw themselves as more responsible for contact, felt more confident that they were meeting parent expectations, and reported more frequent parent-initiated contacts. The low-contact group reported a stronger sense of support from parents. There was no difference between the groups related to principals' support or encouragement of parent-involvement activities.

Teachers have reported having the most contact with parents of children who had learning or discipline problems or parents who were already helping in the school (Becker & Epstein, 1982). After statistically controlling for student academic and behavioral characteristics, parents' education, and other variables, the researchers found that teachers with more black students used more parent involvement techniques. Becker and Epstein also found that teachers were able to work with parents who were not well educated. The belief that poorly educated parents cannot help seems more of a consequence of not having tried. The researchers concluded that "when the school conditions are poor, when learning problems are severe, when many students need more help than the teacher has time to give, teachers may be more likely to seek help from parents and to assist parents in workshops to provide the help they need."

Although most teachers say they need and want parents' assistance, their attitude towards the use of parent involvement techniques is not closely related to their use of those techniques (Becker & Epstein, 1982). Support from the principal and other teachers is also unrelated to a teacher's use of or opinion towards parent involvement. Teachers can develop parent involvement techniques without peer support but prefer working with support.

An innovative attempt to communicate with parents occurred in a study in which a 1st grade teacher recorded academic and nonacademic information on a telephone answering service (Bittle, 1975). Prior to initiating the telephone system, only five parent-initiated contacts occurred in a 30-week period. In the class of 21 1st graders, the average daily number of phone calls was 20.5. When the teacher included assigned spelling words in the telephone message, the average number of spelling errors decreased from 35 percent to 6 percent, although previously spelling words had been sent home in a note. Compared to a control group, it was found that the experimental teacher saved substantial time and effort in obtaining field trip permission slips and money when explanations and requests were included in the telephone message. Bittle suggested using the messages to prompt face-to-face contact with teachers.

Sunal et al. (1983) found that parents desired contact with their children's teachers. When notes were used as a means of parent-teacher contact, the first note produced limited response, but repeated notes increased the level of response. Parents seemed to need to become accustomed to the idea of getting notes from a teacher and to writing return notes.

Edlund (1969) reported that a specific program involving the use of a daily checklist completed by the teacher and sent home to the parent was effective with students in increasing the number of accurately completed class assignments. The amount of time spent in appropriate social behaviors also increased.

The degree to which parents are involved in meaningful ways with their children is an important factor in the effectiveness of parent involvement programs. Gillum, Schooley, and Novak (1977) compared three school districts involved in performance-contracting programs serving culturally different children. All three had parent involvement components. In two of the districts, parent involvement was left to the school principal's discretion or included one or two poorly attended large-group meetings. The third district specified more intensive parent involvement. Parents attended inservice workshops where they learned how to help their children accomplish curriculum objectives. Parents received individualized help in working on program goals. Results indicated that students in all three districts scored higher than would have been expected without the special program. However, the group with the highest parent involvement showed the largest gains.

Parent Training

Certain programs have focused upon increasing parenting skills. Mize (1977) evaluated the effects of the Systematic Training for Effective Parenting Program (STEP) on a sample of parents drawn from four elementary schools using the Individually Guided Motivation System. All socioeconomic levels were represented, with the majority of people being blue collar workers. Parents were asked to contract for biweekly meetings with their children; during these sessions they discussed accomplishments of the past few days and spent time sharing thoughts and ideas. They also spent time each week on reading-related activities. In turn, teachers contracted for semi-weekly conferences with parents. Cooperating parents who were participating in the STEP were found to:

- Have more conferences with the teachers
- Spend more time in reading activities with their children (three hours in two weeks compared to six minutes by the control group)
- Have more positive attitudes towards education.

Children in the experimental group scored nearly two standard deviations above that of children in the control group on the Coopersmith Self-Esteem Inventory. They were also rated by their teachers and self-rated, on two separate attitude measures, as being more motivated to learn and as having more positive attitudes toward schools. Additionally, they gained 12 months in reading achievement and comprehension, compared to a one-month gain by the control group.

In a project described by Smith and Brahce (1963), parents were involved in discussion groups that emphasized their role as a model for their children. Parents listened to their children read and also read to them. They provided regular study times. Children in the experimental group showed a significant increase in reading test scores over children in the control group.

Programs that assist parents to develop interest in, and positive attitudes towards, learning have been found to produce positive gains in the children's achievement. Schools can help parents to function in their role as proactive educational models.

Parents as Decision Makers

Parents have become increasingly involved with the schools in an advisory capacity, as members of Parent Advisory Councils mandated by Title I regulations, and as change agents who have organized on the local level to effect changes in the schools. The effect of parent involvement in this capacity has not been comprehensively evaluated. It is particularly difficult to measure the effect of parent participation in an advisory capacity. Often the groups are established to satisfy federal requirements but have little or no meaningful input on any level (Hightower, 1978; Steinberg, 1979). A major weakness of these councils is "that they have been initiated at federal and state levels with little involvement of parents or administrators at the local level and rarely provide resources for implementation or monitoring" (Steinberg, p. 57).

Lightfoot (1980) reported on parent involvement in an elementary school where parents successfully negotiated with teachers "for more academic work" (p. 13). Berlin and Berlin (1973) described the results of efforts of a group of parents whose children were near expulsion from school. The parents observed in classrooms, collected data to be presented to the school board, and were eventually effective in changing school administration and teaching personnel.

The role of parents as decision makers in school governance, instruction, and curriculum development is not well supported by teachers (Williams, 1981). In a six-state regional survey of elementary teachers, Williams found support for other forms of parent involvement, such as tutoring, with the reservation that teachers should give parents ideas about how to help. Teachers noted that their schools generally did not provide opportunities for parents and teachers to work together on such activities. In a companion survey of elementary principals, Williams found support for parent participation in children's home learning but not in the decision-making role. Principals also felt that parents lacked the training needed for active participation in children's home learning. Although successful and positive instances of parents working in the role of decision maker have been reported, they are rare and apparently have not encouraged teachers and principals to develop this role in parents.

Volunteers in School

Parents not only accept other parents as volunteers in schools, they strongly believe the use of volunteers influences positively student achievement and student attitudes (Sunal, et al., 1983). Parents approve of volunteers who do the following: (1) make classroom materials at home, (2) prepare snacks, (3) construct learning centers, (4) tutor in the classroom, (5) read to students, (6) assist with field trips, and (7) make bulletin boards. Sunal et al. reported that parents also were willing to be involved in demonstrating their hobbies and heritage to children, be interviewed by students, respond to student surveys, and participate in similar activities.

Home-school relations are complex and not completely satisfactory, judging from the number and variety of efforts to improve communication and cooperation. Research has indicated that relationships between parents and schools can be improved through involving parents in an active role in their children's learning. There appear to be some limiting factors to strong parent involvement, and high levels of involvement are not common in schools. What are these factors which act as barriers to increased parent involvement in the schools?

LIMITS TO PARENT INVOLVEMENT

Research has demonstrated that the school can successfully involve parents in educating their children. While most parents are willing to be involved, they may be hesitant to do so unless the teacher contacts them. Once they become accustomed to contacts by the teacher, they are likely to begin initiating other contacts. Interaction can be furthered by volunteer and tutoring programs in which parents are heavily involved. Involvement by parents affects positively students' achievement and attitudes. Unfortunately, parent involvement has not yet been successfully incorporated into all schools. In a needs assessment, Spriggs (1980) found that "teachers and parents do not seem to be coordinating and communicating well about student learning." She further stated: Parents felt that teachers were not interested; parents were typically excluded from schools; and parent-teacher conferences were dreaded rather than seen as part of a useful and helpful process. Lightfoot (1980) attributed this sense of mistrust between parents and teachers to misperceptions. She contended that both lower-class black parents and middle-class white teachers value education; however, they have misperceptions of each other which do not allow them to recognize this shared value system. Because of this mistrust, parents and teachers rarely come together to try to work out their problems and conflicts. When they do talk, they miscommunicate. Lightfoot (1978) also suggested that difficulties are to be expected when teachers and parents try to communicate, because the parent's basic concern for one child may conflict with the teacher's responsibility for group progress. This conflict creates disagreement over the means of attaining common goals. The result is limited communication and involvement as the school only slightly accommodates itself to family needs.

A variety of conditions exist that may operate to limit home-school communication and parent involvement in schools. Moles (1982) suggested that many parents face competing demands of work and family life, come from different family backgrounds, and feel mistrust and anxiety when dealing with school staff. Teachers have related difficulties in that they face competing demands at school and home, have little training in working with parents, and are unsure of how to relate to culturally different families.

Barriers to home-school cooperation were identified in two inner-city junior high schools (Tangri & Leitch, 1982). Teachers pointed to competing home responsibilities, fears for their personal safety at evening events, the perception that parents do not transmit educational values, and low expectations regarding parents' follow-up efforts. Parents reported barriers including family health problems, work schedules, having small children, fears for their safety, late notice of meetings, and not understanding their children's homework.

Tangri and Leitch found that both parents and teachers realized that most communication between them was negative. Teachers complained about poor student performance; parents, in turn, complained about events in school. Both also realized that schoolwork was often not understood by parents. Although parents tried, they could not help with schoolwork. Recognizing that these problems existed, both parents and teachers suggested workshops for parents interested in becoming familiar with course assignments.

Research has indicated the potential for child achievement and child development that can result from high levels of parent involvement in the schooling process. This potential is being achieved in many schools, but, because of the barriers which exist, there is still considerable work to be done in this area.

SCHOOL PROGRAMS WITH PROMISE

Some schools and school systems have developed programs to increase parent involvement among low-income and poorly educated adults. These programs recognize barriers that limit involvement, and they make an effort to overcome them. A variety of strategies has been explored for helping parents contribute to their children's schooling.

Chicago's Parents Plus program brings parents into the school once a week, where they learn how they can help at home with current schoolwork. They also participate in workshops that expand their homemaking and community-related skills. Other school programs are less ambitious but similar in some ways. Schools encourage "make it and take it" sessions where parents make inexpensive educational aids and learn how to use them at home. Calendars, with a learning activity for each day, are given out in some schools, while notebooks with general tips are used in others.

The Home and School Institute has developed "home learning recipes" which add to children's school learning. They also provide opportunities for family interaction (Rich, VanDien, & Mattox, 1979).

Philadelphia developed the use of telephone hotlines. These help students with homework problems. They also provide parents with educational advice and news on school events.

Collins, Moles and Cross (1982) identified 28 urban programs that involved parents in improving the school performance and social development of their children. Half the programs were aimed at low-income families and the others worked with the broad range of children with educational problems. The various programs involved parents through individual conferences, workshops or classes, and home visits or telephone calls. Academic achievement, attendance and social development were program goals. While most programs involved parents in home tutoring, many stressed the parents' role in children's socialization, and many assisted parents in planning home and community educational experiences. The programs reported that results included reduced absenteeism, higher achievement scores, improved student behavior, and more confidence and participation among parents.

Summary

Although we have only just begun the task of comprehensively involving parents in education, Moles (1982) suggested that some themes describing these efforts are beginning to emerge.

1. There is strong interest in parent involvement among parents, teachers and school administrators.

2. Educators need to re-examine prevailing beliefs about parents and their capabilities and interests.
3. There is strong interest in parent involvement beyond the early elementary years.
4. Research on parent involvement is incomplete and evolving.
5. Certain projects of parent involvement seem most useful, including: a sense of shared ownership and a realistic assessment of needs; commitment; and the development of resources that can be built when teachers and parents are included in a program. Staff training and orientation in relations with culturally different people, conferencing techniques, and other aspects of dealing with parents are also important. Finally, clear specification and communication of parent and staff roles are needed.
6. Specific efforts may be needed to break through barriers to parent involvement. These could include: personal contact to recruit parents; training parents who are asked for detailed assistance; evening and weekend meeting times to encourage working parents' participation; recognition of parents' contributions; and using school system computers to generate individualized student information and prescriptions for parent assistance.

A conceptual framework for parent involvement was developed by Cervone and O'Leary (1982) as a means of viewing levels and kinds of involvement (Figure 1). This continuum stretches from activities in which the parent is the passive recipient of information to activities in which the parent is an active partner in the educational process. Parent involvement falls into five categories along this continuum:

1. Reporting Progress (passive)
2. Special Events
3. Parent Education
4. Parents Teaching
5. Parents As Educational Decision Makers (active)

Within each of the first four categories, a specific set of activities can be defined which range from passive to active. The category "Reporting Progress," for example, contains passive activities such as "good news notes," occasional notes from the teacher that parents do not have to answer. It also contains active involvement strategies such as "home-school notebooks," weekly exchanges of information between parents and teachers. This is, then, both a horizontal and vertical continuum. The degree of passivity–activity is determined by the level of commitment required of the participating parent. The fifth category, "Parents As Educational Decision Makers," is not subdivided into examples in Figure 1 because any involvement of parents in decision making is active. It is implied that parents are equal and active participants in the evaluation of their children's progress and of the learning situations existing in the school.

A parent involvement program must provide a continuum of activities. Not all parents can be active partners in their children's education. A good parent involvement program will try to keep communication ongoing and open with these parents. At the same time, it will offer other parents the opportunity to extend their participation. Teachers must also consider how they will move

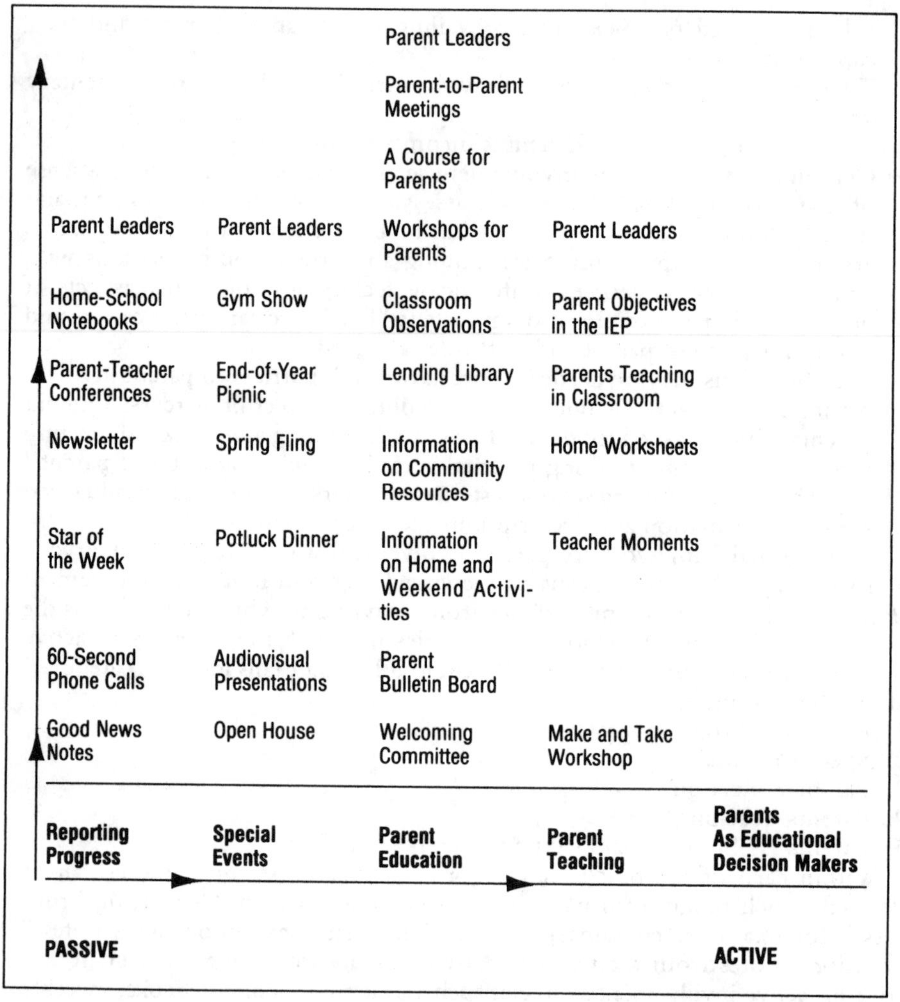

Reporting Progress	Special Events	Parent Education	Parent Teaching	Parents As Educational Decision Makers
		Parent Leaders		
		Parent-to-Parent Meetings		
		A Course for Parents'		
Parent Leaders	Parent Leaders	Workshops for Parents	Parent Leaders	
Home-School Notebooks	Gym Show	Classroom Observations	Parent Objectives in the IEP	
Parent-Teacher Conferences	End-of-Year Picnic	Lending Library	Parents Teaching in Classroom	
Newsletter	Spring Fling	Information on Community Resources	Home Worksheets	
Star of the Week	Potluck Dinner	Information on Home and Weekend Activities	Teacher Moments	
60-Second Phone Calls	Audiovisual Presentations	Parent Bulletin Board		
Good News Notes	Open House	Welcoming Committee	Make and Take Workshop	

PASSIVE → ACTIVE

SOURCE: "A conceptual framework for parent involvement" by B. Cervone and K. O'Leary. (Nov. 1982). *Educational Leadership*. 40, p. 49.

FIGURE 1
Parent Involvement Continuum

parents along the continuum to increasingly more active roles. Many parents will need to be prepared for involvement. Finally, teachers must determine the level of parent involvement that they can work with comfortably. It's important to ensure that the teacher begins comfortably, because success is more likely in a situation which does not strain the teacher's capabilities. Just as with parents, however, effort should be expended to prepare the teacher to move along the continuum towards increasingly active and equal parent participation.

Implications

The social studies program has at its core a concern for assisting children in understanding social relationships and in using that understanding to live satisfying, productive lives with other people. The social studies is, therefore, a natural vehicle for the involvement of parents. Parents are the first and major teachers of children; they build the attitudes with which children approach social relationships. The schools must build upon the interests, knowledge, and attitudes that children bring from home.

Spriggs (1980) and Lightfoot (1980) suggested that the schools often do not communicate clearly with parents, nor do they perceive the parents' values accurately. Such miscommunication and misperception make it difficult for a social studies program to begin with the child, for misperceptions of the child's family results in misperceptions of the child. Involvement by parents in the social studies program should enable parents and teachers to work together, to explore each other's traditions and values, and to begin to communicate. With that communication, a truly "social" studies program can be built.

Communication with parents and with adults who do not have children in the schools should occur frequently in relation to children's activities in social studies. Gallup (1984) found that parents liked to be informed about school happenings. The pollsters identified several traditional means of communication preferred by parents. These included the school newspaper. Parents appear to view a school or classroom newspaper as a useful means of communicating current school events to the home. As such, it fits well into the social studies program. Adults with no children in school identified the local newspaper as their primary source of information about the schools (Gallup, 1984). Articles in local newspapers can describe social studies activities occurring in the schools, such as a social studies fair or a historical play. Open-houses at schools, targeted at non-parent adults and displaying student work, are another means of publicizing programs and informing people.

Parents can make an impact in social studies through tutoring their children. Prior to the beginning of tutoring, parents should be invited to a general meeting with the teacher. The program can then be explained, and examples of specific activities can be presented. The general meeting should be followed with individual meetings with each parent. Specific strategies for working with each child can be explained and examples of specific activities can be presented. Parents should feel that their contribution would be of great benefit to their children. They should also feel they can contribute to a discussion of strategies that work best with their children. A home visit by the teacher should be considered as a most appropriate setting for this discussion.

Where can tutoring be of major help to the child? Possibilities include work in such areas as: (1) vocabulary, (2) test preparation, (3) study guide use, (4) reading list usage, (5) working on key questions, (6) discussing evaluation criteria, and (7) completing unfinished work in response to homework notes. Each should be discussed with parents separately. Tutoring might best begin in one area and then expand, an area at a time, as tutoring in the first areas proves to be successful. Parents should understand the purpose of the tutoring in a specific area and also what the child should be able to do as an end result.

Vocabulary tutoring can occur after students have been introduced to new vocabulary through work in the classroom. Tutoring at home is then a sharing between parent and child. It may function well when parent and child develop together definitions for vocabulary words.

Test preparation is another tutoring function. The tutor should be encouraged to make up questions related to subheadings in chapters of the textbooks. When the child is unsure of the answer, the tutor should read with the child to determine whether the text answers the question. If all else fails, tutor and student should write out the question for discussion at school with other students and the teachers. The tutor should urge the student to provide feedback to the tutor following the discussion.

A study guide developed by the teacher can follow up the initial review of material which occurs in test preparation tutoring. The study guide should emphasize: (1) concepts or specific points the teacher thinks are important, (2) concepts of specific points that students do not seem to understand or remember, and (3) ideas that developed in the test preparation tutoring phase and that contribute important viewpoints to the material under study.

Tutors can also help students choose items from reading lists provided by the teacher. Then, they can assist in reviewing the material read by using a few open-ended questions, such as "What was the most interesting thing/part in this book?" The teacher should suggest two or three questions. Some tutors will use these questions as a "starter" and follow up with additional questions that occur to them. Other tutors will not be as creative but will provide some review for the student by using the recommended questions.

An alternative, that can be introduced after tutors have some experience with reading lists, is to ask the tutor to help the student to develop a short, two-item or three-item reading list. This list does not have to identify books read, but rather books which seem to fit a particular topic and may be suitable for inclusion on a class reading list. The source of the book, such as the nearest public library, should be given. These individual lists can be combined into a class list from which students can select a book to read. After reading the books, they can critique the list by describing whether it was as appropriate as it initially seemed to be.

After tutors have used comprehensive study guides, the teacher can provide key questions to be discussed after a day's lesson. These should review the day's material, and they can also attempt to initiate some discussion regarding the next day's material, thus providing a preview. Daily work makes large-scale reviewing a much simpler task.

As narrative assignments, such as projects, reports, or reviews, are completed, tutors should be provided with straightforward evaluation criteria. Sharing evaluation criteria takes the ambiguity out of an assignment. It also helps to focus the efforts of a tutor who otherwise may not be quite sure of what to do.

Finally, homework notes could be used for students who forget to complete unfinished school work at home, or who otherwise need a little push to finish assignments. Tutors should be notified to check the notes daily and to ensure that the work is done. These notes should be simple or they will become a burden which is not worth the effort required. A useful format is a dittoed paper which lists the days of the week and then follows each day with a line for each subject area of concern. A page number or question number or other comment may be quickly jotted down. This line can be initialed by the tutor when the work is completed. A one-week paper is best. When papers are used for more than one week, they may become tattered.

In addition to tutoring, parents can make all sorts of things at home for use in the social studies program. They can make games, dress dolls in period costumes, create folk toys, construct models, draw maps, put together coin collections, prepare reference packets of newspaper materials, and put micro-computer programs on disks or tape.

Snack-making is another common parent task! Recipes for local traditional or ethnic foods, such as cornbread or crepes, can be sent home for preparation. The prepared foods are then returned to the school for sharing. A popular alternative is to cook in the classroom, with electric frying pans often substituting for a stove. Parents shop or collect the necessary ingredients and then assist students with the cooking.

Learning centers or interest centers often flourish when entrusted to parent volunteers, especially when their developers visit the classroom and introduce the centers to the students, suggesting ways of manipulating objects in the centers, and, in general, sparking student interest. Such centers can describe the quilt-making process, set up a small-scale production line, work on reading road maps, and focus on other activities.

In-classroom tutoring can serve as remediation or as enhancement. Parents can be especially valuable assets to the program in the role of enhancers. As enhancers, they are put in contact with students who share similar interests with them, or who wish to learn a skill that they have, such as doughnut-making or gardening. Parents often accomplish much remediation as they work with children; such remediation occurs through tutoring activities that are fun, challenging and capable of fostering a student's positive self-concept.

Reading to students is usually most rewarding because children enjoy being read to. Parents can be asked to choose a book related to social studies topics under study. Taping stories is also a means of building a classroom collection and of utilizing the talents of parents who read well or who are good storytellers. Puppetry is a related activity, and parents can present puppet shows or help children to develop them. Puppets can be developed for use by students in acting out their emotions or working through their problems.

Parents are frequently used as field-trip chaperones. In some areas this is a popular task, especially in rural regions where there are few opportunities to visit a variety of places. For example, a trip to the regional Coca-Cola bottling plant or to the state legislature might be quite interesting to adults. Beyond their use as chaperones, parents can be considered as coordinators. A field-trip committee could suggest new ideas for trips. Parents often have influence that teachers do not have and may, for example, be able to talk the local garage manager into welcoming children and permitting them to spend an hour with his mechanics. When parents know what concepts and topics the social studies program is addressing, they can often suggest intriguing field-trip ideas and take on much of the burden of planning those trips.

The development of bulletin boards is another area in which parent volunteers can be used to enchance the program. The teacher can design the boards and ask the parents to construct them from the plan. Designs produced by parents are more likely, however, to extend the curriculum in new directions, for parents build upon experiences that the teacher may not have.

Parents can also accomplish newer tasks if the teacher is ready to take advantage of the abilities and accomplishments of a parent volunteer. For example, the parent who enjoys using a microcomputer, and possesses some expertise in using it, may be able to assist children in working with a microcomputer as part of the social studies program. The parent might also help in reviewing software for potential purchase, or in adapting programs for better classroom use. An alert teacher, making a sustained effort at contacting parents, often uncovers great varieties of expertise among parents that would be of value to the social studies program.

The concept of volunteering is accepted by parents. However, it creates some problems when volunteers do not show up when expected, gossip in the classroom about students, do not follow directions, or generally behave irresponsibly. These problems should be addressed openly. If the irresponsible behavior continues, an effort should be made to shift the volunteer to other tasks. Shifting usually solves the problem. If it does not, other tasks that are to be completed at home should be offered to the volunteer. There are few parent volunteers with whom a pleasant accord cannot be reached, but the teacher does have to be prepared to work with some volunteers for a time before the most suitable tasks are found for them. Most volunteers will contribute much to the social studies program if they are properly prepared and if their abilities are effectively utilized.

There are many more possibilities for parent involvement in the social studies program. As we have seen, Cervone and O'Leary (1982) suggested a multi-phase, passive-active continuum for parent involvement (see Figure 1). This continuum contains a variety of activities, all of which can be utilized in the social studies program, and it leaves open to the teacher the possibility of including other activities. The critical factor is the teacher's willingness to involve parents. When the teacher is willing, a second factor becomes important. This is the teacher's readiness to accept different levels of involvement among parents while simultaneously encouraging each parent's movement to a more active level of involvement. If the social studies program is to be the study of our social world, parents must be involved in it, for they are the dominant feature of the child's social world. Only with a significant degree of parent involvement is the social studies program truly "social" studies.

REFERENCES

Anselmo, S. (1977). Parent involvement in the schools. *Clearing House, 50*(7) 297–299.

Barth, R. (1979). Home-based reinforcement of school behavior: A review and analysis. *Review of Educational Research, 49*(3), 436–458.

Becker, H., & Epstein, J. (1982). *Influences on teachers, use of parent involvement at home* (Report No. 324). Baltimore: Johns Hopkins University Center for Social Organization of Schools.

Berlin, R., & Berlin, I. (1973). *School's training of parents to be effective teachers of their own and other nonlearning children.* (ERIC Document Reproduction Service No. ED 099 110)

Bittle, R. (1975). Improving parent-teacher communications through recorded telephone messages. *Journal of Educational Research, 69*(3), 87–95.

Brookover, W. (1979). *School social systems and student involvement: Schools can make a difference.* New York: Praeger.

Cervone, B., & O'Leary, K. (1982). A conceptual framework for parent involvement. *Educational Leadership,* 40(2), 48–49.

Dobson, R., & Dobson, J. (1975). *Parental and community involvement in education and teacher education.* (ERIC No. ED 100 833)

Duncan, L. (1969). *Parent-counselor conferences make a difference.* (ERIC No. 031 743)

Edlund, C. (1969). Rewards at home to promote desirable school behavior. *TEACHING Exceptional Children, 1*(4), 121–127.

Etheridge, G., Collins, T., & Coats, B. (1979). *Home-school relations: Together we stand or divided we fail.* Paper presented at the International Congress on Education, Vancouver, British Columbia. (ERIC No. ED 151 713)

Fairchild, T. (1976). Home-school token economies: Bridging the communication gap. *Psychology in the Schools, 13*(4), 463–467.

Gallup, G. (1980). The 12th annual Gallup poll of the public's attitudes toward the public schools. *Phi Delta Kappan, 62*(1) 33–48.

Gillum, R., Schooley, D., & Novak, P. (1977, April). *The effects of parental involvement on school achievement in three Michigan performance contracting programs.* Paper presented at the annual meeting of the American Educational Research Association, New York City. (ERIC No. ED 144 007)

Hightower, H. (1975). *Educational decision-making: The involvement of parents; myth or reality.* Paper presented at American Educational Research Association, Toronto, Canada. (ERIC No. ED 154 086)

Hofmeister, A. (1977). *The parent as a teacher.* Paper presented at the 56th Annual Faculty Honor Lecture in the Humanities, Logan, Utah. (ERIC No. ED 161 541)

Hubbell, N. (1979). Some things change—some do not! In R.S. Brandt (Ed.) *Partners: Parents and schools* (pp. 75–79). Alexandria, VA: Association for Supervision and Curriculum Development.

Ingram, J. (1978). *The relationship between school-community relations and student achievement* (Tech. Rep. No. 463). Madison, Wisconsin: University of Wisconsin Research and Development Center for Individualized Schooling.

Keeves, J. (1975). The home, the school, and the achievement in mathematics and science. *Science Education, 59*(4), 439–460.

Lightfoot, S. (1978). *Worlds apart.* New York: Basic Books.

Lightfoot, S. (1980, Spring). *Exploring family-school relationships: A prelude to curricular designs and strategies.* Paper prepared for "Toward being at home in school: Parent involvement in curriculum decision making." Symposium sponsored by the American Educational Research Association.

Mager, G. (1980). The conditions which influence a teacher in initiating contacts with parents. *The Journal of Educational Research, 73*(5), 276–282.

McKinney, J. (1975). *The development and implementation of a tutorial program for parents to improve the reading and mathematics achievement of their children.* (ERIC No. ED 113 703)

Mize, G. (1977). *The influence of increased parental involvement in the educational process of their children.* (Tech. Rep. No. 418). (ERIC No. ED 151 661)

Moles, O. (1982). Synthesis of recent research on parent participation in children's education. *Educational Leadership. 40*(2), 44–47.

National Education Association. (1981). *Nationwide teacher opinion poll.* Washington, DC: National Education Association Research Memo.

Nedler, S., & McAfee, O. (1979). *Working with parents: Guidelines for early childhood and elementary school teachers.* Belmont, CA: Wadsworth.

Parker, F., & Mccoy, J. (1977). School-based intervention for the modification of excessive absenteeism. *Psychology in the Schools, 14*(1), 84–88.

Rich, D., VanDien, J., & Mattox, B. (1979). Families as educators of their own children. In R.S. Brandt (Ed.), *Partners: Parents and schools* (pp. 26–40). Alexandria, VA: Association for Supervision and Curriculum Development.

Schaefer, E. (1971). Toward a renovation in education. *National Elementary Principal, 51*(1), 18–25.

Schiff, H. (1963). *The effect of personal contactual relationships on parents' attitudes toward and participation in local school affairs.* Unpublished doctoral dissertation, Northwestern University.

Sheats, D., & Dunkleberger, G. (1979). A determination of the principal's effect in school-initiated home contacts concerning attendance of elementary school students. *The Journal of Educational Research, 72*(6), 310–312.

Shelton, D., & Dobson, R. (1973). *An analysis of a family involvement-communication system in a Title I elementary school.* Final Report. (ERIC No. ED 082 091)

Smith, M., & Brahce, R. (1973). School and home: focus on achievement. In H. Passow (Ed.), *Developing programs for the educational disadvantaged.* New York: Harper & Row.

Spriggs, S. (1980). *Children and families in Appalachia: The status, needs and implications for R&D activities.* Charleston, WV: Appalachia Educational Laboratory.

Sunal, C., Strong, M., Wilmoth, E., & Fassig, B. (1983). *Improving school-family relations.* Paper presented at meeting of National Association of Elementary School Principals, St. Louis.

Tangri, S., & Leitch, M. (1982). *Barriers to home-school collaboration: Two case studies in junior high schools* (Final Report, the National Institute of Education). Washington, DC: The Urban Institute.

Valentin, C., & Alston, H. (1978, July). *Survey of parents' expectations of public schools and aspirations for their children's education* (Project Report). Houston Independent School District.

Walberg, H., & Marjoribanks, K. (1976). Family environment and cognitive development: Twelve analytic models. *Review of Educational Research, 46*(4) 527–551.

Williams, D. (1981). *Final interim report: Southwest parent education resource center.* Austin, TX: Southwest Educational Development Laboratory.

CHAPTER 11

ADVOCATING EARLY CHILDHOOD SOCIAL STUDIES

Carole Hahn

That the basis of adult beliefs, abilities, and behaviors is established in childhood is a maxim accepted by educators, parents, and the public alike. Those groups also agree that a major purpose of schools is to prepare youth to be good citizens. Yet, the acceptance of those two abstract assumptions does not mean that social studies is taught to most primary grade children. To the contrary, national studies have documented the absence of social studies in many early grade classrooms (Gross, 1979; Hahn, 1985). Teachers, principals, parents, and recently even school boards and state legislatures have emphasized language arts and arithmetic in the primary grades—at the expense of social studies. Several authors in this book have mentioned the decline in elementary social studies.

Many social studies educators complain to one another about this sad state of affairs, but do little about it. If we are to reverse the trend, we must become more active advocates in professional circles and public arenas. We must make clear both the costs of neglecting social education and the advantages of providing consistent, carefully sequenced social studies instruction in the early years. The evidence for such a position has been presented throughout this book. Now it is up to social studies educators to synthesize the research, to translate the implications into language that is meaningful to the public, and to plan effective strategies for delivering our messages to all who influence primary grade curriculum and instruction.

In order to be effective advocates for early childhood social studies, we need to direct our efforts in at least three different directions simultaneously. First, we need to nurture a general climate that supports social studies for young children by continually keeping the topic on the minds of the public and in the forefront of the profession. This can be done through constant attention to media and public relations opportunities and through sustained efforts by state and local social studies councils.

A second front on which we must act is at state capitols. We must carefully monitor pending legislation and possible policy changes that could affect early childhood social studies. We must be able to activate a network of individuals who will write letters, make phone calls, or testify at committee hearings. This is an area in which the profession must become more involved, because increas-

ingly decisions are made at the statehouse which affect what does—and does not—get taught in the nation's classrooms.

In addition to fostering a general climate that is supportive of early childhood social studies, we must also become assertive advocates for specific changes that will benefit early childhood social studies. This chapter will briefly recommend how to become stronger advocates through the media and through government relations. It will focus on suggestions for developing a plan of specific action based on research concerning educational change (Becker & Hahn, 1977; Hahn, 1977; Havelock et al., 1971; Rogers, 1983).

PUBLIC RELATIONS, THE MEDIA, AND STATE SOCIAL STUDIES COUNCILS

In *Citizenship and the Critical Role of the Social Studies,* Parker and Jarolimek (1984) emphasized that social studies educators must become advocates in the media, before the school board, and to legislators because the existence of social studies and, along with it, the future of democracy are at stake.

Individual teachers, supervisors, and representatives of state or local councils should get to know members of the press and continually issue news stories to them. Jarolimek and Parker advise "selling" a story with a "grabber"—a human interest angle, a special event, or an interesting photograph. A solid story behind the grabber gives one a chance to inform the public about the ongoing, carefully planned social studies program. A story about 1st graders studying another culture in depth or about the school that won a contest for "Making

History Come Alive" are both opportunities to alert parents to what their young children could be learning.

School boards, legislatures, and mayors ought to be presented with resolutions from local or state social studies councils asserting the importance of early grade social studies. Such resolutions can call for a "Social Studies Week" in which elementary schools sponsor events to draw attention to their programs. In some cases, resolutions may be needed to reassert the need to allocate daily time for social studies instruction.

Individuals on state education committees and on state and local school boards who are the most likely potential advocates for early grade social studies ought to be identified and kept continually informed about what is going on in primary grade social studies in their constituencies. They should also be told that children who participate in strong social studies programs do well on basic skills tests because they have the necessary knowledge about people, places, and events to comprehend the reading passages (see Gary R. McKenzie's chapter in this bulletin). Similarly, those policymakers should be aware that teaching about other cultures in the first three grades fosters the development of positive attitudes toward other peoples as well as toward social studies (see Lynda Stone's chapter and Jantz & Klawitter's chapter).

State councils should develop "road shows" about the need for early childhood social studies. A slide-tape presentation and questions for group discussion could be given to PTAs, school boards, or service clubs. Evidence from this book may provide a good basis for such activities.

All of these techniques will help to call early childhood social studies to the attention of the public. A booklet produced by the Early Childhood Advisory Committee of NCSS (NCSS, 1985) recommends the following as examples of projects that can be undertaken by a local social studies council to highlight social studies in the primary grades: a social studies fair at the shopping mall, a school-wide festival, a living history museum, or a social studies book week culminating in a parade.

While reaching out to the public, we must not forget that our own colleagues often overlook the importance of early childhood social studies when they are planning state council programs. The NCSS booklet mentioned above recommends that state councils:

- Encourage elementary teachers to make presentations at state conferences.[1]
- Publicize state conferences in local elementary schools.
- Recognize outstanding elementary teachers at state conferences.
- Establish a special interest group for elementary/early childhood educators.
- Select keynote speakers who are able to address topics of interest to early childhood educators as well as to secondary teachers.
- Extend complimentary memberships to elementary school administrators.
- Encourage local school districts to adopt social studies as the inservice theme for elementary schools one year.
- Promote social studies related themes at other statewide conferences, such as those for principals and supervisors, or those in reading and science education.

• Encourage elementary/early childhood teachers to submit articles to state professional journals.[2]

It is clear that there is much that we can do to make our colleagues and the public aware of early childhood social studies. Such advocacy through public relations is needed, but alone it is not enough. We must also become stronger advocates within the process of governmental decision making.

GOVERNMENTAL RELATIONS

Legislative liaison committees of state social studies councils should be created to monitor legislation before the state legislature and to determine potential effects of legislation on social studies, including giving attention to the primary grades. Such committees ought to alert state council members about pending bills so that letters or telegrams can be sent to the appropriate people at the most effective times. Similarly, local social studies councils ought to designate someone to monitor local school boards and to alert council members to matters that could affect early childhood social studies either positively or negatively.

The California Council for the Social Studies has developed a legislative handbook that contains much useful guidance for state councils that are just beginning to act in this area.[3] Among other recommendations, the handbook suggests the creation of a legislative committee of state council members to rally support from across the state and the designation of a legislative representative to monitor legislation, testify at hearings, and talk with legislators. A budget that supports government relations activities is also recommended. The California Council sponsors an annual legislative day in which members of the state council meet with their own state legislators to talk about issues affecting social studies. Such programs can be a good defense to protect and promote early grade social studies.

DEVELOPING A PLAN OF ACTION

The remainder of this chapter is for readers who not only believe that social studies is an essential component of the early grades curriculum, but who also want to convince others of its importance. This section is intended to be used, not merely read. If the reader will write responses to the questions that are raised, he or she will be able to develop a specific plan of action for building support for early childhood social studies in his or her particular locale. The following section builds on the research on educational change (Becker & Hahn, 1977; Hahn, 1977; Havelock et al., 1971; Rogers, 1983). If the guidelines presented here are followed, efforts to promote change will have the greatest likelihood of succeeding. In particular, careful assessment of roles, messages, and timing will be useful in developing plans to promote early childhood social studies.

Goal Setting

First, one must identify a precise goal. If one were successful in building support for early childhood social studies, what would the result be? Would the state mandate a higher minimum time allocation, such as 45 minutes per day for social studies? Would the social studies curriculum guide for the school system include more economic or more international content in the primary grades? Would a textbook series incorporate the research on how children are challenged by lessons in anthropology? Would primary grade teachers demonstrate more positive attitudes toward the variety of experiential activities they have been using to teach history? Would parents and other community members be more involved in the social studies program in their local school? The reader should now pause, reflect upon his or her situation and upon the possibilities suggested in this bulletin, and write down the particular goal for which he or she would be willing to work.

Goals for educational change can rarely be achieved by individuals working alone. To be successful, one needs to identify others with whom to work. The research on educational change suggests that potential advocates, gatekeepers, and opinion leaders can be most helpful.

Involving Others

An *advocate* is someone who sees it in his or her best interest for an idea, program, or policy to be adopted. The advocate is often the champion who moves an idea through the appropriate channels. The reader may be the key advocate for improving early childhood social studies, or he or she may be able to identify a potential advocate within the school board, at the county office, or in a school. If as a coordinator, teacher, or professor, one is an outsider to the system one wants to influence, then it is crucial to identify a potential inside advocate. If that person can be convinced of the need for the goal, then he or she can be instrumental in convincing others of the need for change.

The reader should now reflect upon people within the "target system" (whatever groups must accept the goal) who are likely advocates for early childhood social studies because it facilitates their own goals. These people may have previously shown interest in improving early childhood social studies. They may have expressed concern about multicultural education or basic skills. Or, if they supported another idea that is compatible with the goal, they are likely advocates. The reader should now write the name of the individual or individuals who might become advocates. Note also the evidence that suggests they would be receptive to the goal and willing to work to achieve it.

Opinion leaders are the second set of people to be identified. Opinion leaders are the informal leaders who influence the attitudes and beliefs of people within their group. They may or may not occupy an official leadership role. They are accepted as "one of us" by members of their social system. They are not likely to deviate much from group norms, nor to take great risks in trying new things. Because others respect the opinion leader, his or her support is crucial to the acceptance of a new idea. On the other hand, if the opinion leader opposes the idea, it is likely to be set aside.

In identifying the opinion leaders within groups, pay particular attention to who is influenced by whom. Take some time to observe the way in which group members interact. Once having determined who the key opinion leader is within the PTA, the education committee of the state legislature, the primary grade teachers in a particular school, or whatever group needs to be involved, consider what that person's attitude is likely to be toward your goal. Is there any way in which the opinion leader might be convinced that the goal is compatible with any of his or her needs, interests, or values? Also, consider whether you are the best person to do the convincing. Is there someone else who could better persuade the opinion leader to support the idea? Sometimes it is most effective to approach an opinion leader indirectly.

The third set of individuals who should be involved in a plan of action is usually the easiest to identify. They are the *gatekeepers* or *legitimizers,* the persons whose official approval is needed. They tend to have both status and power in a system. They usually play a passive role in the decision-making process, but they can kill an idea if they are not consulted. If a professor wants to talk to local principals about early childhood social studies, he or she may first need to get the approval of an assistant superintendent. A principal's approval may be necessary before a teacher can invite parents to an informational meeting. At the state level in particular, bureaucrats often need to be involved. If you are an outsider to a social system, you ought to ask who the legitimizers are whose approval is needed to move your idea forward. Now write down the names of the legitimizers. Note how they can help or hinder your efforts, and how you might persuade them to help you.

While advocates, opinion leaders, and gatekeepers are especially needed to give support to a plan to improve early childhood social studies, there are other people who must also be convinced to make changes. The reader should now list the other individuals or groups who should be involved in the plan. Consider the following roles: teachers, administrators, supervisors, parents, community members, students, leaders of local and state professional associations, members of school boards, members of the legislature, college professors, officials of state departments of education, authors, curriculum developers, members of curriculum or textbook committees, publishers' representatives, and leaders of related interest groups such as the president of the state historical society, the coordinator of an international organization, or a leader in the League of Women Voters. Consider anyone who could potentially support or be a barrier to the acceptance of your plan.

Persuading Others
Once you have diagnosed the key roles to be involved in your plan or action, it is time to consider the most effective messages for persuading people to accept your goal. Research on the diffusion of educational innovations indicates that people are most likely to accept new ideas, products and programs when they perceive them to be compatible with their own needs and values and when they believe that the benefits are observable (Hahn, 1982; Rogers, 1983). People are also most likely to adopt the innovations they perceive as less complex; programs which may be difficult for teachers of students to understand or use are unlikely to be adopted. For each person on your list, reflect upon what his or her concerns seem to be and note ways in which that person could be persuaded that your goal is compatible with one of his or her own needs or values. In this book, McKenzie has suggested that social studies can improve

reading test scores, and Stone has noted that culture studies can reduce ethno-centricism. Other chapters have demonstrated that young children can learn powerful concepts from economics, anthropology and sociology. These arguments and others may be compatible with values of decision makers and people who influence others.

Consider also the ways in which each person might perceive the proposed change to be too complex or difficult, and think of ways to reduce that possible difficulty. For example, giving students many opportunities to participate in decision making has been advocated by Parker and Jarolimek in this book, but some teachers may feel that this is difficult to do. Remember: it is not some objective reality that is important here, but rather how the innovation is *perceived* by different individuals. Try to put yourself in the person's place and consider how he or she might view the new policy, program, or idea. This enables one to plan different messages tailored to particular individuals. Not everyone is persuaded by research, so it may be necessary to present arguments in addition to the ones suggested in this bulletin.

People do not make changes unless they feel a need for change. If people are satisfied with early childhood social studies, they will not be receptive to changing it. A local needs assessment may be helpful, or the reader might share some of the data in this book that document a general need.

Closely related to the content of messages is the channel that one uses to deliver the messages. Again, research on the diffusion of innovations will be helpful (Havelock et al. 1971; Rogers, 1983). Mass media channels of communication, including brochures, radio spot announcements, slide-tape presentations, and speeches are particularly helpful in creating awareness about and interest in innovations. A state social studies council or coordinator might want to put together a brochure or a presentation that uses the evidence presented in this bulletin and translate it into a message that is relevant to a general audience in the state.

One must realize, however, that mass media techniques alone are not likely to convince people to accept a new approach to early childhood social studies. As people move from the awareness to the persuasion stage, they pay more attention to and put more confidence in face-to-face contacts. By personally talking with someone who has used the approach or who is knowledgeable about the idea, people can raise questions about their particular concerns. The reader should now look over the list of people to be persuaded, and consider who could best deliver personal communication about the idea to the various people listed.

Opportunities and Timing

The *Wingspread Workbook for Educational Change* advises that "an important aid in getting a new idea, product, or practice implemented is to list all the occasions or situations in which individuals and groups within your system are likely to be open to suggestions regarding your particular innovation" (Becker & Hahn, 1974, p. 45).

Examples of opportunities include occasions when books are selected for adoption, when teachers are hired or resign, when curricula are revised, when the year's inservice meetings are planned, when faculty meetings are held, when budgets are prepared and materials ordered, when Parent Night at school is planned, when the legislature is in session, when professional conferences are held, or when children are involved in a social studies project that is newsworthy. Consider these and similar occasions when one might inject information about early childhood social studies, persuade a colleague, or suggest an alternative to current practice that would lead to improvement in social studies in the primary grades. Consider informal opportunities like discussions in a teachers' lounge or at social events. The reader should now list the occasions that might be used to help achieve the goal. Note also who might be reached at each opportunity and what message they would be most receptive to hearing.

Putting It All Together

The reader should now have completed an assessment of occasions, roles, and communication techniques that are related to achieving his or her goal for early childhood social studies. It is now a good idea to make a time line for the period ahead of you on a large sheet of paper. Sequence the occasions across the top of the page, and list the people in various roles down the left-hand margin (or the reverse). Make a grid and, within the cells, describe the action that is needed. Read through all of the diagnosis to be sure that nothing is overlooked; add ideas that occur at this stage. Your grid may look something like the one shown. It can be generated by an individual, or a small group, such as a committee.

The final step of the plan is to build in time to monitor the success of the strategy as it unfolds. Scheduled monthly meetings with a few other advocates might help.

Clearly, it is going to take much time and energy to be effective advocates for early childhood social studies. Yet, if we do not devote ourselves to this cause, no one else is likely to do it for us, and social studies may be squeezed out of the early grades altogether. Whatever efforts we make now to revitalize early childhood social studies will strengthen citizenship education at all levels. Action now is a wise investment in the future.

	Summer '87	**Fall '87**	**Winter '88**	**Spring '88**
Occasions:		Inservice meetings	State legislature textbook selection	Social studies conference ordering materials
		PTA meetings		
People:				
Harbin	Keep informed of grades 1–3 social studies activities			
Stein			Monitor legislative committee— call state network	
Brown	Organize grades 1–3 PTA program			
Wong	Send list of names for textbook reviewers			Get newspaper coverage of state conference
Self	Call Harbin— volunteer to do inservice	Do inservice		
	Call Brown about PTA	Find speakers for state conference		

NOTES

[1]The Wisconsin Council for the Social Studies added to its state conference one day devoted to elementary social studies and then publicized this arrangement throughout the area. Three hundred elementary teachers attended!

[2]For details on these and similar ideas, write to the NCSS office for a copy of *Publicizing and Encouraging Elementary School Studies: Strategies for State and Local Councils,* 1983.

[3]For a copy of the California Social Studies Legislative Handbook, write to the California Council for the Social Studies, 616 Juanita Way, Roseville, CA 95678.

REFERENCES

Becker, J., & Hahn, C. L. (1977). *Wingspread workbook for educational change.* Boulder, CO: Social Science Education Consortium.

Gross, R. E. (1977, May). The status of the social studies in the public schools of the United States: Facts and impressions of a national survey. *Social Education, 41,* 194–200, 205.

Hahn, C. L. (1977). Research on the diffusion of social studies innovations. In F. P. Hawkins et al. *Review of research in social studies innovations: 1970–1975* (pp. 137–177). Washington, DC: National Council for the Social Studies.

Hahn, C. L. (1982, March). *Adopting curriculum innovations: Testing the applicability of Rogers and Shoemaker's theory to textbook adoption.* Paper presented at the annual meeting of the American Educational Research Association, New York.

Hahn, C. L. (1985). The status of the social studies in the public schools of the United States: Another look. *Social Education, 49,* 220–223.

Havelock, R. G., et al. (1971). *Planning for innovation through dissemination and utilization of knowledge.* Ann Arbor: University of Michigan, Institute for Social Research Center for Research on the Utilization of Scientific Knowledge.

National Council for the Social Studies (1985). *Publicizing and encouraging elementary social studies: Strategies for state and local councils.* Washington, D.C.: NCSS. (ERIC Document Reproduction Service No. ED 253 476)

Parker, W., & Jarolimek, J. (1984). *Citizenship and the critical role of the social studies.* Washington, DC: National Council for the Social Studies.

Rogers, E. M. (1983). *Diffusion of innovations.* New York: The Free Press.

INDEX